Advance Praise

"Elizabeth Howell's new book provides a masterful synthesis of the vital revolution in trauma theory and practice over the last 25 years. In this illuminating, indispensable guide she weaves together the powerful insights of multiple disciplines with those of her own personal transformation as a relational trauma therapist. Dedicated to exploring the painful and complex reality of her subject, Howell's book is an invaluable guide to the newly hopeful field of trauma therapy."

—Jessica Benjamin, psychoanalyst and author of
Beyond Doer and Done To and *The Bonds of Love*

"Elizabeth Howell writes from her heart, guided by her deeply felt and valued relationships with her patients, clearly cherished as her most important collaborators. Her original thinking shines through as she adds her own views and creatively spells-out and interprets the work of both psychoanalytic thinkers and traumatologists, an integrative feat few writers have achieved. Sit down with Howell, as I have, and enjoy her company. You will be delighted!"

—Richard A. Chefetz, M.D.,
Private Practice of Psychiatry, Washington, D.C.

"Howell's distinctive blend of trauma-informed clinical compassion, academic and analytic questioning reaches a new peak here. She exposes the trauma caused by Freud's creation of the Oedipus complex and the damage of one-person psychology. At the same time she offers hope through comprehensive non-dissociative theorizing, backed as always by solid clinical evidence. Gently, authentically, and relationally argued this is a powerful seminal bombshell of a book—albeit an elegant one."

—Valerie Sinason, Ph.D., British psychoanalyst and author

"At the heart of Elizabeth Howell's courageous thesis is the question: can contemporary psychoanalysis adapt to trauma and dissociation informed psychotherapy? She pulls no punches in offering scholarly yet confronting responses to offer a belated resolution to the 100-year trauma debate raging between Freudian 'repression' and Janetian 'dissociation'. Therapists and patients alike will greatly benefit from Dr. Howell's parsimonious definition of trauma as *that which causes dissociation.* This radical reconceptualization has powerfully reshaped the future direction of trauma therapy as her clinically based discussions amply illustrate."

—**Dr. George Halasz, Adjunct Senior Lecturer, Monash University, Melbourne, Australia, and child and adolescent psychiatrist**

"Clear, well-written, engaging. Valuable for clinicians at all levels."

—**Lucie Grosvenor, LCSW, Executive Director, Psychoanalytic Psychotherapy Study Center**

Trauma and
Dissociation Informed
Psychotherapy

Trauma and Dissociation Informed Psychotherapy

RELATIONAL HEALING AND THE THERAPEUTIC CONNECTION

Elizabeth Howell

W. W. NORTON & COMPANY

Independent Publishers Since 1923

Note to Readers: Standards of clinical practice and protocol change over time, and no technique or recommendation is guaranteed to be safe or effective in all circumstances. This volume is intended as a general information resource for professionals practicing in the field of psychotherapy and mental health; it is not a substitute for appropriate training, peer review, and/or clinical supervision. Neither the publisher nor the author(s) can guarantee the complete accuracy, efficacy, or appropriateness of any particular recommendation in every respect. Names and identifying details have been changed for all clients discussed, and some individuals presented are composites.

For information about permission to reproduce selections from this book, write to Permissions, W. W. Norton & Company, Inc., 500 Fifth Avenue, New York, NY 10110

For information about special discounts for bulk purchases, please contact W. W. Norton Special Sales at specialsales@wwnorton.com or 800-233-4830

Manufacturing by Lake Book Manufacturing, Inc.
Production manager: Katelyn MacKenzie

Library of Congress Cataloging-in-Publication Data

Names: Howell, Elizabeth, author.
Title: Trauma and dissociation-informed psychotherapy : relational healing and the therapeutic connection / Elizabeth Howell.
Description: First edition. | New York : W.W. Norton & Company, [2020] | "A Norton professional book." | Includes bibliographical references and index.
Identifiers: LCCN 2019030136 | ISBN 9780393713732 (hardcover) | ISBN 9780393713749 (epub)
Subjects: LCSH: Psychic trauma. | Dissociation (Psychology)
Classification: LCC RC552.T7 H69 2020 | DDC 616.85/21--dc23
LC record available at https://lccn.loc.gov/2019030136

W. W. Norton & Company, Inc., 500 Fifth Avenue, New York, N.Y. 10110
www.wwnorton.com

W. W. Norton & Company Ltd., 15 Carlisle Street, London W1D 3BS

1 2 3 4 5 6 7 8 9 0

CONTENTS

Acknowledgments xiii

Preface xv

Introduction xix

1. *How Freud Buried Trauma 3*

2. *Trauma as Dissociation 25*

3. *Ubiquity of Trauma and Dissociation:*
The Effects on Minds and Bodies 45

4. *The Clinical Dyad as a Wounded Dyad 59*

5. *Dissociation, Repression, and the Unconscious 77*

6. *Disorganized Attachment as Dissociation 97*

7. *The Conundrum of Self-Criticism and*
Self-Attack 111

8. *Structural Models of the Psychological Organization*
of a Traumatized Person 135

9. *Exit from the Closed System as the Therapist*
Becomes Real 157

10. *Conclusion: Toward Psychological Healing 171*

Endnotes 187

References 189

Index 215

ACKNOWLEDGMENTS

I WISH TO EXPRESS thanks for the generous contributions of time, energy, and thought to colleagues and friends who kindly read chapters of this book. I especially thank Jennifer Leighton, who read and commented on every chapter with suggestions about what to add and what to elim inate; Sheldon Itzkowitz, who read and commented on most of the chapters, sometimes contributing just the words or phrases that I hadn't thought of when my mind was too tired or blank; Margaret Hainer, on whom I can always count to find any logical errors and whose helpful chapter readings made me sharpen my concepts; Orit Badouk Epstein, for her helpful readings and comments on attachment theory; Billie Pivnick for her careful reading and astute comments on these same chapters, and Valerie Sinason, for her insightful readings of several chapters and her helpful suggestions for rearranging certain sentences and words. I thank Onno van der Hart for his helpful comments on my views of *inside out* versus *outside in* approaches to psychic organization and healing.

I thank my husband, Patrick Flanagan, for painstakingly accurate copyediting of every chapter and for his many helpful suggestions.

Finally, but not at all least, I am highly appreciative of my editor, Deborah Malmud, for her continuous and generous commentary, from beginning to end, about what to edit out, what to add, and how to enhance to flow of this book.

PREFACE

IT'S AN AMAZING THING to find oneself in the midst of changing times. As a clinical psychologist first in graduate school and postgraduate training in the 1970s and then in analytic training in the 1980s, I was trained mostly in the Freudian model, intermixed with a sprinkling of interpersonal thinking. In undergraduate and graduate school I learned that Freud was a genius for being able to analyze himself and that Sándor Ferenczi, who disagreed with Freud about child sexual abuse and the importance of really listening to the client, was crazy. Today, those ideas are reversed in my mind: learning about oneself comes from allowing self-impressions to be filtered through others, and Ferenczi, not Freud, was the more important genius. The relational and postmodern perspective shows how, because we are always embedded in relational fields, the idea of being able to completely analyze oneself outside of that embeddedness is an illusion. Furthermore, the dissociative structure of mind is guaranteed to cloud one's vision of oneself.

In the 1990s, I was teaching clinical and abnormal psychology to graduate and undergraduate students. In the clinical psychology course, I used a Freudian textbook. At the same time, I was becoming increasingly fascinated by the trauma literature that was starting to appear, especially books written and edited by Richard Kluft. For me, the trauma literature explained much more about people's problems than did the Freudian literature that I was teaching. I did not know how to integrate the two bodies of largely incompatible theoretical systems. In addition to my slipping in some Kernberg and some Kohut to the class material, I also began to think aloud in the class about trauma and dissociation. Then one day, as I was teaching about Freud's defense mechanisms—including *isolation of affect* (which involves separating oneself and one's thoughts from feelings) a student raised her hand and asked, "Isn't that the same as dissociation?" I had been thinking the same, but I had not had the courage to say it out loud, so I thanked my student and told her that I believed she was right.

I found a key to the integration of psychoanalytic thinking and the world of knowledge about dissociation in the writings of Philip Bromberg. His work became a guiding light to me in my work with clients and in my thinking. First, I sat at his feet; and now, if I may presume, I stand on his shoulders.

Around the same time, I was a member of the Women's Institute, a collective of women psychotherapists in New York City. At one point we decided to separate into subgroups to study particular topics, after which we would come back together and report on our research. I joined the group on masochism. As I was reading the old and new literature on masochism, I realized that the symptoms of "masochism" were symptoms of trauma. This was quite an amazing discovery to me. I wrote two papers on the topic.

Also in the same time frame, I had three clients who had dissociative identity disorder (DID), although I did not realize their diagnoses at the time. It was not until one client called me on the phone in great distress to tell me that someone was hitting her that I began to realize the reality of DID. In response to my inquiry as to who was there, she said "no one," but she continued to insist that someone was hitting her. Before long I began to put it together and realized that a dissociated part of her, an alter, was hitting her; but that she experienced this as another person hitting her.

In 1995, I presented a paper at the International Society for the Study of Trauma and Dissociation (ISSTD) on masochism as a trauma disorder. As I learned more and more about trauma and dissociation at conferences and workshops, I felt that my *real* education in psychology and mental health treatment had just began. This was after my PhD in clinical psychology, my 2-year postdoctoral program, and 4 years of analytic training. As I learn more and more about trauma and dissociation, I feel that my education continues. Particularly important to me has been learning about the multiple self-state model of the self, including the dissociated self-state model, formulated in psychoanalysis by Philip Bromberg, Stephen Mitchell, and others, but also powerfully ratified by Frank Putnam's research on discrete behavioral and mental states.

Along with many others, I have developed different ways of understanding how certain problems of living develop in the matrix of trauma and dissociation, in ways that may open up avenues to healing. In the following pages, I will describe how I think of trauma and dissociation and why I think it is an apt language for psychotherapy.

In this book I will describe why I define trauma as what causes dissociation, why I think problematic or psychopathological splitting originates in a process that Sándor Ferenczi (1949) called "identification with the aggressor," why I view a particular form of dissociation of self due to attachment problems as tantamount to superego, and other ways that I view the importance of dissociation.

It is impossible to fully capture in words the kinds of information and affect that flow back and forth within people and between people, including between client and therapist. We work as theorists to find better theoretical models to help explain why what is happening is happening. As clinicians, our goal is to be able to helpfully respond to what our clients tell us, even when we can't fully cognitively understand what is happening in them, in us, and between us.

I think that the increasing recognition of trauma and dissociation, as they become more visible, are here to stay, even though societal and personal denial may try to slow it down.

INTRODUCTION

WE ARE ON THE cusp of a major change in the way clinicians understand the human mind. From about the late 1980s to the present, there has been an explosion of interest in trauma in the mental health field. However, it is not just knowledge about trauma that is increasing. We are also learning how the human mind is dissociatively structured. In fact, one could say that the meaning of psychological trauma is that it causes dissociation of the mind.

Many different ways of looking at the self coalesce in the new trauma–dissociation model. The trauma–dissociation model departs from the older, often implicit, medical model that in theory identified a specific pathogen with a specific disease, in which the practitioner as a person is removed from the person of the patient, and in which the practitioner's *treatment* fixes the patient's *disorder*. We are departing from models that primarily stress psychic determinism and unconscious agency while ignoring or obfuscating the real and lasting damage of exogenous trauma. We are leaving behind a one-person model in which psychodynamics primarily emanate from forces and fantasies within the person, and moving toward an embrace of a two-person model that recognizes relational interactions. The trauma and dissociation informed approach transforms ways of understanding psychopathology, or problems in living. Personality disorders can be understood as dissociation-based, and much of psychosis as posttraumatic. What used to be understood as neurosis, as emanating from harsh superego, may be understood as attachment-based dissociation.

This change in focus applies to the entire mental health field, insofar as it applies to nonorganic problems in living. The Freudian model of repression and personality structure implies agency, while the trauma model recognizes helplessness. Other approaches to psychotherapy—for instance, cognitive behavioral therapy that may appear uninfluenced by Freudian dogma—are often permeated by Freudian concepts such as ego/id/superego and repression.

Our inner world is not so much a cauldron of id impulses fueling sexual and aggressive fantasies, as it is peopled with many versions of ourselves, usually coinciding with differing emotional states and experiences, as well as with representations of our relationships with attachment figures. These are to varying degrees connected or disconnected from each other. In the new model, the practitioner and the client are both traumatized and flawed human beings who affect each other in the mutual process called psychotherapy, which is intended for the healing of the client. Healing occurs, not so much from treatment of maladies, from *dis-eases* being cured, or even repression lifted, but from the client becoming able to speak and hear herself or himself—including dissociated parts of the self—in the presence of someone who is intently listening as well as emotionally attuned. The listener then becomes a witness to the client's experience. Healing involves accepting, acknowledging, and mourning parts of the self that have been dissociated and hold the trauma.

This new shift in thinking about the human mind emphasizes relationality and the importance of human connectedness. From birth, humans are relationally embedded, and development proceeds, for better or for worse, in the nexus of relationships. We have learned who we are from the words, feelings, gestures, tonality of language, attitudes, and overall relationships with early significant others and from the culture in which we live. In this relational matrix, the need for attachment is a major force dictating what stays in consciousness and what aspects of relationships must be dissociated. Current concepts of relationality were presaged by the work of feminist writers. Notably, Jean Baker Miller and Carol Gilligan in the 1970s and 1980s valorized the concepts of interdependence and relationality.

Relationality implies a two-person model of development and of psychotherapy. The two-person model recognizes the existence of perpetrators and abusers, a reality that by its very structure the one-person model could not assimilate. Most of our clients come to us because of difficulties derivative in some way of relational and developmental trauma.

Trauma is rooted in helplessness. Recognizing trauma and dissociation means recognizing vulnerability.

Dissociative self-states are understood to be parts of the self that contain affect, thought, and memories of real interactions so overwhelming to the child that they can not be assimilated into ongoing narrative memory. The traumatic affective overwhelm causes a dissociative response in the brain. When a child's mind is overwhelmed by events that cannot be assimilated, such as those that betray the child's love and trust, normal processes of dissociation cordon off these experiences, resulting in dissociated self-states that encapsulate the unbearable thoughts, affects, and memories. As a result, the mind only partially knows itself and its past.

The dissociative damage done by relational trauma often makes people feel worthless, disempowered, and shamed. It confuses people about other people's and their own intentions, and it creates *blame-self* and *blame-other* patterns of thinking. The bulk of therapeutic work is to help clients to demystify and transform interpersonal trauma from unthinkable to thinkable, unknowable to knowable, and unbearable to bearable. Such work helps a person to become able to connect traumas with the rest of experience and then to know that they are past. This happens when these experiences can be shared in a safe relational setting. The crucible of therapeutic action exists, then, not only in the traumatized, dissociative self of the client, but also in the relationship with the therapist.

Trauma and dissociation underpin a cascade of new ways of thinking. We now recognize that trauma is encoded in the body and that trauma is often *unspeakable* until or unless this can be decoded and then symbolized. We understand how trauma impedes the processing of experience into narrative memory. The neurobiological result of trauma is often the sensorimotor, rather than the narrative registration of unendurable experience. Traumas cause emotional dysregulation, bodily dysregulation, and can become blank spaces in the continuity of remembered experience.

Discoveries in neurobiology, in the organization of patterns of physiological, emotional, and mental states of the self (or self-states), and in developmental research have contributed to a model of self that is highly influenced by context, in which unity of self is not taken as a given.

This book discusses different aspects of trauma and dissociation informed psychotherapy in the following chapters.

Chapter 1: How Freud Buried Trauma. By repudiating his earlier seduction theory (a trauma theory) and replacing it with his Oedipal and repression-based theory of psychoanalysis, Freud placed a roadblock in the way of understanding and healing much of human emotional suffering. He turned practitioners' attention away from the trauma thinking that had been explicated by Pierre Janet and that he himself had previously endorsed. Like a modern church that covers over a Greek temple, his new theory of psychoanalysis basically buried the reality of exogenous trauma.

For many psychologically minded people, the 20th century opened with Freud's monumental and elaborate theoretical edifice built on the premise of psychic determinism and repression: Freudian psychoanalysis. This exciting new approach to emotional healing grew in popularity, but Freud's privileging of fantasy over reality, his embrace of his new Oedipal theory, and his for-the-most-part denial of exogenous trauma had consequences: (1) the widespread theoretical and cultural denial of real-life, exogenous trauma in psychoanalysis and the culture at large, and (2) the consequent suffering of many human beings who remained confused about or disbelieved their own experience.

As the 21st century moves forward, trauma and dissociation have become undeniable, and better ways of healing them are increasingly formulated and applied.

Chapter 2: Trauma as Dissociation. This chapter addresses how the meaning of trauma may be understood as *that which causes dissociation*. This conceptualization clarifies the meaning of trauma. It underscores the serious damage that trauma, especially trauma that is early, chronic, and severe, causes to the developing brain and mind, to the capacity to regulate one's own affect, and to the capacity to relate to others. Both the benefits and the harm of dissociation are discussed. Methods of dissociation-informed trauma treatment are discussed.

Chapter 3: The Ubiquity of Trauma and Dissociation. This chapter addresses the ubiquity of trauma and dissociation, as well as the direct and indirect effects on people's minds and bodies. The mind/body link, along with bottom-up and top-down therapies is discussed. The meaning of the prevalence of adverse childhood experiences (ACEs) with relevance to trauma and dissociation is discussed. Trauma is correlated with and predicts physical disease as well, which itself takes a toll on mental health. The chapter also highlights the diagnostic professional confusion about trauma and dissociation.

Chapter 4: The Clinical Dyad as a Wounded Dyad. Given the high prevalence of trauma and dissociation, clinicians themselves are not immune. Despite many years of blindness by mental health professions to the fact that clinicians are part of the treatment they deliver, the profession is beginning to recognize that the medium for the delivery of individual psychotherapy is a *wounded dyad*. Psychotherapy can no longer be adequately compared to a physician treating a disease, to a form of treatment in which both the clinician and the client are absent as people.

In this chapter, I present a clinical vignette that describes an enactment between my client and myself. This enactment concerned ways that each of us had dissociated the meaning of how the client thought about important events in her life. The identification and resolution of this mutual dissociation resulted in increased progress in the therapy.

Chapter 5: Dissociation, Repression, and the Unconscious. This chapter discusses the usage and meaning of the terms, *repression, dissociation*, and *the unconscious*, with an emphasis on their relevance to trauma. Repression and dissociation are explained and differentiated, with case examples. The meaning of the unconscious and subconscious is discussed, and corresponding new categories of the repressed unconscious and the dissociated unconscious are suggested. A case vignette of a client with DID illustrates how dissociative structure works and can be worked with in therapy. Finally, the merits of *inside-out*, as opposed to *outside-in* approaches to psychotherapy work are discussed.

Chapter 6: Disorganized Attachment as Dissociation. Disorganized attachment is described as a major contributing factor to dissociative problems. Attachment dilemmas, dissociative multiplicity, and how alternative behavior systems can be used defensively to stand in for attachment deficits are discussed. The resulting fractured personality organization is the broken psyche of an overwhelmed child. The chapter addresses psychotherapeutic approaches to these dilemmas.

Chapter 7: The Conundrum of Self-Criticism and Self-Attack. This chapter addresses the contribution of attachment dilemmas as they pertain to how people may overly criticize themselves, subject themselves to danger, and fail to adequately value themselves. I examine how different theoretical constructs describe the relationship of attachment dilemmas and self-blame, ranging from Ferenczi's identification with the aggressor, to Fairbairn's internal saboteur, to Freud's superego, to the impact of shame. Case examples illustrate ways of dealing with these dilemmas.

Chapter 8: Structural Models of the Psychological Organization of a Traumatized Person. This chapter describes different structural models of the dissociated psyche. A common aspect of these models is that the posttraumatic personality is structured around dissociated traumatic experiences. They have a common emphasis on the exile of the traumatic experience into dissociated parts of the self. They differ in the precise form of the sequestration and in the contents of what each author considers the most traumatic and potentially traumatizing experiences to be avoided. Yet, an important commonality is that major parts of the self, even though differently described by the different theorists, have their own autobiographical sense of "I."

Chapter 9: Exit From the Closed System as the Therapist Becomes Real. Trauma and dissociation create a closed system, in which internal dividedness replicates the external interpersonal distance between the client and early attachment figures. The important challenge is how to help clients find a way out of the closed system and be able to see their way into trust, relationality, and nurturing interpersonal connections.

Chapter 10: Conclusion: Toward Psychological Healing. This chapter concludes the book with new research and ways of thinking about the traumatized dissociative self and the process of healing. It is suggested that a more apt myth for our time of ubiquitous trauma is that of Osiris. Osiris was the god of the Nile who was cut up (divided) and but pieced back together and brought back to life by the love of his wife Isis. The Osiris myth connotes dissociation and psychological healing. It is contrasted to the famous story of Oedipus, who murdered his father and married his mother, and that is the centerpiece of Freud's psychoanalysis.

But Freud did not include that the story begins with the crime of child sexual abuse. The chapter retells the missing part of the story.

The Osiris myth is a more fitting (and a more hopeful) story for trauma therapy and for our time. The Osiris myth also intersects with the cutting-edge research and thinking of Frank Putnam who, articulating the multiple self model via developmental research, documents the human vulnerability to context-dependence and fragmentation. Putnam's research shows how humans start out life with multiple behavioral states, and how, even though we are often not aware of it, state shifts characterize our lives.

The chapter ends with an illustration from dream work: how a previously hidden, shamed, self-critical, child self-state of a client was contacted, and how healing ensued.

Trauma and
Dissociation Informed
Psychotherapy

CHAPTER 1

How Freud Buried Trauma

Freud sought for, created theories that he hoped would surpass all others and secure his stature in this world as a great man . . . In his self-analysis he discovered—or invented—his Oedipus complex which he instantly promoted to a universal law.

—Louis Breger (2000, p. 3)

CONTRARY TO SOME PUBLIC opinion, Sigmund Freud did not discover the unconscious. The importance and impact of Freud's brilliant and voluminous body of work is undeniable. Freud did *popularize* the concept and scope of unconscious determinism. Through the force of his compelling analyses of problems stemming from unconscious sexuality and aggression; his formulations of repression and of conflict and defense; his opus on dreams, fantasy, symbolization; his formulations of transference, countertransference, and resistance; and much more—along with his ambition and his political canny with respect to having disciples spread the news of his work—he changed the narrative of intellectual and psychological culture for well over a century. The hegemony of Freudian theory also eclipsed the equally important body of knowledge about trauma and dissociation that had preceded him.

Notably, Freud placed a roadblock in the way of understanding and healing much of human emotional suffering when he abandoned his trauma theory and advanced his Oedipal-psychosexual theory. As he marched forward with his discovery of repression, the cornerstone of his overarching theory of the mind, he mostly left by the wayside recognition of trauma and trauma's corollary, dissociation. This had important consequences for psychological theory and for many people's lives for most of the last 100 years.

The Freudian psychoanalytic emphasis on the Oedipal complex, repression, and the unitary unconscious has occluded our being able to think more clearly about the ways that psychodynamics and mental structure are trauma-based and perpetuated by dissociative processes. The question of how this happened and what the broader consequences have been is the subject of this chapter.

Early Studies of Dissociation and the Unconscious

The idea of the unconscious has been present in Western culture for at least five centuries. As early as the 1500s the notable Swiss physician Paracelsus suggested that an "unconscious" could cause disease and used hypnosis therapeutically (Ellenberger, 1970). It was not until the late 1700s, via the discoveries of Franz Anton Mesmer, that a scientific study of "second consciousness" and dissociative phenomena began (Fromm, 1987). Using what he called a "magnetic" method (in current parlance—*hypnosis*), Mesmer demonstrated that he could remove disease symptoms by contacting another state of mind. He and his followers discovered that the induction of "magnetic sleep," or hypnosis, could elicit the appearance of "a (new) personality, with a continuous life of its own" of which the subject was unaware (Ellenberger, 1970, p. 145). In the scientific literature on mesmerism, discussion of amnesia and switching between identity states was common (Middleton, Dorahy, & Moskowitz, 2008).

According to the psychiatrist and historian, Henri Ellenberger, "The entire nineteenth century was preoccupied with the problem of the co-existence of these two minds and their relationship to each other" (1970, p. 145). As an example of how familiar and widespread the concept of the unconscious was in the 19th century, Frederick Douglass, the acclaimed orator who had escaped slavery, spoke in 1840 of "unconscious racism." This was 16 years before Sigmund Freud was born in 1856! Clearly, by the late 1800s, when Freud began to write, the intellectual climate in Western culture was rich with the ferment of discoveries about the unconscious.

In particular, knowledge of dissociation and dissociative states of mind became invaluable in the treatment of hysteria, the primary psychological malady of the time. Hysteria included many kinds of psychological distress, such as what today we understand as somatoform disorders; borderline disorders; Posttraumatic Stress Disorder (PTSD); histrionic disorders; chronic and complex trauma disorders and dissociative disorders, including volatile mood states; and switches of identity. A diagnosis primarily applied to women (although there was continued debate about whether men could be hysterics), the term *hysteria* derived from the ancient Greek word, *hystera*, which meant uterus. The early Greek belief was that a wandering uterus caused hysterical symptoms. Even though the medical meaning of hysteria changed over time, it remained a diagnostic term from the 1700s until the late 1900s, when it was eliminated from the *Diagnostic and Statistical Manual*.

In the 1800s in Paris the eminent physician and neurologist Jean Martin Charcot observed "a sudden trauma could evoke a spontaneous hypnotic-like state, during which autosuggestion occurred" (Dell, 2009, p. 727), and he demonstrated that he could produce physical and psychological symptoms with hypnosis. Charcot linked trance states, hypnosis, and the psychological disease of hysteria, but he maintained that there was a physiological basis for hysteria. So compelling were Charcot's experiments that they attracted the interest of a young Sigmund Freud to study in Paris with him, as well as that of his contemporary, Pierre Janet. Janet greatly extended the implications of Charcot's findings through his own work with patients at the Salpêtrière Clinic (where Charcot also worked), outlining in the mid to late 1880s the linkage of trauma, dissociation, and hysteria. Janet described the essence of hysteria succinctly and relevantly to current knowledge of dissociation as *"psychological misery*, i.e. a reduction of the individual's integrative capacity" (Van der Hart, 2016, p. 48), but as also characterized by a retraction of the field of consciousness and highly dissociated states of mind and body. He successfully traced his patients' impaired functionality and great emotional distress to preceding traumatizing events in their lives, which had been dissociated. Thus, for Janet, psychological healing aimed at integrating previously dissociated traumatic experiences with the rest of a person's life.

Pierre Janet's Pioneering Work

Although his body of work has only recently been resurrected (primarily by Henri Ellenberger in 1970 and more recently by Onno van der Hart) in the mental health field, Pierre Janet, Freud's contemporary and predecessor, was a well-known and highly respected clinician and writer in his time. Predating Freud, Janet emphasized the importance and impact of forgotten trauma, as well as the idea of unconscious (or "sub-conscious," in Janet's terminology) determinism. As his early publications on hysteria (1885, 1886, 1887, 1888, 1889) preceded Freud's by a few years, he was the first to explain the linkage of trauma and dissociation and apply this linkage in detail to the understanding and treatment of hysteria. Janet was also the first to codify a psychodynamic depth psychology. His descriptions of how dissociated parts of the mind interact with each other constitute a theory of psychodynamics. Janet also documented how he used catharsis therapeutically (Van der Hart & Friedman, 1989, 2019).

Called "the founding father of the field of posttraumatic stress" (van der Hart, 2016, p. 44), Janet described what we now call PTSD, and he originated the still state-of the-art, phase-oriented trauma treatment.

The key premise of Janet's trauma and dissociation theory is the basis of trauma theory today: when people are overwhelmed by what he termed vehement, often terrifying emotions, they cannot assimilate or link the experience with the rest of their personal history. The overwhelming experience of trauma interrupts the coherence of experience, such that the synthesizing functions of the psyche fail.

Janet described how extremely heightened emotional arousal, often today thought of as *hyperarousal*, impedes the integration of traumatic memories, separating them from conscious awareness. Aspects of these traumatic memories contribute to what he called subconscious "fixed ideas," which are dissociated fragments of past experience that are irrelevant to the present. The cause of these fixed ideas, which can powerfully organize symptoms, is usually a traumatic event that the mind cannot assimilate. Because they are not available to consciousness, these dissociated fixed ideas can be triggered intruding into consciousness and influencing behavior and thought. In his linkage of traumatic residues to fixed ideas and to multiple, subconscious centers of experience (which, unaware of each other, often conflict with one another), Janet described their psychodynamic power (Janet, 1889, 1907, 1925; Van der Hart, 2016; Van der Kolk & Van der Hart, 1989).

Janet has also been called the grandfather of body psychotherapy (Boadella, 2011, cited in Ogden [2019]). His cases demonstrated how traumatic memories are encoded and stored in the body and how these traumatic memories contain sensorimotor and affective components. Janet described how in sensorimotor difficulties such as vision or speech the "subconscious and automatic motion is retained, whereas the voluntary motion is lost" (Janet, 1907, p. 206).

Especially relevant to today's somatic therapies and current neuroscience is Janet's explanation of how motor and mental actions that could not be completed in a traumatizing event result in symptomatology: "Such patients . . . are continuing the action, or rather the attempt at action, which began when the thing happened; and they exhaust themselves in these everlasting recommencements" (Janet, 1925, p. 663). Patients are subconsciously attempting to complete the action that belongs to and was intended to resolve a past traumatizing event. However, the overwhelming trauma prevented the possibility of a competent completion that would yield a sense of triumph, and this failure *to complete the action* generates exhaustion and a loss of will. Rather than being able to prevail, escape, or otherwise "perform any of the actions characteristic of the stage of triumph" (1925, p. 669), they are stuck in a psychobiological state of submission, exhaustion, or collapse. Current clinicians such as Bessel van der Kolk, Peter Levine, Babette Rothschild, and Pat Ogden have advanced popular therapeutic methods for helping traumatized people *to complete the action*—thereby regaining a feeling of effective action—and to integrate the trauma into autobiographical memory.

Studies on Hysteria

When Josef Breuer and his protégé, the young Sigmund Freud, wrote *Studies on Hysteria* (1893–95), they were writing in terms of concepts of dissociation that were currently in use at that time. As had Janet, they articulated a trauma theory and therapy based on the concept of a secondary consciousness. In *Studies on Hysteria*, Breuer and Freud presented their understanding of and methods for alleviating the symptoms and distress of hysteria. Notably, in their "Preliminary Communication," the first chapter of *Studies*, they linked these symptoms to dissociation, to the existence of a "second consciousness":

> The longer we have been occupied with these phenomena, the more we
> have become convinced that *the splitting of consciousness which is so strik-*
> *ing in the well-known classical cases under the form of "double conscience"*
> [footnote: the French term "dual consciousness"] *is present to a rudimen-*
> *tary degree in every hysteria, and that a tendency to such a dissociation, and*

with it the emergence of abnormal states of consciousness (which we shall bring together under the term, "hypnoid") is the basic phenomenon of this neurosis. (Breuer & Freud, 1893–95, p. 12, italics in the original)

Emphasizing the importance of this dissociation, Breuer and Freud stated that "the basis and *sine qua non*" (without which not) of hysteria is "the existence of hypnoid [dissociative] states" (p. 12). (*Hypnoid states* was a term that Breuer adopted from Charcot [Breger, 2000], referring to somnambulistic, trance states.) Hypnoid states are characterized by intense ideation that is cut off from the rest of consciousness, similar to hypnosis. Linking trauma, dissociation, and hysteria, the authors stated that behind the symptoms was a trauma. Breuer and Freud stated that the hysterical symptoms corresponded to traumatic memories that had become pathological because they had been cut off from associational contact with the rest of consciousness and had been "denied the normal wearing-away processes by means of abreaction and reproduction in states of uninhibited association" (Breuer & Freud, 1893–95, p 11). They announced the cure they found: remembrance and abreaction. Symptoms were healed when the memory of the trauma could be discharged, abreacted, in words or action, or both. When the "strangulated affect" (p. 17) of the idea "can find its way out through speech" (p. 17), it can be associated with the rest of consciousness and the symptoms recede.

The central case history of *Studies* was of Breuer's patient, Anna O., whose real name was Bertha Pappenheim. In fact, in these early years (1893–95) Freud credited Breuer for the beginnings of psychoanalysis on the basis of his understanding of Anna O.'s dissociative symptoms. In response to Breuer's intense, caring, listening, and collaborative presence (Breger, 2011), this highly intelligent, highly disturbed, and highly dissociative patient developed "the talking cure" which she called "chimney sweeping" (Breuer & Freud, 1893–95, p. 30), of the mind. Her traumatizing family relationships that were too painful for her conscious awareness could only be expressed symptomatically, somatically, and symbolically: "By helping her put her affectively charged experience into words, Breuer reversed the process, making conscious what had up to that point been kept out of awareness" (Breger, 2011, p. 36). Anna O. probably had dissociative identity disorder (DID); she exhibited different identity states that were amnestic for each other and in which she spoke different languages, such as English, German, and French. While she was ill, she had complained to Breuer that she had "two selves, a real one, and an evil one" (Breuer & Freud (1893–95, p. 24). Despite its difficulty, Breuer's treatment of Bertha Pappenheim (Anna O.) was a highly successful trauma treatment. Pappenheim went on to become a powerful social worker. She was active in furthering women's rights and in aiding women who were victims of prostitution.

According to Louis Breger (2000, 2011), it was Breuer's collaborative work with this patient that provided the most formative and ultimately most useful ideas for the theory that Freud later claimed as psychoanalysis: "Throughout his work with Bertha, Breuer developed two concepts that became staples of psychoanalysis: the unconscious mind and the symbolic expression of psychological conflicts" (Breger, 2011, p. 35). Breger (2011) adds, "Work in the last thirty to forty years reveals that, in large measure, Breuer's ideas were more valid than Freud's" (p. 118). Ironically, this early period in which dissociation was so prominently studied and which was the birthplace of psychoanalysis was retrospectively called the *pre-psychoanalytic* period by Freud and his followers (Davies, 1996).

According to Michael Fitzgerald (2017), "Pierre Janet and Joseph Breuer were the true originators of psychoanalysis. Freud greatly elaborated on their findings. Freud initially admitted these facts but denied them in later life" (p. 358). Noting the similarities between Janet's concepts and those of Freud, such as Janet's "function of reality" and Freud's "reality principle," Ellenberger (p. 539), wrote: "Indeed, it is difficult to study the initial periods of Janet's psychological analysis and Freud's psychoanalysis without coming to the conclusion expressed by Regis and Hesnard, that 'the methods and concepts of Freud were modeled after those of Janet, of whom he seems to have inspired himself constantly until the paths of the two diverged' "(p. 539–540).

After their paths diverged, the weight and popularity of Freud's brilliant and grand sweeping theories, in which he used myth and metaphor so skillfully, along with Freud's abilities as a multilingual empire builder, had the effect of burying much of the earlier emphasis on dissociation and Janet's important work. Ellenberger compared Janet's work to the ancient city of Pompeii, covered by volcanic ashes: "The fate of any buried city is uncertain. It may remain buried forever. It may remain concealed while being plundered by marauders. But it may perhaps also be unearthed someday and brought back to life" (p. 409).

Freud Identifies Child Sexual Abuse as the Cause of Hysteria

In *Studies on Hysteria*, Breuer and Freud (1893–95) said that although they had found the cure for hysteria, they had not discovered its etiology. Soon after the publication of *Studies,* in a new paper, "The Aetiology of Hysteria" (1896/1962), Freud stated that he had found the original cause of hysteria: child sexual abuse. He was so sure of himself that he referred to his discovery as the *"caput Nili "* (the head of the Nile) in neuropathology (Freud, 1896/1962, p. 203). As Peter Gay (1988) put it, this discovery was for Freud, "the solution of a thousand-year-old problem the source of the Nile" (p. 93). Freud wrote that "Sexual experiences in childhood consisting of stimulation of the genitals, coituslike acts, and so on, must therefore be recognized, in the last analysis, as being the traumas which led to a hysterical reaction to events at puberty and the development of hysterical symptoms" (pp. 206–207). Freud (1896/1962) was clear and passionate in his exposition of his discovery that the original cause of hysteria was sexual abuse by a relative or trusted caretaker:

For the idea of these infantile sexual scenes is very repellent to the feelings of a sexually normal individual; they include all the abuses known
to debauched and impotent persons, among whom the buccal [inside
the mouth] cavity and the rectum are misused for sexual purposes . . .
on the one hand, the adult . . . who is armed with complete authority
and the right to punish . . . and on the other hand, the child, who in
his helplessness is at the mercy of this arbitrary will, who is prematurely
aroused to every kind of sensibility . . . all these grotesque and yet tragic
consequences reveal themselves as stamped upon the later development
of the individual and of his neurosis, in countless permanent effects.
(pp. 214–225)

Freud stated that he had successfully traced back the symptoms to
sexual abuse in 18 patients and that he had corroborated it in 2 of them.
In my view, Freud's presentation of this formulation was courageous:
his thinking was taking him toward the identification and potential
accountability of sexual perpetrators. Did he not surmise, on some level,
that the supposedly upstanding abusing parties, whether fathers, family
friends, or relatives of these patients, would not be pleased? Or was his
passion and pride in his discovery more important?

The New Narrative: Psychosexual and Oedipal Theory

The answer is not clear. Within less than a year and a half, after the
presentation of "The Aetiology of Hysteria" (1896/1962), Freud dramatically changed his views of the child's dilemma. He switched course,
abandoned what has been called his *seduction theory*, and replaced it
with his new psychosexual and Oedipal theories, neither of which had
corroboration in real life.

Many reasons have been offered for Freud's change of position. Freud,
himself (1896/1962), felt that his formulation presented in "The Aetiology of Hysteria" had been ill-received and that when he confronted

them with "the truth," his peers abandoned him. He wrote to his friend, Fliess, that the "donkeys gave it an icy reception" (p. 189). Several weeks later, he wrote again to Fliess, saying, "The word has been given out to abandon me, and a void is forming around me" (Masson, 1984, p. 10). However, according to Ellenberger (1970) "in the literature of that time no expression of hostility is to be found" (p. 490).

In the intervening 17 months between Freud's presentation and change of course, his father died, and his letters to Fleiss indicated that he thought his own father might have molested his siblings (Masson, 1984). Among the official views that Freud gave for abandoning his formulation was that given the numbers of hysterics, there just couldn't be that many perpetrators: "in all cases, the father, not excluding my own, had to be accused of being perverse" (Masson, 1985, p. 231, quoted in Brothers, 1995, p.8). Freud was probably unaware of the extent to which many sexual perpetrators tend to have multiple victims, sometimes even in the thousands (Salter, 2003), and that therefore there is not a one-to-one correspondence between numbers of perpetrators and victims.

Many have weighed in on the reasons for Freud's change of direction, including aspects of Freud's own internal conflicts (Breger, 2000, 2011; Brothers, 1995; Davies and Frawley, 1994; Freyd, 1996; Gay, 1988; Kupersmid, 1993; Ahbel-Rappe, 2006; Pines, 1989; Salyard, 1988; Tabin, 1993). At best, the reasons appear to have been complicated. Even Jeffrey Masson, author of *Assault on the Truth*, who had access to the Freud archives, could not give a simple and clear-cut answer. Nonetheless, after reading Freud's letters, Masson (1985) believed that the seduction theory was correct and suggested that Freud changed his theory for reasons of fear of social unacceptability.

Continuing to endorse his seduction theory might well have thwarted Freud's professional ambition. Both Fitzgerald (2017) and Breger (2001, 2011) have independently noted that, even as a young adult, Freud had a thirst for fame and envisioned himself as a hero. Gay (1988) noted that the midwife at his birth predicted to his mother that her son, Sigmund, would be a great man because he was born in a caul (a piece of the amniotic sac attached to the newborn's head or face, often believed to be a sign of specialness). Breger (2000) suggests that Freud's need to undo his own early traumas, including the economic humiliation of his father's business failures, along with the rampant anti-Semitism with which he had to cope, influenced his need to place his stamp on history as the conquistador of the human mind. "As Freud's drive for fame grew, he needed a single, overarching law to fulfill his wish to be a great man, and he fastened on sexual conflict and the Oedipus complex" (Breger, 2011, p. 100). Coincidentally, and, perhaps, conveniently, this new theory repudiated the earlier seduction theory, which was henceforth mostly unavailable for further examination, elaboration, and correction.

In his new theory, Freud replaced the formulation presented in "The Aetiology of Hysteria," that sexual *traumas* were repressed, with the formulation that sexual and Oedipal *wishes* were repressed. With almost surgical severance, he reversed his earlier conviction about the trauma of child sexual abuse and instead linked the symptoms of neurosis to internal conflicts about fantasied and wished for sexual relations with the parent of the other sex. (Although Freud did at various points allow that childhood sexual abuse can occur and can have lasting damaging effects, he viewed this as more of an anomaly than the norm.[1]) Now the cause of neurotic symptoms was endogenous (generated from the inside), initiated by the child's own fantasy, rather than having been caused by exogenous (external) trauma.

Effects of the "Either/Or" Polarization Regarding Sexual Trauma

By first saying that sexual trauma is the root cause of all hysteria and then saying that in most cases it did not happen at all—that, instead, the child wished for sexual relations with the parent—Freud's self-contradictions lead to a false dichotomy for the issue of trauma: Did the sexual abuse happen or did it not happen? This preoccupation had the effect of diverting attention away from the importance of the general reality of exogenous trauma, sexual or otherwise. Freud was wrong in saying that child sexual abuse is the source of hysteria because by saying so he was diverting attention away from other serious traumatic experiences, such as attachment trauma, developmental trauma, other forms of relational trauma, natural disasters, war, famine, and more, as well as combinations of all of these. Unfortunately, the highly charged argument about the primacy of sexual abuse as the sole cause of the symptoms of hysteria created a polarization such that trauma and dissociation as the actual and fundamental cause of such symptoms was overlooked.

The following section on Holocaust trauma vividly illustrates this point.

Holocaust Trauma Overshadowed by Oedipus

During and in the wake of World War II many of Freud's followers became more doctrinaire and less receptive to traumatizing realities because of the need to preserve the psychoanalytic movement in the face of Nazi threats (Kuriloff, 2013). In a way that may seem at first counterintuitive, rigidified adherence to Oedipal doctrine contributed to an odd form of Holocaust denial. During the Holocaust in Germany and Austria, as psychoanalytic institutes were taken over by the dogma of the Nazi regime and as Jewish members were expelled or murdered, psychoanalytic teachings were endangered (Kuriloff, 2013). Emigrating Freudian psychoanalysts understandably felt the need to preserve the status quo of theory. Tragically, though, for many, their own experiences of the Holocaust had often been so unendurable that they were dissociated and unavailable to integration. Unable to process their own traumas, many of these analysts were unable to do this for their patients or to revise their theories (Kuriloff, 2013). According to Dori Laub, who cofounded what are now the Fortunoff Archives of Holocaust Testimony at Yale University, "Among the immigrant psychoanalysts, many who had fled from the terrors of the Holocaust, Orthodoxy became an armor, the theory became their armor, to leave no opening for some memory, some recognition of what had happened to creep in" (cited by Kuriloff, 2013, p. 43).

In a moving roundtable discussion titled *"Last Witnesses: Child Survivors of the Holocaust,"* four psychotherapists, Dori Laub, Sophia Richman, Clem Lowe, and Eva Metzger Brown described how their experiences as children during the Holocaust affected their lives and their own analyses (see Brown et al., 2007). The general theme was that their analysts were more interested in their Oedipal complexes than in the terrifying and traumatic experiences they had endured and that had severely damaged them. As Clem Lowe, stated, "For many of us, the event of the Holocaust was not really important [to our early analysts]" (Brown et al., 2007, p. 32). Sophia Richman, another Roundtable member, said of her first analyst:

> What he wanted to focus on was Oedipal issues. And I talked about my [Holocaust] experience but I talked about it in a very detached way. I was really in a very dissociated state, without realizing that that's what it was. I would talk about it very mechanically, like these were the facts, this is what happened, this is my childhood. But there was no feeling. I was like a robot . . . And he . . . wasn't able to do anything with that. (p. 33)

The stories abound of how doctrinaire psychoanalysts could not help their patients who were Holocaust survivors because they were blinded by the theory of Oedipus. Perhaps if there had not been such a polarization about sexual abuse, which had the effect of diverting attention from exogenous trauma, the horrific traumas that these survivors experienced and reported would have been easier to recognize.

Further Consequences of the New Narrative: The Client's Self-Blame

Freud established a new narrative of the progression—and meaning of that progression—of human life. In the new narrative, incestuous desires made the child become the guilty culprit rather than the victim. This not only completely reversed his earlier formulation about child abuse, but it changed the narrative about the mind that had been emerging at that time, such that recognition of the impact of trauma and dissociation was largely eclipsed. Oddly, Freud's highly diminished attention to exogenous trauma did to the history of the knowledge of the mind what trauma itself does to human memory: it left a blank spot surrounded by incoherent pieces of knowledge and a multitude of incomprehensible broken shards of experience.

Freud's repudiation of his earlier formulation that child sexual abuse is the *cause of hysteria,* along with the consequent polarization of the issue, contributed to too many therapists' disbelief of the real experiences of many patients who had been abused by caregivers. It especially promoted many survivors' disbelief of their own memories and minds. Many of my clients who were sexually abused as children and adolescents have told me that the idea that their own memories are false (according to Freud's Oedipal theory, their memories were false distortions of their wishes) makes them doubt their own minds and has increased their symptoms.

Ratification of the Child's Egocentric Beliefs

Freud's neglect of trauma and dissociation in his new narrative based on the Oedipus complex and psychosexual stages did more than call into question the reality of child sexual abuse by providing an alternative explanation. Not only did people who had suspicions or memories of having been abused doubt themselves. Not only did it make people reluctant to reveal their knowledge of their experiences in a world that would interpret it otherwise. The new theory also had the effect of ratifying the child's own early developmentally appropriate egocentric beliefs and attachment-based psychic defenses against acknowledging their abuse.

As Piaget, who was influenced by Janet's thinking (Ellenberger, 1970), has noted, the preoperational thought of early childhood is not yet logical, nor does it encompass another's point of view. In this developmental period children often think something happened because they caused it. Thus, if they are abused, it is because they did something wrong. If something bad happens, the child made it happen. Add to this that perpetrators often tell children just that: they are being hurt because they have been bad or because they wanted it.

Ratification of Attachment-Based Defenses Against Acknowledging Abuse

Even more importantly, the Oedipal theory of the child's fantasy and wish *ratifies* the child's attachment-based self-blaming defenses. What is a child to do when the abuser and the attachment figure are one and the same? The child preserves attachment (and this enhances sanity and survival) by blaming the self and dissociating the aspects of self that know of or have strong emotions about the abuse. Sándor Ferenczi (1949) described how abused or frightened children preserve the good aspects of the parent or caregiver in consciousness by taking the burden of badness of the aggressor into themselves, thereby maintaining what he called the "situation of tenderness" with the aggressor. In sum, the mind modifies itself with self-blame to accommodate attachment relationships with frightening but needed and usually loved attachment figures.

Thus, when official theory and the abused child's defenses dovetail, we need to be on the lookout for possible iatrogenic effects of such theory. For example, one person I know who was sexually abused as a child and an adolescent renamed herself Kate in her late adolescence, after the play

Kiss Me, Kate (based on Shakespeare's play, *Taming of the Shrew,* about how a husband tames his unsubmissive and cantankerous new wife). Her adoption of the new name suggested that *she* was the one who needed taming, rather than her abusive father. Later, she named her dog (as an object of identification and affection) Electra, after Electra in the Greek play, who murdered her mother. As an intellectual adolescent, she took the Oedipus themes to heart: she was a shrew and a murderess at heart, rather than a victim of her father's inappropriate and callous sexual behavior. (When he was still a member of Freud's inner circle, Carl Jung named the female counterpart of the Oedipus complex the Electra Complex, following from the *Oresteia,* the ancient Greek trilogy of plays by Aeschylus. According to the *Oresteia,* Electra, together with her brother, Orestes, murders their mother, Clytemnestra, to avenge Clytemnestra's murder of her husband (and Electra's and Orestes' father) Agamemnon.) Kate was so caught up in her unconsciously self-blaming myths that she was not able to think clearly about what her father had done to her until middle adulthood. Until then she was unable to understand that her inner world was not just about her feeling of guilt, but that it also involved someone else who had egregiously harmed her.

In the Oedipal Theory There Is No Room for an Abuser

Freud's psychosexual and Oedipal theory does not leave room for the existence of a perpetrator. It is a one-person psychology, focusing primarily on the drives, defenses, and fantasies of the individual. Here the child is the sole guilty one with respect to sexual and aggressive impulses. In contrast, trauma–dissociation theory is a two-person theory that is inherently relational and does leave room for an abuser.

Unfortunately, the Oedipal theory also gives cover to pedophiles. The proposition that children fabricate their memories of abuse was also used in the acquittal of Ernest Jones, Freud's disciple, biographer, and the last remaining member of Freud's secret committee and palace guard.

Jones, who had been previously dismissed from several positions because of allegations of sexual abuse, was brought to trial for sexually abusing children in his care. In this trial, the evidence, including semen stains on a tablecloth, as well as the children's almost identical testimonies, seemed irrefutable, but Jones was acquitted, in part because the children's testimony was not deemed admissible (Kuhn, 2002).

Freud's Neglect of Trauma and Dissociation in His New Narrative Prevented the Development of a Richer Theory

By turning away from the seduction theory, Freud essentially ceased addressing real trauma, but he also reduced the construct of the mind to one consciousness and one unconscious. Although psychoanalysis owes its origins to the study of dualism and multiplicity—for example, Breuer and Freud's (1893–95) early observations of "double consciousness" in hysteria—Freud abandoned this concept, preferring instead that of one *unitary* unconscious. As Grotstein (1999) observed, psychoanalysis has "suffered from Freud's failure to grasp the deeper significance of . . . dual consciousness of dual 'I-ness . . ." (p. 36).

In addition, by turning away from dissociation, Freud prevented himself from developing a more universal and overarching theory—one of repression *and* dissociation, one in which the psyche is structured by the willful defense of repression as well as by dissociation, including both dissociative integrative failure brought on by trauma and dissociation used as a defense. (I discuss these two types of dissociation, as well as repression, in Chapter 5.)

Full Circle and Moving On

When the student, Sigmund Freud, asked his teacher, Martin Charcot, whether his clinical innovations fit with existing theory, Charcot answered: "Theory is good, but it does not prevent things from existing." Charcot's response became one of Freud's favorite quotations, one he even repeated in his eulogy at Charcot's funeral (Freud, 1893, p. 13). This is the spirit of my response to some of Freud's theories: these theories are in many ways good, but this does not prevent other things from existing. Despite Freud's brilliance and monumental discoveries, his exclusive emphasis on the Oedipal complex and repression has too long prevented the recognition of how psychodynamics and mental structure are trauma-based and perpetuated by dissociative processes.

It is as if Freud laid a huge boulder across the flow of a large babbling brook and created a huge reservoir of many, often interconnected, interesting thoughts and theories about the nature, limitations, and prospects of humanity. However, some rivulets from the old brook, which was filled with knowledge and theory about trauma and dissociation, continued on into current history; these rivulets have grown into rivers.

Currently we have cumulative knowledge about war trauma, attachment trauma, and other developmental and relational trauma, the recognition of everyday trauma to women and children (as well as men), and increasing information about how trauma is processed in the brain and encoded in the body.

The symptoms of hysteria, the supposed woman's disease that Janet and the early Freud addressed, emerged in full force among the soldiers of World War I, but the name was changed to *shell shock*. Charles Myers, a World War I physician, psychologist, student of Janet's, and author of *Shell Shock in France, 1914–1918* (1940), observed that recovering wounded soldiers often exhibited two disconnected patterns of behavior. He called these the emotional personality (EP) and the apparently normal personality (ANP). (Myers's observations were later incorporated into Van der Hart, Nijenhuis, and Steele's (2006) "theory of the structural dissociation of the personality," which is addressed in Chapter 8.

After the Vietnam War, with the high numbers of psychologically damaged soldiers returning home, the effect of trauma and traumatic dissociation was undeniable. PTSD became an official psychiatric diagnosis, replacing the earlier terms *shell shock* and *battle fatigue*. With the advent of the Women's Movement, writers such as Laura Brown (1991) and Judith Herman (1992) observed that war-damaged soldiers were not the only traumatized and ravaged victims of harm, but that women and children are traumatized by assault, rape, and child abuse *in a way that is not outside the ordinary*. Soon, the abuse and neglect of children, along with their frequent posttraumatic, somatic, and dissociative consequences, became more accessible to public consciousness, almost a century after Freud's abandonment of his seduction theory.

Current knowledge and theory has resurrected the importance of trauma and dissociation. Well over a century ago, Pierre Janet (1907) wrote of how "vehement emotions" evoked by trauma impede the integration of memory. Because they cannot be integrated, aspects of traumatic memory remain separated from the rest of consciousness; they periodically and seemingly inexplicably intrude into experience as flashbacks, involuntary movements, anxiety, fogginess, or unformulated panic that may be quickly re-dissociated. Today we know much more of how traumatic experience is processed in the brain and how this differs in significant ways from the encoding and integration of nontraumatic experience.

Extending Janet's emphasis on how trauma is encoded in the body was left off, Babette Rothschild (2000) wrote:

> The body remembers traumatic events through the encoding in the brain of sensations, movements, and emotions that are associated with trauma. Healing . . . necessitates attention to what is happening in the body as well as the interpretations being made in the mind. Language bridges the mind/body gap, linking explicit and implicit memories. Somatic memory becomes personal history when the impact of [trauma is]] so weakened

that the events can finally be placed in their proper point in the client's past." (p. 173)

Bessel van der Kolk (2014) has eloquently said, "the body keeps the score." He and others such as Onno van der Hart (2006, 2019), Bruce Perry (1999), Lenore Terr (1990, 1994), Pat Ogden (2019), Ellert Nijenhuis (2000), Babette Rothschild (2000), Peter Levine (1997, 2015), and Robert Scaer (2001) have described the power of somatoform dissociation. They have written of how localized but otherwise inexplicable body pain may be a reexperience of traumatic injury in that very body part. In essence, the trauma prevented the experience from being integrated into narrative memory; hence, the traumatic memory remained encapsulated in unintegrated sensorimotor modalities. Allan Schore (1997, 2003ab, 2009, 2019) has been most notable for his work explaining the links between what we experience and how the brain works, between the phenomenological and the neurological. In Chapter 2, I discuss in more detail how trauma impedes the processing of experience into narrative memory.

Other significant developments have been in the area of the therapeutic relationship. Breuer's success with Anna O. was largely attributable to his interaction with her in the development of what she dubbed "the talking cure" (Breuer & Freud, 1893-95). Our current knowledge of trauma and dissociation has helped us to understand aspects of the therapeutic relationship and the therapist's listening stance in important new ways. We now know how crucial it is to listen for dissociated emotion, along with validating the reality and importance of feelings and emotion. In addition, affect changes are key indicators of dissociated self-states. We are more aware of how profoundly the body holds trauma, and we watch for somatic changes, such as changes in breathing and posture, knowing that we must work with the body and bodily sensations as well as the verbal mind to be effective. Not only do we emphasize verbal interpretation less; but as trauma clinicians, we are cognizant of how interpretations can be experienced as intrusive and unhelpful by the traumatized client. And, finally, trauma therapists are acutely aware of the necessity of the client's feeling of safety in the relationship. All of these are necessary for healing, including the work of memory integration and mourning. The latter includes not only the traumas themselves, but also ways that the client was harmed or may have harmed others that resulted from the traumas.

CHAPTER 2

Trauma as Dissociation

Trauma has been and continues to be at the epicenter of human experience.

—Peter Levine (2015, xix)

TRAUMA AND DISSOCIATION ARE part of who we are; they are embedded in all of our lives. Trauma alters for the worse the mind, the brain, and the body. From early on in people's lives, trauma, stress hormones, and dissociation influence and organize our bodies and minds. The severity, chronicity, and timing of when traumas occur in our lives affect the neurobiological organisms that we are, influencing the endocrine system, the immune system, the gastrointestinal system, the cardiovascular system, and the nervous system, all of which are intertwined and influence each other. Trauma is directly and indirectly intertwined with dissociation. The hardest thing to really know about trauma and dissociation is that they are not just another thing—not added in, not just add-on concepts.

To see how dissociation is embedded in our lives, let's look at our everyday language, which reveals common aspects of divisions in the experience of self. People say that they are, or someone else is, "coming unglued," "beside myself," "in a state," or "falling apart." Often people are exhorted to "pull (themselves) together," implying that parts of the self are separated and not working together. Or, more positively, one might say something like, "She brings out the best part of me." This linguistic evidence often goes unnoticed as dissociation.

What is dissociation? Dissociation means dis-associating, making and keeping apart things that would normally be connected. Dissociation is both a process and a structure. As a process, dissociation refers to a variety of things, such as hypnosis, the absorption of getting lost in a book or movie, going into a trance, or blocking out emotion in overwhelming, stressful circumstances. As a structure, dissociation refers to ways that experiences, including emotion, thought and memory, become walled off and inaccessible to each other and to the rest of the self. Dissociated parts of the self, or dissociated self-states, can exert powerful, but often hidden forces on thought and behavior that is often inexplicable to the consciously experiencing self.

In many ways, dissociation is hidden. It is often hard to notice in others and even more so in ourselves. In peri-traumatic dissociation (the dissociation that occurs around the time of the trauma and right after) one may become blank and hazy at the time and then later become unclear about and perhaps not remember the things, or all the things that happened. Sándor Ferenczi (1949) described how the victims of childhood abuse go into a trance and become "automata" and robotic. When some reminder of a trauma appears—or another similar trauma occurs—a similar haze may emerge, and it may be so rapid that one just lets it pass unnoticed. This may then create a kind of blank space in memory and emotions, including deficits in the ability to recognize, process, and regulate emotions, leading to a profound lack of knowledge about ourselves. In effect, there is lack of awareness of what we don't understand; if we don't remember, then we can't remember what we don't remember.

Trauma creates gaps in how experience, memory, emotions, and bodily feelings are usually knit together. An analogy might be a hole in your sweater. The connecting threads of the fabric that were knit together are gone in a certain place. They don't support and intertwine with each other anymore. You have to be careful, because further stress on the fabric might tear the hole further, causing more threads to unravel. Trauma causes the disassociation of things that should be connected. It is hard for people to be aware of an image, emotion, thought, or memory that is not available to consciousness, even though it should be. It is hard to know about this lack of connection, often including amnesia—unless there is some corroborating evidence for missing memories from another person or other environmental evidence. How does this come about? What is trauma?

What Is Trauma?

Trauma to the body means, literally, a wound. Even though there are similarities, trauma to the mind is more complex. Currently, the word *trauma* is used in so many different ways and sometimes so profligately that its meaning is in danger of being lost. As just one example, sometimes the words *abuse* and *trauma* are used interchangeably. Abuse is not always overwhelming or traumatic, but it often is.

Trauma studies have proliferated, and are now much a part of our discourse, but there is a lack of clarity about the definition of trauma itself. We speak of early trauma and later trauma, cumulative trauma, relational trauma, and developmental trauma. We speak of "big T" trauma and "little t" trauma (Shapiro, 2001), and of massive and everyday trauma. Psychological trauma overwhelms a person's orientation to a former reality, installing instead its own brutal and fear-based rules. Trauma overwhelms what a person's mind can comprehend. It makes one's sense of self, of subjectivity, irrelevant to its powerful sweep. As David Spiegel (1990) vividly contextualized the meaning of trauma:

Trauma can be understood as the experience of being made into an object; the victim of someone else's rage, of nature's indifference, or of one's own psychical and psychological limitations. Along with the pain and fear associated with rape, combat trauma, or natural disaster comes a marginally bearable sense of helplessness, a realization that one's own will and wishes become irrelevant to the course of events, leaving either a view of the self that is damaged; contaminated by humiliation, pain and fear that the event imposed; or a fragmented sense of self. (p. 251)

In traumatic experiences, key processes that affect the well-being and the functioning of a person have markedly changed. As Richard Chefetz (2015) states:

Traumatic experience has occurred when there has been sudden or cumulative experience that alters the developmental trajectory of an individual through changes in the organization or constitution of their self-states, the ability to have emotional experience, the capacity to think and balance associative and dissociative processes, the capacity to live in relationship with self and others, and the maintenance of an enduring sense of self, all of which is reflected in altered neurobiological function (p. 191).

One Person's Trauma Equals Another Person's Distress

How is trauma measured and observed? In an effort to identify experiences or events that would be objectively considered to be traumatic, the current *Diagnostic and Statistical Manual of Mental Disorders, Fifth Edition, DSM-5;* 2013, American Psychological Association, pp. 271), provides specific requirements for Criterion A, the stressor event of Posttraumatic Stress Disorder (PTSD), that is, the trauma. These include personal direct exposure to a life-threatening event or to the death or threat of death of a close friend or relative, serious injury to the self or to a loved one; indirect exposure (in the sense of learning that a close friend or close relative was exposed to trauma); or repeated indirect exposure to frightening and aversive aspects of a trauma. The *DSM-5* definition does not include indirect exposure through media such as television or other media platforms.

However, reliance on objective criteria fails when we consider certain kinds of interpersonal experiences that do not include exposure to death or violent injury. For example, mortification by shaming or bullying that is a far cry from the atrocities of war, or the horror of a massive natural disaster, can cause so much hyperarousal that the brain cannot process the events and lead to neurological damage (Teichner, et al., 2003). There is also the issue of cumulative trauma, of a cascade of destabilizing experiences that build on each other, each amplifying the effect of the last. As Chefetz notes, "a sledgehammer will drive a nail into a piece of wood in one powerful blow, and it's also true that a thousand small blows will drive that nail just as deep." (personal communication, May, 2015).

Another notable problem with the *objective* view of trauma is the issue of resilience. Not everyone is affected in the same way by the same objectively measured event. Some seem to weather relatively unscathed the same events that overwhelm others, causing posttraumatic stress. Furthermore, those who are less resilient may be seeing the experience through the lens of a past trauma. As a result, many trauma experts prefer to define as traumatic that which is overwhelming to the individual or to the individual's defenses.

Others dispute the subjective approach, noting that without an objective measure of trauma, anything that is merely upsetting might be described as traumatic. One unfortunate result of this dilemma is that the current connotations of the word include both of these highly different meanings, referring either to an objectively catastrophic event or to something that feels subjectively very upsetting. Such overinclusiveness then can drain the word of any meaningful specificity.

Clearly, trauma is not an *event*; rather, it is about how a person processes the event. Can we get more specific? I have proposed a definition of trauma that transcends objective and subjective: *trauma is that which causes dissociation,* that is, it causes a blank spot or fissure in experience, causing a deficit in the ability to regulate affect and to make sense of things. This conceptualization has the advantage of bypassing debates about the meaning of objectively defined trauma (which does not result in posttraumatic stress to all of those exposed to it) and subjective trauma (which can run the risk of categorizing anything that is distressing as traumatic) (Howell, 2005).

Recently, Moskowitz, Heinimaa, and Van der Hart (2019), have proposed a similar definition of trauma, as an ongoing "inability to integrate the implications of an event into the existing conceptions of oneself and the world." Their definition is similar to mine in its emphasis on the unassimilability of the traumatic event. One cannot comprehend or make personal meaning of the event, causing a separation of ideations, affects, and somatic reactions. To me, this implies that trauma is something that causes dissociation.

Psychological trauma is overwhelming and cannot be assimilated in the mind. The traumatic experience has torn the fabric of understanding. If the experience cannot be assimilated, it cannot be effectively linked with other experience, even if it is not forgotten. For example, Jane was in a terrifying taxi accident with her young child. Describing her experience she said, "I suffered from severe shock after that accident. Although I remember it all, I thought we were going to die three times in less than a minute. Time slowed down. I was not thinking well afterward. After the initial shock wore off, I was easily triggered. I often found myself slamming on the imaginary brake on the passenger side of a car. I had PTSD symptoms and unresolved emotional distress for nearly a year." Jane remembered what had happened, but for a long time the fear remained in her body although the threat had passed.

The definition of trauma as *that which causes dissociation* holds true across circumstances. An experience is traumatic if it is overwhelming enough to cause a break in the linkage and meaning of experience, in narrative memory, and even in body processing. When an event cannot be assimilated into the rest of the experiencing self, it becomes, as Pierre Janet so well described, a *fixed idea* that is isolated and disconnected from the rest of the self. When the traumatic event cannot be linked with other experience, a dissociation, whether small or large, results (Van der Hart, Nijenhuis, Steele & Brown, 2004). The definition is not circular because dissociation does not require trauma. Dissociation is the larger category, including adaptive processes, such as hypnosis and absorption.

My definition of trauma also helps us to understand how the compassionate presence of another person contributes to resilience. The availability of a trusted other, such as an attachment figure, friends, or a therapist, can effectively widen a person's window of tolerance (Ogden, Minton, & Pain, p. 27) by bearing part of the burden of knowing. This makes the potential traumatic result of a dissociative process less overwhelming and less likely to result in structural dissociation. For example, a girl who was sexually molested by a babysitter told her mother. Her mother hugged and comforted her and took appropriate measures against the molester. The girl suffered relatively few traumatic aftereffects because she did not have to bear and process it alone. Similarly, Dori Laub, who founded the Fortunoff Archives of Holocaust Studies, survived the Holocaust with his mother, who in that setting behaved like a lioness protecting her young (Laub, 2015). He certainly did not escape unscathed, but he escaped with his mind and his heart. He kept a feeling of vitality, and the ability to create meaning and purpose from his experience. In contrast, his mother, who had no one protecting her, was much more emotionally damaged.

Trauma, Dissociation, and Memory

Trauma that is early, severe, and chronic has profound effects on development. It affects brain structure and creates dissociative experiences and psychic fragmentation. Massive terror and massive releases of stress hormones can be devastatingly overwhelming to a person, derailing a sense of psychic equilibrium and sense of self in time. In short, trauma interferes with the registration and consolidation of experience into narrative memory. But this is a complex matter. Trauma results in curious ways of forgetting, remembering, and distorting. As Judith Alpert notes: "When does the 'forgetting' of trauma begin? For some, the unbearable horror is expunged instantly. In fact, it never enters consciousness. Nevertheless, it continues to haunt. For others, the 'forgetting' happens slowly over time"(Alpert, 2001, p. 731–732).

Narrative memory accommodates to new information, attitudes, and context. As a result, it changes somewhat over time. In contrast, because it is dissociated and not linked with ongoing experience, traumatic memory is basically static. Thus, to refer to traumatic experiences as *memory* might be a misnomer (Janet, 1925), even though it might also be the best term we have.

Traumatic experiences are processed differently in the brain. They manifest themselves in procedural and somatosensory modalities, rather than primarily in narrative and declarative memory (Courtois, 1999, 2004; Courtois & Ford, 2009; Chefetz, 2015; Levine, 1997, 2015; Ogden, Minton & Pain, 2006; Scaer, 2001; Terr, 1994; Van der Kolk, 1996, 2014).

Declarative memory (also called explicit memory) is memory for facts and events. Autobiographical or narrative memory is a kind of declarative memory. Declarative memory is contrasted to procedural or implicit memory, which involves motor skills, habits, conditioned emotional responses, and the *how to* (e.g., "I know how to ride a bike, how to stay balanced, and so on"). This implicit knowledge is hard to put into the language of facts.

What happens in the brain in trauma is that extremely high levels of emotional arousal lead to inadequate processing in the hippocampus, which is involved in the organization and integration of experience, thereby contributing to narrative memory. Sensory information is first partially processed in the thalamus and then passed to the amygdala, which is involved in evaluating emotion. The amygdala passes this emotionally evaluated information on to areas in the brain stem (that transform the information into hormones and emotional signals) and then to the hippocampus. The intensity of emotional arousal varies with the strength of the signal from the amygdala which affects the accuracy of hippocampal memory consolidation. Up until a certain point, the stronger the emotional signal from the amygdala, the better hippocampal consolidation into declarative memory will be. However, when the signal from the amygdala is too strong, the integrative function of the hippocampus fails and memories are stored in affect states and nonintegrated sensory modalities such as somatic sensations, visual images, and audible and haptic sensations. As Van der Kolk has noted: "The experience is laid down and later retrieved in isolated images, bodily sensations, smells and sounds that feel alien and separate from other life experiences. Because the hippocampus has not played its usual role . . .these fragments continue to lead an isolated existence Traumatic memories are timeless and ego-alien" (1996, p. 295).

When affective arousal is so high as to be unbearable, the brain shuts down its sympathetic activation, and a dissociative process ensues (Schore, 2009). That is when we see the blank stares on traumatized peoples' faces. When such dissociative processes result in amnesia, there is a fissure in memory and experience, and the traumatic experience lives on in dissociated self-states.

Because dissociated experience has been separated from some other aspects of self-experience and knowledge and does not join in the ongoing streams of narrative memory, its emergence may often be in the form of an intrusion. It is not just discrete memories that are dissociated. Pieces of living experience, including affect, are dissociated. The neurobiological result is often the sensorimotor, rather than narrative, registration of the unendurable experience, although, of course, sensorimotor registration and narrative memory may occur together in cases of unresolved emotional distress. This lack of assimilation results in vulnerability to flashbacks as well as a deficit in narrative memory with regard to the event: "Thus, the core pathology of PTSD is that certain sensations or emotions related to traumatic experiences are dissociated, keep returning in unbidden ways, and do not fade with time" (Van der Kolk, 2002, p. 383).

Even when an event emerges in startling clarity in a flashback, it may be expressed in a sensory way that has no current context and may not be immediately understandable. For example, when Janice began therapy with me, her former therapist told me that he suspected she might have been sexually abused in childhood. I did not directly inquire about it with her, but after she had achieved a sense of safety with me in our work, she began to have ominously toned dream images about a shed in the woods. Then she began to have conscious waking anxiety-arousing intrusive images of squirrels scampering about in the shed. This was followed by dream images of male sexual genitalia. Finally, after two years of our work together, she began to experience full-fledged terrifying flashbacks. In one, she saw herself as a child, being raped from behind by her father, her body completely limp. She went through a period of terror. Once she hallucinated her father's presence in my office. She saw him standing right beside my chair. She asked me in her terror if he was really there—did I see him? I told her that I did not see him, that she was having a flashback. In one way she realized that he wasn't really there, but in another way, the terror she felt was almost overwhelming: she had a foot in the present, even though she was experiencing the past as if it were happening in the present. The hallucination was a fragment of past experience intruding into the present as a dissociated self-state. When she was able to allow herself to stay with these intrusive, dissociated sensory experiences as part of what her life had been—as an aspect of the past—without being overwhelmed and retraumatized in the present, they began to fade. As she spoke more about it, the sexual abuse became more and more integrated into narrative memory. Although she felt shattered by the knowledge, in another way she felt more whole because more of her was integrated. She knew more and more things made sense. Because of her personal courage that allowed her to experience her flashbacks and the overwhelming emotions accompanying them, the formerly dissociated events became better known to her in personal autobiographical memory. The flashbacks became rare rather than frequent because she now understood, accepted the information, and became able to tolerate the emotion.

Even though reclaiming the horrifying dissociated experiences was highly painful and disorganizing for Janice, previous to therapy the PTSD intrusions had caused extreme ongoing pain, and her amnesia had seriously disrupted her ability to lead her life. This does not gainsay what a blessing her dissociative capacity was when her traumas began. It allowed her to go on functioning as a child and adolescent and gain a foothold on adulthood without experiencing a devastating loss of function.

Benefits of the Capacity to Dissociate

Dissociation is a normal and useful capacity of mind and can often be highly beneficial. The very abilities to focus attention, to separate figure from ground, and to engage in deep states of concentration such as absorption are manifestations of dissociative capacities on which we all rely. Most likely an evolutionary survival capacity (Dell, 2009), dissociation has served human beings across time and cultures, from dissociative trances in ritual ceremonies and shamanistic rites of healing, to experiences of spirit possession, and to personal mystical experiences of intense absorption and transformation (Ellenberger, 1970; Hilgard, 1977 James, 1952/1958; Somer, 2004). In times of extreme adversity, dissociation fosters survival. For example, in mountain falls, biological trance-like states have been found to slow down metabolism and preserve life (Dell, 2009).

Dissociation also allows persons undergoing psychically unbearable events to observe the events as if through the wrong end of a telescope, thereby separating themselves from the ongoing experience of the trauma and emotionally distancing themselves. In this way, victims of rape, incest, beatings, serious automobile accidents, natural disasters, and war trauma—to name a few—may in an automatic, involuntary way become numb and do what must be done without disabling emotional interference.

Dissociation can be soothing. It was to the 8-year-old foster child, Travis, who was bruising his body by pinching, as described in Na'ama Yehuda's 2016 book, *Communicating Trauma*. She asked Travis if the pinching helped: "'It makes the noises in my head quiet so I can go to the stars,' he finally said. 'I can understand how sometimes things like that can help,' I [Yehuda] replied. He stared at me, then quietly said, 'When I get sad, my heart gets tight and I can't breathe, so I pinch and I go to the stars'" (p. 84). Travis had found a way to make himself dissociate. Although dissociation in response to trauma is generally first involuntary, highly dissociative patients report that they, like Travis, have found ways to voluntarily *disappear* from ongoing traumatic experiences by going into a trance state, floating to the ceiling or sky, becoming lost in the wallpaper, or going into a mouse hole in the wall.

The ability to dissociate helped me to cope with the disastrous attack on the World Trade Center by Al Qaeda terrorists on 9/11. On that bright, crisp, sunshiny morning of September 11, 2001, I was on my way to work on the subway. On the train I heard from other riders that an airplane had hit the World Trade Center and that there was a fire. Even though I felt somewhat dismissive of what I had heard, imagining that it was just a small plane doing little damage, I exited the subway right before the WTC stop to have a look. The sight was hypnotically stunning: the towers were burning rapidly like matchsticks. People were staring at this spectacle, many appearing to be transfixed. Realizing that it might be dangerous to stay, I pulled myself away and tried to get back on the subway—only to find that it had been stopped. So I walked home over the Brooklyn Bridge as part of a throng of hundreds. From what I could see, everyone was calm and numb, as I was—just focused on getting away to safety. I chatted with a man who had walked down more than 60 flights of stairs from one of the towers, and I asked if anyone was hurt. Illustrating what retrospectively seems a common deep wish to not know the unbearable, or a physiologically based inability to know, along with his shock, he said, "No," and that everyone was fine, and all had made it down the stairs. Even though a black cloud of smoke, debris, and human remains was rapidly gaining on us as we walked, it seemed to me that the mood of numbed calm was pervasive. Even though it was a terrifying time, I believed that *I* was fine. That is, for a day or so.

Soon I began to worry about all the other people in the subway car, those who did not get out when I did. Since the train had been stopped right after I got out, what happened to them? Did they survive? Had they exited at the next stop, right under the Trade Center, with its confusing maze of lengthy exit paths? Were they caught in the smoke and fire? Only later did my anxiety about *myself* set in. I was hypervigilant, agitated, and anxious, and I had intrusive thoughts, all signs of posttraumatic stress. I couldn't stop talking about the incident. To those who didn't understand what had happened, I might have seemed crazy.

Fortunately for me, some people did listen to me, and my posttraumatic symptoms resolved quickly. This contact with empathic others, some of whom had shared similar experiences, helped me to contextualize the past terror within an awareness of my then current safety. If a trusted other is available to help a person process the terror and to realize that it is past and that the present is safe (if that is the case) the shock of the trauma and the dissociative process are much less likely to lead to continuing dissociative outcomes.

As is common in such circumstances, the immediate terror of the situation was blocked out by my mind's automatic, calm narrowing of attention to only the most relevant matters during the trauma, followed later by hyperarousal and frightening, intrusive thoughts.

On 9/11 I experienced the *process* of dissociation. However, when an overwhelming stressful event continues for too long, occurs too frequently, or happens too early in a person's life, and the person is too alone in it, a more chronic *structural* dissociative organization may develop, including affective dysregulation, unrecognized emotions and experiences, continuing depersonalization, and amnesia. This is problematic or pathological dissociation. Although depersonalization that separates the observing person from the experience at the time of the trauma is likely to be adaptive in the moment, its persistence over time is debilitating and, for some, extremely painful. Depersonalization/derealization is common in traumatized people. Clinicians often will not know of a client's depersonalization unless they ask about it. For example: "Do you have a recurring feeling of being detached from your body or thoughts— like you are observing yourself from the outside? Do you have a feeling of being detached from your surroundings or that the world is unreal?" Very often, the answer is "yes."

People Dissociate for a Reason

Generally, people avoid extremely upsetting affect and knowledge. When it is overwhelming, they dissociate. Understandably, becoming acquainted with what one has dissociated is often not a welcome task:

> Confronting trauma face to face, in ourselves and in others, requires an ability to accept that there exists the kind of profound and searing pain that knocks people off their axis of feeling centered and oriented in the world. This is the kind of disorientation that makes people feel they are going crazy until or unless they find a way to make it stop. This is

what dissociation does: it arrests the unutterable horrible feeling of going insane, the feeling that the world makes no sense and that one's mind has no continuity or expectable form. (Howell and Itzkowitz, 2016b, p. 20)

By splitting apart experience, with the result that information does not add up, dissociation actually maintains sanity. Dissociation preserves personal coherence, sense of continuity in time, and sense of sanity by, as Philip Bromberg (1998) noted, "hypnoidally unlinking the incompatible states of consciousness and allowing access to them only as discontinuous and cognitively unrelated mental experiences" (p. 260).

Does Successful Trauma Treatment Reduce Dissociation?

The answer is a qualified yes. Often, trauma treatment and dissociation treatment might be considered the same thing, but it's complicated. There are different forms of trauma treatment, but specifically dissociation-focused treatment is often necessary for significant amelioration of dissociative disorders. Bethany Brand and colleagues (2019) summarize several studies that found that trauma treatment that did not also focus on dissociation failed to reduce dissociative symptoms even though depression and general psychiatric symptoms were reduced. Since one of the major issues in dissociative disorders is the rigidified separation of memory, affect, and experience, integration is a key goal. In addition, not all trauma treatments are sufficiently attentive to the potentiality of iatrogenic retraumatization by overwhelming affect.

An example of trauma treatment that was also dissociation treatment was the work with Janice, who was discussed above. As Janice was able to process a multitude of traumatic horrors in psychotherapy, she had more access to greater realms of her experience, and her dissociative barriers weakened. Her ability to live her life improved because she was less likely to be triggered or absorbed into dissociative states of mind. This required a titration of the amount of traumatic experience that is experienced at any one time.

Preventing Retraumatization

A key issue in working with traumatized people is how to foster the toleration and ultimate integration of traumatic experiences without causing retraumatization. Stated in the language of neuroscience, Van der Kolk says the challenge is "how to process trauma so that it is quenched rather than kindled" (2002, p. 388). (Kindling is a kind of increased and changed-in-kind sensitization due to repeated trauma and amygdalar stimulation.)

Exposure to dissociated memories and affects in treatment that is too soon, too rapid, or too intense may be retraumatizing. Exposure therapy in which the client is flooded with stimuli that trigger reexperience of the dissociated traumatic material that is then abreacted (experienced and expressed with intense affect and painfully mourned) was often successful with war veterans in the 1980s and 1990s (Chu, 1998). However, when the same methods were applied for people with complex PTSD and dissociative disorders, a number of unnecessary breakdowns and hospitalizations ensued. Unlike the Vietnam veterans who were more likely to have suffered their trauma as adults and were therefore more likely to have an underlying fairly integrated personality structure, those traumatized in childhood were more likely to be destabilized by exposure therapy.

How to work with complex trauma and stay within the window of what is tolerable for the client is a key issue. As it was, Janice had an intuitive sense of the best pacing for herself, and that made it easier for me. This is not true for all clients with complex trauma. Some incoming clients have the idea that they want to get it all over with as quickly as possible, without realizing the potential for retraumatization; some are so dissociated that they are prone to go into retraumatizing abreactions on their own in, and out of, the treatment setting.

Phase-Oriented Treatment

A phase-oriented treatment approach, originally formulated by Pierre Janet, is helpful and often necessary. Janet's model of phase-oriented treatment included three basic stages: (1) stabilization and symptom reduction, (2) treatment of traumatic memories, and (3) personality integration and rehabilitation (Van der Hart, Nijenhuis & Steele, 2006). Following Janet, therapists such as Putnam (1989); Herman (1992); Chu (1998); Courtois (1999, 2004); Courtois and Ford (2009); Kluft (1999); Van der Hart, Van der Kolk, and Boon (1998); and Van der Hart, Nijenhuis, and Steele (2006) have modified some specific emphases, the number of phases, and particular language, but have retained the basic idea of phase sequence, with safety first.

Reducing and Controlling Affect Intensity

Richard Kluft (2013) and Catherine Finc (1993) developed a technique called "fractionated abreaction," in which the therapist deliberately breaks down any planned trauma work into smaller pieces. Kluft's "rule of thirds" (1993) is generally wise to follow: intense emotional or uncovering work should be completed in the first two-thirds of the therapy session. This leaves the remaining one-third for restoring equilibrium.

Another method that Kluft (2013) describes for the creation of a feeling of control over affect is using an imaginary rheostat. Instead of controlling electric current, it controls self-assessed affect intensity. The clients are first asked to raise the level of their anxiety a small amount, perhaps 2 degrees. Once they have achieved this, it is now clear that they have some control over their affect. Following this, they are asked to lower the level of affect intensity.

A method commonly used in trauma work with dissociative clients and in EMDR (eye movement desensitization and reprocessing) is safe place imagery. The client is asked to remember or imagine a safe place. If the work begins to generate too much intensity of affect, the client can be asked to go to the safe place for solace.

Another technique for mitigating the intensity of the traumatic memories is to instruct the client to imagine that she has a television remote in her hand and that the traumatic experience is being played on the screen. The client can then mute, drain the picture of color, or move the figures farther away in the visual field. Other techniques involve the principle of connecting the traumatic event with safety (what a safe treatment relationship does in itself). An example is for the client to imagine a split screen. One screen shows the traumatizing event, or a part of it; the other one depicts an image of safety. The client can alternate between the screens.

Dissociation-Focused Treatments

Many such safe treatment approaches have been written about in the form of a co-guide for clients and therapists to use together. I often recommend and use *Coping with Trauma-Generated Dissociation: Skills Training for Patients and Therapists* (2011) by Boon, Steele, and Van der Hart.

A state of the art method of treatment for dissociative disorders and dissociative identity disorder, in particular, has been developed by Bethany Brand at Towson University and her colleagues (2009, 2012, 2013, 2016, 2019). This involves a combination of ongoing support for the client-therapist dyad, online psychoeducation, and progress reporting. The data on her work shows that trauma therapy for DID is highly effective. Findings in the latest (2019) study included large improvements in adaptive capacities and emotion regulation and medium improvements in PTSD symptoms, with the greatest improvement occurring in the highest dissociation group. There was also a reduction in suicide attempts. Brand and her colleagues see emotional dysregulation due to trauma as key. Therefore, increasing the capacity for toleration of intense and painful affects and for emotional regulation is foundational to recovery.

Finally, a method from Richard Schwartz's internal family systems model (1995) that I have found particularly helpful is to ask one internal part to step aside, so as to allow other parts of the self to feel more freedom of expression. For example, there may be parts that punish, criticize, or dominate the part of the person usually experienced as *the self*, in executive control most of the time. Asking certain parts of the self to step aside allows other parts to reflect more clearly. For example, in one instance, I asked a client if she would ask a fearful and obsessive part of herself that she called "the good girl," and who was usually experienced as herself, to step aside. At first she was quite anxious about this possibility. But when she did ask that part to step aside, an angry aspect of her came forward who did not want to be ruled by her obsessions and other peoples' unnecessary demands. Allowing this more agentic part of herself in expanded her sense of who she was and could be. As a result, she felt greatly relieved of her sense of burden and need to perform perfectly.

Relational Approaches to Trauma

One of the most interpersonally damaging aspects of the traumatized and dissociatively structured mind is the reduced capacity for an interlinked diversity of self-other configurations and internal role-relationships (Ryle, 2003). That is, people who have been chronically traumatized and are predominantly fearful have often had to concentrate their energy and attention into narrowed and constrictive forms of thinking and interaction (not necessarily with full conscious intent). These forms of thinking seem to flow through a relatively small number of mental-emotional and expressive channels and are often focused on control of the other. These forms of interaction, such as fierce and often unexpected demands for love or engaging in devaluing behaviors, are hard to formulate and name in the moment, with the result that they can blindside the clinician and others. One way relational psychotherapy heals trauma and dissociation is by helping clients get to know their internal diversity, allowing them to experience more reflectiveness and ambivalence. Different self-other patterns of being and relating can be experienced in the relationship; intense feelings of each partner for the other can be allowed and experienced; and with empathy, caring, and de-shaming, the therapist can function as a relational bridge to the client's dissociated states of mind (Bromberg, 2011). This helps the client achieve greater diversity and clarity of mind and become less confused.

Human beings are context dependent not only to similar situations, such as specific triggers, but also to current interpersonal situations of powerful forces in human interactions. Most of us are vulnerable to the universally interpersonal evocative pulls of love, power, emotional attachment need, shame, guilt, and so on (Ryle, 2003). Enactments of these issues frequently occur between people, including between therapists and clients. When these universal issues interact with an impoverished mental diversity and rigidified channels of experience in either or both parties, therapists need to know themselves well enough, be present enough, and be non-defensive enough to help the client achieve greater self-knowledge and greater self-acceptance, along with reduced dissociation.

CHAPTER 3

Ubiquity of Trauma
and Dissociation

The Effects on Minds and Bodies

*[I]t would take a bold man to claim that his ego was so perfectly inte-
grated as to be incapable of revealing any evidence of splitting . . .*
—Ronald Fairbairn (1944/1952, p. 8)

UNTIL AROUND 1980, TRAUMA was considered rare, dissociative disorders
even rarer, and dissociative identity disorder (DID) almost nonexistent.
Following the return of traumatized Vietnam veterans in the United
States and the new diagnosis of posttraumatic stress disorder (PTSD),
it was recognized that for many, such as noncombatant war survivors;
battered women (and men); and abused, bullied, and beaten children
trauma can be an experience of everyday life, not at all not outside the
ordinary (L. Brown, 1991; Herman, 1992).

Using *DSM-5* criteria, the exposure to traumatic events in the United
States has been estimated at 89.7 %; exposure to multiple traumatic
events is the norm. The lifetime prevalence (the proportion of the population that has had this disorder at some time in their lives) of PTSD
is 8.3% (However, these figures are slightly lower than those yielded by
DSM-IV because of changes in criteria [Kilpatrick et al., 2013]). Dissociative disorders are currently found to have a lifetime prevalence of

9–18% internationally, and dissociative identity disorder (DID), which is the most severe of these, a 1–1.5% prevalence in the general population (Şar, 2011). In outpatient treatment, rates of dissociative disorders range from 12–38% (Brand, Lanius, Classen et al., 2009). Dissociative disorders continue to be highly underdiagnosed. This is especially true of DID clients who spend an average of 5–12.4 years in the mental health system before being correctly diagnosed (Spiegel et al., 2011). The prevalence of dissociative disorders, even though it may be underestimated, attests to the pervasive damage of relational trauma.

Trauma and Dissociation Are Everywhere

Philip Bromberg (2006), who has described "the dissociative nature of the human mind," persuasively tells us that developmental trauma, the kind of trauma that affects the developing child, is ubiquitous:

> Developmental trauma is a core relational phenomenon and invariably shapes personality in every human being. It contributes to every human being's potential for affect dysregulation, which is always a matter of degree even in those for whom secure attachment has led to relative stability and resilience. We all are vulnerable to the unanticipated experience of coming face to face with our own "otherness," which sometimes, albeit temporarily, feels more "not-me" than our minds can deal with. This is part of the human condition. The big difference between people is the extent to which the sudden affective hyperarousal touches an area of unprocessed developmental trauma and is not only unpleasant, but mentally unbearable and thus unavailable to cognition. (2011, pp. 32–33)

Similarly, Ronald Fairbairn believed that we are all schizoid (i.e., dissociative): "some measure of splitting of the ego is invariably present at the deepest mental level . . . this would not hold true, of course, in the case of a theoretically perfect person whose development had been optimum; it is difficult to imagine any person with an ego so unified and stable at its higher levels that in no circumstances whatever would any evidence of splitting come to the surface in recognizable form" (pp. 7–8, 1952).

Enlightened trauma and dissociation informed psychotherapy then not only recognizes the pervasiveness of trauma, but also embraces the reality of the dissociatively structured mind. Psychotherapy that incorporates an understanding of dissociated self-states, as well as how trauma is dissociatively stored in the body, offers a prospect of genuine healing as the client becomes increasingly able to assimilate dissociated traumatic experiences.

The Mind/Body Link: Psychoneuroimmunoendocrinology

There is a high correlation between animal defense states to predation and human posttraumatic and dissociative disorders (Moskowitz, 2004; Nijenhuis, Vanderlinden & Spinhoven, 1998, 2004; Perry, 1999, Schore, 2003ab, 2009). Van der Hart, Nijenhuis, and Steele in their book *The Haunted Self* (2006) describe similarities between human behavior following terror and animal states responsive to predation, such as fight/flight, freezing, and a hypoaroused state they label "total submission." Not surprisingly, somatoform dissociation is highly correlated with what Van der Hart calls "psychoform" dissociation, or mentally experienced dissociation. Forms of physiological response to threat and to trauma are in our genes.

The concept that trauma is stored in our bodies is not just a theory. In some cases it is highly visible. For example, one of my clients who was physically and sexually abused, including being pimped, from age 11 to age 15 reported frequent scary gasping for breath, with her throat filled with mucous, after a flashback of being strangled. She often suffers immobilizing back pain without any current injury. However, the pain is in a particular location on her back where she was severely beaten.

Sometimes I have seen her face swollen up in a way that had no medical explanation—on the side of her face that was brutally hit. The anesthesia that she developed in her feet due to having to spend long hours doing laundry in an unheated basement in northern winters sometimes reappears, such that she loses sensation in her feet and is vulnerable to falling unexpectedly and with distressing frequency.

It has often been stated that the fight/flight (and more recently, freeze) response was, but is no more, adaptive in earlier human evolution when people had to respond to frequent threats of predation. The idea is that although these early kinds of response to threat are in our genes, they are often triggered inappropriately (and then often bottled up) in situations when such dangers do not exist, leading to mental distress and physical disease.

Gabor Maté, author of *When the Body Says No* (2003), suggests an alternative view:

> The fight-or-flight alarm reaction exists today for the same purpose evolution originally assigned to it: to enable us to survive. What has happened is that we have lost touch with the gut feelings designed to be our warning system. The body mounts a stress response, but the mind is unaware of the threat. We keep ourselves in physiologically stressful situations, with only a dim awareness of distress or no awareness at all . . . We no longer sense what is happening in our bodies and cannot therefore act in self-preserving ways. The physiology of stress eats away at our bodies not because it has outlived its usefulness but because we may no longer have the competence to recognize its signals. (p. 36)

A significant part of Maté's message is that all too often people in so-called civilized societies have suppressed, repressed, and dissociated their body signals of distress in accommodation to attachment needs and fears of social reprisals. The problem is that if one is unaware of affect, which starts in the body, the achievement of affect regulation will be difficult.

The ability to self-regulate is what Maté, following Ross Buck (1993), calls "emotional competence."

Maté emphasizes that the psychological is inseparable from the nervous system, immune system, and endocrine system. He calls this psychoneuroimmunoendocrinology, "the name of the discipline that studies the interrelated function of the organs and glands that regulate our behavior and physiological balance" (2003, p. 87).

It is not surprising then, that approaches to how to work with complex trauma include verbal psychotherapy as well as sensory- and body-based psychotherapy.

Top-Down and Bottom-Up Therapies

Top-down verbal therapies focus on cognitive and verbal interpretation of experience. However, top-down approaches may mask information from our bodies and emotions. In contrast, bottom-up processing involves sensorimotor reactions, bodily states, sensations, and affects. A variety of body-based psychotherapies (Levine, P., 1997; Ogden, 2019; Ogden, Minton & Pain, 2006; Rothschild, 2000) are useful for identifying and healing traumas that have remained in the body as well as calming down the nervous system. Working with the body releases emotion, and connecting this with the rational connects "the rational and emotional parts of the brain" (Van der Kolk, 2015, p. xvii).

Because trauma interferes with the modulation of the ventral vagal nerve (as will be discussed in Chapter 7), the traumatized person may fall back upon phylogenetically less advanced brain structures for strategies of fight, flight, freeze, or dorsal vagal collapse. One thing that body-aware therapists do, then, is enable ventral vagal modulation, such as attention to the body and breathing. Simple attention to body sensations may work as a gentle exposure, helping a person to become comfortable with these feelings, rather than seeing them as trauma-linked threats.

Simple breathing exercises can help shift the autonomic state and body states of affect. However, just asking someone to take deep breaths can invite hyperventilation. I often use a breathing method in which a person breathes in a deep breath for the count of four, holds for the count of four, breathes out for the count of six, holds for the count of two, and then repeats for six to ten repetitions. There are many excellent variations on this pattern. Because the person is counting and watching the breath, hyperventilation is unlikely.

Eye movement desensitization and reprocessing (EMDR) (Shapiro, 2001) involves helping people remember their emotions, body sensations, thoughts, and views about themselves relating to the trauma while undergoing bilateral stimulation. In my view, EMDR works because in addition to bilateral stimulation that is thought to aid neurophysiologically in memory integration, it lessens dissociative structure by helping the person to process trauma. Originally, Francine Shapiro, who developed EMDR, asked clients to watch her hand as it moved back and forth in front of the client's face, with the eyes tracking the movement; bilateral stimulation has been found to be effective using nonvisual methods, such as tappers or audio. EMDR brings up associations to the trauma, which first heightens affect, and then generally diminishes it.[2]

A proviso for EMDR is that like exposure, EMDR has the potential to trigger highly dissociative clients into traumatized states of being. It must be used carefully with heightened vigilance for the possibility of emerging unmanageable affect.

In practice, top-down and bottom-up processes are often intertwined. Even in bottom-up approaches, or in EMDR, both sensations and words, both top-down and bottom-up, are framed by each other. Sensitive therapists use both approaches simultaneously, consciously or unconsciously, modulating their voices and modifying body positions in response to the client's need for closeness or distance. Using imagery and metaphor, therapists speak to somatic and affective states.

Allan Schore (2003ab, 2009, 2019) and Daniel Siegel (1999, 2004, 2007) have addressed how right-brain processes, including perception of facial expression, body posture, and eye contact are millisecond processes, often bypassing the more time-consuming left brain (and verbal) processes. When this out-of-awareness right-brain-to-right-brain interaction goes well, it promotes secure attachment in the therapy process. Schore (2019) writes and speaks of right-brain-to-right-brain (of therapist and client) resonant regression to process early dissociated affects. This resonant healing bond promotes psychological growth.

Adverse Childhood Experiences (ACE)

The damage of relational and developmental trauma often shows up in the body and in disease. The extremely high correlations between developmental trauma and adversity with later physical disease indirectly attest to the prevalence of trauma. Although abuse and adverse childhood experiences are not necessarily traumatic in the sense of causing dissociation, they often are. They are part of the picture when we talk about trauma. It is not just that trauma causes dissociation; it also damages physical health. In fact, many problems treated by mental health professionals, such as obesity, are actually physical problems. Let's examine the studies of adverse childhood experiences.

Vincent Felitti and Robert Anda and colleagues (1998) studied how childhood adverse events later impact physical health. They collected data on over 17,000 Kaiser health plan members in middle-class San Diego, including their current health data as well as self-reported childhood abuse and other adverse events in addition to current risk factors such as smoking and substance abuse. Basing their definitions of categories of adverse events on prior studies of the correlations between obesity and childhood trauma and adversity, the researchers asked the participating adults about the following experiences before the age of 18 years:

1. Recurrent emotional abuse
2. Recurrent physical abuse

3. Contact sexual abuse

4. Physical neglect

5. Emotional neglect

6. Substance abuse in the household

7. Mental illness in the household

8. Mother treated violently

9. Divorce or parental separation

10. Criminal behavior in the household, or incarceration

(Harris, 2018, p. 37; Shonkoff et al., 2012)

Each category counted in scoring as one point, with a possible maximum score of 10. The basic results were consistent with other studies of the prevalence of adversity, maltreatment, and trauma: over 67% of their population had at least one ACE. About 40% had two or more ACEs, and 12.6% had reported four or more ACEs.

The astounding thing about the results of this study was the consistent high correlation with later health outcomes. There was a dose-response relationship between the number of ACE categories and later poor health; that is, the more adversity, the greater adult illness. Compared to someone with no ACEs, a person with one or more ACEs is twice as likely to develop an autoimmune disorder; a person with four or more ACEs is twice as likely to develop heart disease and cancer, twice as likely to be obese or overweight, and 32.6 times as likely to have been diagnosed with learning or behavioral problems. A person with seven or more ACEs is three times as likely to develop lung cancer and three and a half times as likely to develop ischemic heart disease. And finally, ACEs are related to telomeres, which sit at the ends of DNA strands, protecting them. Shortened telomeres are associated with shortened longevity. For every ACE, a person's "odds of having short telomeres increased by 11%" (Harris, 2018, p. 89).

Not unexpectedly, increased ACEs are also correlated with a person's engagement in health-damaging or risky behavior such as smoking, drinking, sexual promiscuity, physical inactivity, and overeating. Four or more ACEs predict that a person is 2.5 times more likely to smoke, 4.5 times more likely to be dependent on alcohol, and 10 times as likely to use drugs intravenously, as compared to a person with zero ACEs (Harris, p. 70). Thus, it might appear that the poor health outcomes associated with increased ACEs are attributable to the risky behaviors also associated with increased ACEs. However, that would be an erroneous conclusion. According to Nadine Harris, author of *The Deepest Well: Healing the Long-Term Effects of Childhood Adversity*, "It turned out that 'bad behavior' accounted for only about 50% of the likelihood for disease" (2018, p. 41).

All of these outcomes stem from a dysregulated stress response. The presence of imminent danger, such as a tiger lunging at you or someone around you waving a knife, signals the release of endogenous stress hormones, norepinephrine (adrenaline) and cortisol. The release of norepinephrine causes heightened alertness and focus, along with increased heart rate and blood pressure. However, norepinephrine levels that are too high cause the brain to partially shut down. Heightened stress activates a complex circuit of feedback loops involving the HPA axis (the hypothalamus, the pituitary, and the adrenals) prompting the release of cortisol from the adrenals (Yehuda, 2000). The increased cortisol supports survival by shutting down systems not immediately necessary in times of emergency, such as the immune system, pain perception, and digestion. When acute stress or adversity is a single event, high levels of stress hormones appropriate to the event are released for that event and then generally subside. However, the long-term consequence of high cortisol secretion is harm to the brain and to health. When the stress is recurrent, stress hormones stay high, wreaking havoc with the endocrine system, the inflammatory system, the immune system, the gastrointestinal system, the cardiovascular system, and the neurological system. Increased cortisol influences the body to crave high sugar and high fat foods, as well as increasing blood sugar, blood pressure, and inflammation, and inhibiting reflective thinking (Harris, 2018). PTSD has been associated with HPA dysfunction, implicating the effect of early life stresses on long-term development and function (Bremner & Vermetten, 2007; Simeon & Abugel, 2006; Yehuda, 2000).

Toxic stress influences epigenetic modification of DNA genetic instructions, changing neuroendocrine expression. Chronic stress is associated with loss of neurons and neuronal connections in the hippocampus (which is involved in memory) and the medial prefrontal cortex (PFC) (Shonkoff et al., 2012). MRI studies have shown measurable changes in the brain. Increased cortisol is also associated with decreased hippocampus size. A number of studies have found smaller hippocampal size and volume among adults who were physically or sexually abused (Nijenhuis, 2003). One study found that for persons with fully evident dissociative identity disorder (DID), hippocampus size is decreased by 25%, and for those with a nonspecified dissociative disorder, the hippocampus size was decreased by 15% (Ehling, Nijenhuis, & Kirke, 2003). Vermetten, et al. (2006) found that women with DID had 19.2 less hippocampal volume and 31.6 less amygdalar volume than healthy controls. The good news is that after successful and integrative psychotherapy, much of this decrease was recovered.

In response to the lack of a surge of enthusiasm about the ACE findings, Harris (2018) asks: "Why were people so resistant to the science of adversity . . . ? Because when you bring it down to the level of cells, to the level of biological mechanisms, then it's about *all* of us. We are all equally susceptible when adversity strikes. And that is what a lot of folks *don't* want to hear. Some want to stand back and pretend that it is just a poor-person problem" (p. 194). In contrast, Harris comments that if a study came out showing that eating cottage cheese tripled your chances of cancer, "the Internet would break and the dairy lobby would hire a crisis management firm" (p. 40).

Harris's answer is similar to the answer to a similar question about trauma and disease in general. For example, about twenty years ago when my brother was dying of lung cancer, the first thing many people would say was: "Did he smoke?" (In fact, he had quit about 10 years previously, which at that time was thought to erase any damage, even though we know differently now.) In other words, many people were eager to attribute a cause that would eliminate danger to themselves. To make it the other person's fault makes the idea that "it couldn't happen to me" more consistent with personal needs for feelings of safety.

Here we return to how hard it is to accept the reality, not only of trauma, but of widespread trauma. Our psychiatric diagnostic system manifests an inconsistent treatment of the issue of trauma.

Professional Confusion About the Effects of Trauma and Dissociation on Problems in Living

Largely because the phenomenon of dissociation has itself been so dissociated within the mental health field, the *DSM* itself is full of inconsistencies with regard to the influence of trauma and dissociation. As Luxenberg and colleagues (2001) explained, "trauma-related disorders, including dissociative disorders, continue to be grossly underdiagnosed. This underrecognition can be best understood in light of the multiplicity of symptoms with which these patients present that may not be readily recognized as being related to their traumatic experiences" (p. 377). It would seem simpler and far clearer to note the underlying importance of trauma and dissociation in many disorders that are otherwise classified.

For starters, posttraumatic and dissociative symptoms have often been confused with psychosis. Indeed, the symptoms listed by Schneider (1939/59) as pathognomonic for schizophrenia are actually more descriptive of DID (Kluft, 1987; C. Ross, 1989). Behavior that might appear to an outside observer to be delusional or hallucinatory may well be a reliving of a traumatic event that has not been assimilated. Terrifying flashbacks, visual, auditory, or somatic are often mistaken for psychotic symptoms (Moskowitz, 2008). For example, my client Sheila reports that she often awakes from sleep with her hands and legs flailing. Upon inquiry, she was reenacting an unassimilated memory of fighting off a rapist. If she had been seen doing this in a hospital, for instance, her behavior would likely have been understood as psychotic.

Another issue is the diagnosis of borderline personality disorder (BPD). *Borderline* originally referred to problems that were on the borderline between psychosis and neurosis. Although the term has been retained, current meanings of the term are varied (Howell, 2002, 2019). More accurate terms have been suggested such as "complex trauma" (Herman, 1992) and "chronic relational trauma disorder" (Howell, 2019; Howell & Blizard, 2009).

Although BPD was early considered to be on the schizophrenia spectrum, it is being increasingly understood as an outcome of trauma (Gunderson & Sabo, 1993; Herman, 1992; Howell, 2002; Kroll, 1993; Putnam, 1997; Ryle, 1997b; Zanarini, 1997). Research on BPD has found both abuse and neglect to be highly significant risk factors (Zanarini, 1997). Difficulty with affect regulation, recognized as an essential component of BPD, is also among the key signs of PTSD (Schore, 2003(ab)). BPD has been found to be significantly related to PTSD (Mclean & Gallop, 2003). However, newer research associated with the development of the World Health Organization's International Classification of Diseases (ICD-11) (Cloitre, Garvert, Brewin, Bryant, & Maercker, 2013) has found only limited overlap. As McWilliams (2011) notes, "It is probable that . . . borderline psychology is not a single entity and is multidetermined, like most other complex psychological phenomena" (p. 54). The negative connotation of the term BPD makes its use undesirable.

In my view, the splitting that is often associated with the aforementioned, pejorative BPD diagnosis (Kernberg, 1975)—characterized by alternating good and bad perceptions of self and other—is dissociative and has similarities to state switches in DID (Howell, 1999, 2002). In splitting there is an affective switch in consciousness. (The person once considered an angel is now the devil.) Even though the person retains a continuity of memory and will likely acknowledge a dramatic shift in behavior and affect, the meaning is disavowed. Since there is no amnesia for the switch in BPD, it is a partial, not a full, dissociation.

Adding to the commentary on the inconsistencies and confusions about trauma disorders and dissociative disorders, Colin Ross, in his (2009) electronic publication, "Expert Commentary: How the Dissociative Structural Model Integrates DID and PTSD," observed the presence of dissociative features in many disorders:

> When the [dissociative] intrusion is a physiological sensation, in *DSM–IV–TR* language we call that *somatization*. When the intrusion is an impulse to pluck hairs out of your head, or a sudden intrusion of a rage state, we call that an *impulse control disorder*. However when the intrusion is an impulse to wash your hands repeatedly, we call the impulse a *compulsion* and diagnose OCD. . . .When a flashback episode intrudes, we call it a *dissociative flashback episode* and diagnose an anxiety disorder. When the intrusion is an auditory hallucination, we call that *psychosis* according to DSM–IV–TR. When the same symptom occurs in DID, we call it a dissociative symptom.

CHAPTER 4

The Clinical Dyad as a Wounded Dyad

The ordinary response to atrocities is to banish them from consciousness.
—Judith Herman (1992, p. 1)

TO VARYING DEGREES, we are all traumatized and dissociative. How could it be otherwise, then, that the clinical dyad is a wounded dyad? None of us has escaped developmental trauma. If experiences of some events are too overwhelming to be taken in as part of who one is, then these experiences become dissociated pieces of ourselves that are unavailable to conscious inspection and are often invisible to us in daily life, despite their power within us. These pieces of ourselves that are blank to our conscious experience, whether we call them fixed ideas, complexes, or just dissociated parts of ourselves, powerfully drive perception, cognition, and behavior. In this way, we all have dissociative minds.

This view of the clinical dyad as a wounded dyad is a dramatic change from the old paradigm. We have gone from a view of the therapist as a blank screen derived from the medical model of a physician objectively treating an objective illness in an objective patient, who is an object of study and treatment and who is also objectified, to an understanding of a messier two-person dyad, that while existing for the benefit of the client, involves the subjectivity of each party in substantial ways. Now we are thinking very differently about the process of psychotherapy. The old paradigm did not chart out this new territory.

As with all changing models, remaining residues from the older model hold unsolved problems. Among the many issues to be disentangled in this new paradigm are weighty interactions of universal psychic trigger points—of domination, submission, need, humiliation, hatred, longing, and so on—of patterns of wounded subjectivities that might not always rise to conscious awareness. In this murky area, shame and blame are often endemic and intense. Even though a coparticipant, the client is in a role evocative of dependency—often of hypnotic dependency. The wounds of the two parties—some known and acknowledged, some not—inevitably interact in ways that are beneath or beyond our awareness and in ways that are bigger than either party. In the inevitable enactments, we as therapists must recognize, metabolize, and deal with our own blind spots of dissociated parts of ourselves. It also behooves us to recognize that our clients may accurately notice these. Such client observations should be carefully considered and not be passed off as transference distortions.

From the One-Person Model to the Two-Person Dyad

In the medical model and the Freudian model the issue of concern was *one person*'s psychic structure, dynamics, and problems. The therapist is understood to be like a medical doctor who addresses a person's dis-ease. The therapist's personality and blind spots are not involved. This positivist view that one can see the other objectively, devoid of the contextualization of one's own eye, is in distinction to a view that the result of an observation cannot be separated from the process. The latter interactive view is more consistent with the two-person model.

The one-person perspective, in which one person's psychic determinism and defenses are the focus, is ultimately egocentric. In contrast, a two-person trauma model suggests shared humanity and social obligations.

The two-person model (not really limited to two persons, but that is the best way to say it for now) acknowledges that developmentally a person is formed in the context of relationships, and that likewise, individual psychotherapy is a two-person relationship. In the two-person model the client's healing is the result of a joint process, a process that involves resonances, rhythms, and interactions of self-states, including dissociated self-states of each of the parties. This interactive process potentially yields an almost infinite number of patterns that seem to settle into certain grooves that can hopefully ultimately be recognized and then worked with. Needless to say, this process is bigger than that of just two people. Intersubjectivity theory (Benjamin, 1990; Stolorow, Atwood, & Orange, 2002) adds to the importance of experiencing and claiming one's own subjectivity, the recognition that people are embedded in a psychological field in which their subjective worlds interact. A primary growth-promoting aspect of the two-person model is the developing appreciation of how one interacts with others. Related is the importance of empathy, a concept underscored by Kohut (1959, 1971 1984). As Jennifer Leighton (2016) notes, "Kohut's 1959 treatise on empathy was a major voice in the articulation of the new relational paradigm: If we are to know and heal our patient, we must immerse ourselves in his experience and the context of his development" (p. 129).

One of the patterns that the two-person model allows for is examination of the inherent authority structure of psychotherapy.

The Authority Structure

Even though it is not the intent of the psychotherapy enterprise, the design of the authority structure mimics or repeats that of the parent-child relationship (Newton, 1973). The effect, which is often unconscious for therapist as well as client, deserves to be clarified. This is not just another way of talking about transference. It is beyond the transference to a particular person and pertains to the structure and roles of authority situations. A key issue is that of the therapist's authority and power in the therapy relationship. It is easy to mistake the illusion of personal authority for the role-related mantle of professional authority, easy to assume that the authority belongs to us, as therapists, personally, *even as we speak the languages of mutuality, co-construction, and intersubjectivity.* Although it is the therapist's role to set the frame and guide the treatment, it is easy for him or her to unconsciously hide behind the cloak of the authority of the role. Despite the therapist's training in an area of expertise, the role of expert should not be collapsed with the role of authority. President Truman is rumored to have said something to the effect of "Remember when you applaud, it is not for me, but for the presidency." An important question for therapists to ask of themselves is whether they attribute more knowledge and acumen to themselves in the role of therapist than they would in other situations.

Roles are powerful identity-shapers. A telling example of the power of roles is Philip Zimbardo's Stanford Prison Experiment (Zimbardo, 2007), a social psychology experiment in which students in the study were assigned roles of prisoner or prison guard. The students, especially those assigned to the role of guards, enacted their roles more intensely than anyone would have expected—the guards, often with violence and sadism.

Familiar roles are evoked in congruent situations. An unpalatable but sometimes-told example of how abuse in the psychotherapy relationship can be influenced by role-confusion is sexual exploitation by a middle-aged male psychiatrist (or therapist) of a young, culturally or personally disempowered, dependent female. Boundary violations still occur even by allegedly well-analyzed therapists (Gabbard & Lester, 1995). I have been told by more than one prospective client that her previous therapist told her that he was having a sexual relationship with her because he thought it would help her. Of course, sexual and other kinds of exploitation may occur with the genders reversed as well. Neither male nor female therapists are exempt. Desire, whether sexual, maternal, paternal, or otherwise is inherent in the relationship. Psychotherapy clients are in an inherently dependent position of seeking relief from an expert. Although the therapeutic dyad is coconstructed, this does not mean that it is equally so. It is not an equal playing field, and the therapist has the job of maintaining the frame.

The Fallacy of Interpretation

One aspect of the influence of authority roles in psychotherapy pertains to interpretation. Many of us learned in our training that correct interpretations are the basis of healing. But how valid is interpretation? How do we, as clinicians, really know what is true and what is unconscious in another person? I submit that we rarely do. Even if such interpretations are correct, they may lead clients away from their own experience. Even though clinicians' moments of insight about their clients' experiences can be enormously helpful, I believe that these insights should be carefully communicated in the context of connectedness rather than from on high, with the arrogance of thinking we *know*. I believe it is better to say something like, "Is it possible that you understood such and such the way you did because of past experience?" than to say "You misinterpreted this in the light of the past, even though you are not aware of it yet." Interpretations carry an inherent shaming potential. Generally it is better to ask questions. Questions invite the client to join us in a joint venture of exploration, as opposed to delivering an interpretation as *the* answer.

The Difficulty of Staying Close to Traumatic Experience

Many traumatized people have felt doubly alone, first from the trauma itself, and second because others have so often distanced themselves from their trauma and developing troubles, increasing isolation and feelings of shame. This is one of the reasons that the therapist's emotional acceptance and responsiveness is so important. Being meticulously close to the client's experience is often the heart of the work. Yet, it is also often one of the most difficult parts of our work with traumatized people.

Judith Herman (1992) wrote, "The ordinary response to atrocities is to banish them from consciousness (p. 1)." In trauma work the clinician is asked to also process the horrors that the client is asked to process. This means that we have to let the horrors being told to us into our own experience, even viscerally. As Richard Gartner (2014) wrote, "After all, who among us truly wants to hear about a child's torturous, overstimulating, and ruinous experiences?" (p. 614). Cultural blindness compounds the individual human blindness to the cruelty, sadism, and unconcern with which many vulnerable children are treated. It is hard for both the client and the clinician to hold the unconscionable in consciousness. Yet, because the unconscionable is so easily dissociated, it becomes embedded in the unconscious. For traumatized clients and their therapists, there is no innocence.

Richard Gartner (2014) has introduced a new concept and term, *countertrauma*. Analogous, but not identical, to counter-transference, countertrauma is specifically a response to the client's trauma. He contrasts countertrauma to "vicarious trauma" (Pearlman & Saakvitne, 1995) in that countertrauma is our own—we are not experiencing our client's traumas, but rather our own traumas, including our own unresolved issues, in response to our clients' traumas. Gartner emphasizes that as we consider processing and verbalization of trauma important for our clients, it is important for us as therapists as well: "We need to discover ways to encode our experience linguistically, to talk about it in detail in an environment that does not pathologize our internal reactions and in so doing, help ourselves feel less shamed and professionally isolated" (p. 614).

Therapists *can* be overwhelmed by clients' traumas. For example, while discussing a case, a supervisee uncharacteristically began making jerky movements with her head and arms—so much so that it was making me dizzy. Finally, I said, "It seems that this has really gotten inside of you, like it feels too much for you." My supervisee then said, "Yes, it is overwhelming." As we discussed what was overwhelming (i.e., traumatic) to her about the situation, she stopped jerking her body.

Being Triggered by Our Clients

When we can take in the client's experience and not be overwhelmed, the client is less in danger of feeling toxic, and we are in a better position to help our clients with their traumas and pain. Avoiding being overwhelmed is not always so easy. Among other things, the clients' experiences may trigger our own traumatic memories, which may not always be well-processed. We must be able to distinguish between what the client is experiencing and what we are experiencing and to contain our own personal reactions as separate. Otherwise, there is risk of an enactment.

Stuart Perlman (2004) exemplifies this dilemma with a vignette of a time when he had gone out to put money in his client's parking meter; he returned to find that she had stabbed herself and was bleeding profusely on his carpet. He wrote:

> This was a powerfully upsetting moment for me. In an instant, many thoughts and images passed within me. I was horrified at the sight of blood. Now, looking back, I realize it triggered a physical re-experiencing in my body of an accident I had when I was ten years old in which I was run over by a car. I could feel the physical impact. All I could see was the blood, the blood of the car accident and the blood dripping from her arm onto my carpet. It felt to me almost as if she had hit me with a physical blow. It made me frightened of her, until I later realized that what I was reacting to was not what she was doing to me but rather included a re-living of the car accident. (p. 101)

What Clients Know About Us

Clients know a great deal about us, but it can feel derailing when they seem to know things about us that we thought we were able to keep private. In another example from Perlman's evocative essay, he describes how a client told him that she could tell if a person has been sexually abused, and she told him that she believed he had been sexually abused after his accident at 10 years of age. Perlman (2004) wrote that at first, he felt within himself a vehement denial, but that following this, he had an experience of being back in a body cast from his neck to his toes, only having openings for his genitals and behind. He remembered his vulnerability and humiliation at how "people would have to wipe me after I defecated and would wash my genitals and behind. Nurses would come in abruptly and pull off the bed sheets and wash me as though I was not a person who had rights over his own body . . . Though . . . I was not sexually abused legally or technically, I felt profoundly violated, helpless, and physically imprisoned" (p.105).

I once had a stunningly similar experience with one of my clients. At the beginning of a session, my client, who did not know I had a sister, suddenly asked me, "Did your sister commit suicide?" I gave her the technically truthful answer, which was "No." (As with Perlman, there was some truth behind my client's question. My sister had lupus and did not want to die, but there were contributing factors to her death.) Even though I was stunned by my client's uncharacteristic intrusiveness, I asked, "Why do you ask?" Her answer was, "She says she took a hit for you." I answered that my sister had indeed taken a hit for me. (My sister had been sexually abused by our father, and I had not; there was no way the client could have known this.) I thanked my client for her communication, and continued on with the session, which was about her. If I had it to do over again, I would have inquired more about the meaning of this revelation to her, including how the interactions between us may have given her the intuition or felt sense or knowledge that something had happened to my sister. I was too stunned, and the best I could do was to recover and do the work.

Right-Brain Knowledge of the Other

Beyond the kind of knowledge that people may have of us that appears not to be explicable in a purely cognitive or sensory way, people know a great deal more about each other in many ways than we or they consciously know. Affects are conveyed procedurally and implicitly by somatic states, by body rhythms, and by facial expression in ways that are not accessible to ordinary verbal consciousness. Allan Schore has written in multiple articles and books of such communication that occurs between people in right-brain-to-right-brain affectively responsive ways. Facial expression, especially, can often be subtle and nuanced to our left-brain minds, occurring so rapidly—in split seconds—that it is unavailable to conscious perception. However, as he notes, these communications are not so nuanced to the right brain, which processes information holistically, and "can appraise facially expressed emotional cues in less than 30 milliseconds . . . far beneath the levels of awareness" (Schore, 2003a, p. 71). Schore emphasizes how this process is bidirectional, involving, "a very rapid sequence of reciprocal affective transactions within the intersubjective field that is co-constructed by the patient and the therapist" (2003a, p. 73). Thus, client and clinician are subliminally in communication almost constantly.

Clients' Awareness of Their Therapists' Murky Psyches

There is another way that our clients know about us that may have to do with intuitive implicit knowledge. The human psyche is murky, obscure, and imperfect. That therapists often desire to be seen in a positive light is understandable. However, as Chefetz (1997) astutely notes: "The patient correctly perceives that within the therapist resides all those potentials for murderous rage, sadistic thought and action, collusive betrayal, and self-object devaluation which the patient knows too well from the past.

The therapist's conscious or unconscious denial of these potentials is, in my experience, the most common source of impasse in the treatment of persons with post-traumatic disorders" (p. 259).

Traumatic Transferences

It should be no surprise then that traumatized people, who have often experienced unconscionable treatment and who have an intuitive knowledge of the cruel potentialities of humans, including their therapists, should have traumatic transferences. The term, "traumatic transference" refers to the (usually) unconscious expectation that "the therapist, despite overt helpfulness and concern, will exploit the patient for his or her own narcissistic gratification" (Spiegel, 1986, p. 72, cited in Loewenstein, 1993, p. 57). This includes more specific instances of dissociated expectations, often accompanied by a perceptual illusion that the therapist is like or is about to do what a former abuser did. A very stark example of the latter was my client with DID, who, right after a switch, asked me point blank if I intended to abuse her. Although it may not be initially apparent, trauma clients may in some way assume that there will be exploitation. Traumatic transferences are more common than one might think and often harder to assess. For example, in some cases a client's overaccommodating behavior toward the therapist might be more than meets the eye. It could be a response to an underlying terror of being punished for being confrontational or disagreeable.

Enactments

The word *enactment* was used in the past to refer to a client's *reenactment* of an earlier experience, relationship, or feeling state. I prefer to use the word reenactment to refer to the one-person aspect of a repetition of earlier experience, and enactment to refer to a joint interaction of client and therapist together, as is common in current relational thinking. Enactment involves mutual dissociation, the enmeshed interaction of dissociated self-states of both persons, dissociatively interacting with the other, expressing a problem between them, but also in each of them, that has not been previously understood (Bromberg, 2006). The release (and the learning) from the enactment occurs when one or both parties develop an insight into their own blind spots. When this can be articulated, clients (and therapists, also) have a wider vista through which to view their own experience.

The following is a description of one of my enactments and the joint recovery and learning from it.

Sally

Sally is a highly intelligent, highly personable, talented, caring, and highly dissociative person. In her early life she was exposed to intense rejection, derogation, and frequent extreme punishments and abuse from both of her parents. She never understood why until later, when she was adult. While we were working together, she took her mother to a spa as a gift. At that time, Sally's mother, under the influence of the onset of dementia, confessed to her that she had never known whether Sally had been her father's biological child. Though married, Sally's mother had had an affair with an Indian man while her husband was away on work duties. Soon after, she had become pregnant with Sally. She told her husband, Sally's father, of the affair. Throughout Sally's childhood both parents had treated her as if she were an alien to them, even frequently commenting on her "olive" skin, which was in fact, observably fair. Only looking backward did it become possible to connect the dots that the mother was ferociously punishing her daughter for her own sins. Following her mother's confession, Sally asked for and received from her father a DNA test, which matched her own. Upon receiving this definitive knowledge, her father became kinder to her.

Sally began her life as a sickly child, even born with the umbilical cord wrapped around her neck. For reasons that she could not divine at that time, her mother would frequently beat her with a hairbrush, even beating her hands, when Sally tried to protect other parts of her body. From a young age, she tried to please her mother by giving her massages (with the hands her mother had beaten). Her mother would scream at her if she had a temperature as a kindergartener, because she would then have to stay home with her child and forego her card game socializing (the school would not admit a child with a temperature into the classroom). When Sally was 8 years old she attempted to strangle herself by hanging herself with her mother's stockings.

In contrast to her siblings, Sally was treated in many ways like a household slave. By the time she was in junior high school, she was not permitted to participate in any after-school activities because she had to come home and cook dinner for the family. Even though there was no financial necessity, she had to sew her own clothes as well as her sister's wedding dress and those of her bridesmaids. Her sister and brother followed in the pattern set by the parents and were allowed to derogate, humiliate, and harm Sally without mercy. When she was a child and a teenager, her father, who had had military interrogation training, would often sit her in a chair for excruciatingly long periods of time while he relentlessly chastised her for being a liar, a thief, and a cheat (none of which was true).

One piece of solace for her was that her father's boss and his wife took a liking to her. They appreciated her intelligence, talents, and creativity. They welcomed her presence, and she gladly spent summers with them in her preadolescence and adolescence. So great was her attachment to and need of these people that she dissociated the boss's nightly visits to her bedroom where he molested her. After the birth of her first child, these memories flooded her, and she developed highly symptomatic PTSD.

Sally learned to cope with her childhood abuse by compulsively looking on the bright side, focusing on the needs of the other, idealizing others, and blaming herself for the cruel treatment she received. She became the family clown and entertainer who could make people laugh with her funny faces. Her "front face" was a cheery one, even as she denied and dissociated overwhelming abandonment, sadness, and disappointment.

In our work together, Sally has told me many times of some wonderful new enterprise of hers that she is sure is going to work out. Only it didn't work out. As this recurred, I began to query her and express doubts about a new person or new plan that she felt was going to be wonderful, only to be silenced by her reassurances that she was aware of all the potential pitfalls and that she had everything under control. Again, things did not turn out. I felt greatly saddened and frustrated, and in my desperation to protect her, even a few times began to act parentally, saying things like "Please show it to me first before you sign it."

Not only was Sally herself idealizing, but she could be highly convincing (including to me) as she described some new project, whether buying a house or dating a man. She told me that she could be extremely convincing to others, and having convinced them, she could then convince herself.

One piece in the enactment that I am about to describe is that, because of my own traumas, I can be idealizing too. My own defensive style, though not as severe, matched hers. I very much *wanted* to believe the wonderful things she was telling me. Early on, once I became better aware of her pattern of high hopes followed by extreme but then denied disappointment, I would (not completely aware of my participation by my own high hopes for her) say things like, "Now that you know how much you tune out your feelings, it is important that you examine things carefully." Later on, catching myself, I would say things like, "We need to examine these things carefully."

In one session, she was telling me of another failed relationship with a man who had seemed wonderful. She told me that he was building a house for her, that they were going to get married, and that she would move to another state to be with him. Concerned, and almost feeling cruel with my question, I asked her if he had put a ring on her finger and if he had promised marriage. Her face fell, suddenly suffused with extreme sadness; she said that he had done neither. Then she poignantly said, "I can take a tiny crumb and make it into a beautiful wedding cake." My response to this painfully sad statement was to process my own shock and tell her that she had had me convinced. She answered affirmatively that she has a knack for convincing people. I then expressed my thought that it was quite a leap for her to be planning on moving and marrying before there had been any discussions of marriage. But in doing so, I was without realizing it, taking distance from her and blaming her in a sense for her ability to previously convince me (which I myself had participated in without much awareness that that was what I was doing). It was then the end of the session, and she said to me that she was not going to end feeling "bummed out."

After she left, I denied to myself for a few minutes the obvious: that she was telling me that *she was bummed out*. Then I became aware of how distant I had felt and been in my last remark, and that I had actually sort of known that a part of her could indeed make crumbs into wedding cakes. I suddenly became aware of my extreme pain about her disappointment and loneliness, and I cried. I realized more focally and viscerally the extreme extent to which her idealization had protected her from the overwhelming abuse, shame, abandonment, and terror she had felt in her family. Her ability to delude herself had saved the day countless times throughout her childhood, enabling her to create an endurable view of an unendurable life setting. I began to realize that I had not gone far enough with her to her loneliness and terror. I realized that the issue was not only that she needed to stop deluding herself now (despite how her self-delusion may in fact have given her the hope to live in her childhood), but also that I needed to stop listening to the part of myself that longed for her to be fine and for her to be taken care of. In short, I needed to start paying attention to, and correct, the parts of me that were resonating with the idealizing, ever-hopeful, parts of her. I had in a vague way known that these things were too good to be true, but I had been unable to *really* know it. When I could finally listen to the truth, it was clear to me.

In the following sessions, I began to ask more about her feelings of terror, shame, loneliness, and abandonment. It was very painful for both of us, but it was much more useful than my saying things like "You have to watch out for your tendency to deny," or even "We have to watch out for it." We went to the experience of the little 8-year-old girl who wanted to strangle herself with her mother's stockings because she felt or knew that she would never be cared for, that she was permanently abandoned, that her mother hated her, and that she would always be disappointed. Now this little 8-year-old part of her, who can finally speak the truth of her feelings, knows that the past is not permanent and that times can change.

When I finally realized how distant I had become in response to Sally's telling me that I had bummed her out by making her aware that there was no wedding cake, and that I had hurt her feelings, I became better able to address her dissociated feelings of hopelessness. She became better able to speak and think about these things in a clear-eyed way. She has mourned her compulsory cheerfulness and her overoptimistic self-deception, and they have greatly diminished. Her presence in sessions has more weightiness to it.

This kind of out-of-awareness resonance, called "dissociative attunement" by Karen Hopenwasser (2008), consists of "systematically self-emergent moments in which multiple self-states are shared by means other than projection" (p. 349). Further, it is a "mutually held state of attunement [that] is neither a do-to-you or a do-to-me experience. It is a synchronized simultaneous awareness of knowing that is non-linear and bi-directional" (p. 351). Sally and I had been simultaneously resonating to the same wavelength of idealization. In being attuned to Sally, I was experiencing much more than my own cognitive and emotional responses to her. Part of being attuned is being in it, experiencing the music and the rhythm of the other's mood, often without knowing. Thus, dissociative attunement involves an affective resonance and empathic attunement that has a life of its own. In this case, it involved the idealizing defense against the attachment trauma as well as the trauma behind it. The counterpoint to Sally's cheerfulness was her wail of despair, which we were both stubbornly refusing to hear. It seemed that in this case, because of my initial difficulties in hearing about her severe pain, I had to hurt her to finally hear her. Once I heard her we were both better able to mourn the pain and the loss that had been too unbearable to enter conscious experience.

Woundedness and Shame

There is no inherent shame in woundedness. It happens to all of us. Yet trauma, especially relational trauma, often carries intense shame. This is especially so for men who carry the extra burden of the cultural mandate that men are supposed to deny vulnerability and to be strong and tough (Betcher & Pollack, 1993; Gartner, 1999; Gilligan, 1982). If the affects of shame about the trauma rise to a certain point of intensity, they can bring about dissociation. Both client and clinician are likely to have some dissociated shame. Thus, a substantial part of trauma work is uncovering, processing, making sense of, and learning from shame. Philip Bromberg (1998) writes that a core piece of unsymbolized traumatic material is the affect of shame, and it rightfully belongs to both parties. He explains that shame can motivate the therapist to maintain affective distance from the shame-filled parts of the client's experience. Such distancing is likely to generate enactments, and shame is often at the heart of these enactments. At such times, certain aspects of the therapist are resonating but not communicating with certain aspects of the client.

This was what happened between Sally and me. We were resonating too much and not communicating enough. It was in part my shame, responding to my perception of her shame in her ultra-idealizing, that influenced me to take a nontherapeutic distance on that fateful day. Finally, we got through to each other, and we are both better.

When Sally read my write-up of this particular section of our work, she was temporarily overcome with sadness. Her ability to process what I wrote about our work together has become a part of the therapy.

CHAPTER 5

Dissociation, Repression, and the Unconscious

What we call the unconscious might usefully include the suspension or deterioration of linkages between self-states, preventing certain aspects of self—along with their respective constellations of affects, memories, values, and cognitive capacities—from achieving access to the personality within the same state of consciousness.

—Philip Bromberg (1993, p. 182)

PEOPLE OFTEN SPEAK OF *repressed memories*, referring to memories of childhood abuse, often sexual abuse. Usually, in this context, the more accurate words to use would be *dissociated memories* or *dissociated experiences*, because such intense experiences of childhood abuse tend to be so overwhelming to the mind as to be traumatic and thus dissociated. (Of course, some people never forgot their memories of abuse.)

Repression and Dissociation

Let's look at the similarities and differences between repression and dissociation. Often people use the words interchangeably, partly because they both have the same consequence: the separation of one realm of experience from another, dividing unconscious from conscious, as well as causing amnesia. Especially early on, Freud often used the word repression in a way that sounded like Janetian dissociation (Davies, 1996), and at times he used the words interchangeably (Erdelyi, 1990, 2001). But later he mostly used the term repression. As a result, repression is often the default term. However, repression and dissociation are two very different processes and appear differently in psychic structure.

First of all, repression is a specific kind of dissociation (Erdelyi, 1990, 1992; Fairbairn, 1929/1994). In both repression and dissociation the mind is divided in a way that creates an unawareness of certain aspects of experience. In both, by observing how people are often unaware of things they did or said—in such a fashion that this could not be related to random forgetfulness—one might infer that there is some cause that makes for this unconsciousness of things that would be expected to be known.

In repression, *specific* memories that were once known and formulated have been put out of mind. In contrast, dissociation refers to aspects of affectively laden experience that have been kept apart, such as subconscious centers of dissociated experience and dissociated self-states, rather than to an exclusion of specific contents. Repressed contents "are experienced as once familiar, rediscovered aspects of mental life . . . [which] have been previously experienced, psychologically digested, encoded, and then forgotten" (Davies & Frawley, 1994, p. 66). When these memories return, they are fully formed.

In contrast, dissociated experiences are not pre-formed. Donnel Stern describes dissociation as *unformulated experience*. Emphasizing its role in defense, he underscores "the unconscious decision not to interpret experience [but] to leave it in its unformulated state for defensive reasons" (1997, p. 31)., Whereas repression is a defense that deals with the unpleasant, dissociation is brought on by experiences that were unbearable and therefore unassimilable. As Philip Bromberg (2006) has explained:

Repression defines a process . . . designed to avoid disavowed mental content that may lead to unpleasant intrapsychic conflict. Dissociation shows its signature not by disavowing aspects of mental *contents* per se, but through the patient's alienation from aspects of *self* that are inconsistent with his experience of "me" at a given moment. It functions because conflict is unbearable to the mind, not because it is unpleasant. (p. 7; emphasis in the original)

Two clinical examples from my practice illustrate the differences between repression and dissociation respectively. The first example is of repression. It involved a client's reporting a dream. Examination of the dream brought to her mind the previous session, in which I had said something that slightly offended her. I had not followed up on it with sufficient empathic inquiry. She hadn't thought about it much until it came up in the dream. As we talked about the previous session, she reported having consciously thought right after the session that she did not want to think about this anymore. When we discussed it, she remembered the entire incident perfectly, and we were able to resolve some of the previously unspoken issues. She had preferred not to think any more about this memory because it was painful, and she then repressed it. Then the dream reminded her of it.

The second example, of the emergence of a triggered dissociated self-state, involved a time a client had an anxiety attack on her way to the session. She had just had lunch with a friend, who had told my client, who is of Polish descent, a joke about how many people it takes to change a light bulb that used a common and derogatory term. This joke, supposedly funny, is like most ethnic jokes humiliating and derogating if it is not told in a way and in a situation that is accepting and inclusive. The joke did not feel inclusive at all to my client. Although she had attempted to laugh, the joke actually humiliated and angered her. At the time she was so subject to heightened shame and rage affect that she could not remember the corresponding WASP joke, which, in its own particular stereotype applied to her friend (and to me). On the way to the session she did recall the WASP joke, but then before she could think more about it, or even enjoy it, she went into a full-fledged panic attack for a few minutes, with extremely high, unnamable anxiety, racing heartbeat, and fear that she would not be able to breathe. By the time she walked in my door, she had recovered. When we talked about it, we realized that the WASP joke also applied to me. Although the retaliatory rage elicited by the Polish joke and then expressed by the WASP joke was aimed at her friend, it also crossed over, in a kind of dream logic or trance logic, to include me in the same category (primarily mixed English, Scottish, Irish, Welsh descent). Her usually dissociated rage state had elicited a terrifying fear state that hit her full force as an anxiety attack, early anxiety about losing a precious source of connection. This client had grown up in a family in which she was highly neglected but also in which even an expression of mere displeasure could elicit abandonment, shame, or punishment. Her dissociation of her emotions about how she had been treated had enabled her to maintain an attachment that she needed as a child to her parents. (This incident could of course also be explained as a harsh superego, a connection that will be explained in Chapter 7.)

Spatial Metaphors

Both repression and dissociation are often depicted in spatial metaphors. A frequently used metaphor for differentiating repression and dissociation, proposed independently by Heinz Kohut (1971) and Ernest Hilgard (1977) is that repression refers to a horizontal split whereas dissociation refers to a vertical split. In repression, the idea is that unwanted memories and conflictual wishes are pushed down into the unconscious, and kept down by counterpressure. They are sometimes described as *buried* until they can be dug up. In the vertical split of dissociation, psychic contents are not buried, but vertically separated in side-by-side presentations.

The vertical split, side-by-side metaphor is in keeping with how dissociated contents often appear contextually, for instance, a neighbor's red sweater may bring to mind an abuser's red sweater, and a person may experience an intruding flash of intense fear. In contrast, the horizontal split is in keeping with the commonly cited ice-berg metaphor, in which conscious and unconscious are like an iceberg, of which we see only the top (conscious) although the much greater mass of the iceberg is beneath and unseen (the unconscious). Freud's topographical model, with the conscious on top, the preconscious in the middle, and the unconscious on the bottom is also consistent with the spatial metaphor of the horizontal split. In this way of thinking, the unconscious is implicitly *down,* a place that where repressed wishes and memories are buried, and where they are kept down by continuous counter-pressure. Overlapping with the id, the repressed aspect of the unconscious is full of banished representations of deadly sins, with thought crimes of lust, hatred, anger, jealousy, and venality, and of some defenses against these.

Even though these visual metaphors of horizontal versus vertical can sometimes serve as a useful heuristic, the concepts are more complex. One of Freud's (1910/ 1957) visual metaphors for repression is actually all on the same plane. Freud gave the example of a classroom with an unruly student who is expelled to outside the classroom door, which is then forcefully blockaded to prevent his return:

> Let us suppose that in this lecture-room . . . there is nevertheless someone who is causing a disturbance and whose ill-mannered laughter, chattering and shuffling . . . are distracting my attention from my task. I have to announce that I cannot proceed with my lecture; and thereupon three or four of you who are strong men stand up and, after a short struggle, put the interrupter outside the door. So now he is "repressed," and I can continue my lecture. But in order that the interruption shall not be repeated . . . the gentlemen who have put my will into effect place their chairs up against the door and thus establish a "resistance" after

the repression has been accomplished. If you will now translate the two localities concerned into psychical terms as the "conscious" and the "unconscious," you will have before you a fairly good picture of the process of repression. (p. 25)

Agency in the Repressed Unconscious

In the preceding illustration, Freud described the agency, the power of repression (the "three or four . . . strong men"), along with the expulsion of unwanted mental contents: the interrupter is banned from the classroom. Just like those young men who put Freud's will into effect, the act of repression is willful. There is a feeling of power about the repressed unconscious, formed as it is by the agency of the person, even if supposedly unconsciously. Even though we may not know our own minds, at least we are the agents of our own amnesia and distortions. As Boulanger (2007) writes, "The Freudian subject by bringing drives under control, achieves, agency . . ." (p. 57).

It is important to notice this bias in favor of personal agency has the potential to blind us to the uncontrollable, potentially humiliating and overwhelming realities of traumatic experiences. Freud's model of repression left us with a version of psychic determinism that was grand and powerful. In contrast, being traumatized involves being completely helpless before forces that are outside ourselves.

Repression and Suppression

Freud described the process of repression as a willful exclusion of information from consciousness. In his essay "Repression," (1915/1957), Freud wrote that the "essence of repression lies in simply turning something away, and keep it at a distance, from the conscious" (p. 147). It involves pushing out of consciousness both unpleasant and unwanted memories and as well as wishes that conflict with internalized prohibitions. As described in *Studies on Hysteria* (Breuer & Freud, 1893–95), it is about:

the kind of memories, such as loss, unrelieved shame, and other situations the patient wished to forget or because social circumstances made a reaction impossible or because it was a question of things which the patient wished to forget, and therefore intentionally repressed from his conscious thought and inhibited and suppresses. (p. 10)

When I was in graduate school I was taught that repression is always unconscious, from the initial *primal* repression to the repeated, or *actual* repression. In the literature, also, repression has often been understood to be an unconscious process, initially and throughout. However, there is a logical problem inherent in the requirement that repression be solely an unconscious process: somehow there would have to be knowing and not knowing at the same time. The repressing part of the ego must repress that it is repressing, and so on. In this way, repression would ultimately require an infinite series of inner homunculi to do the repressing (Erdelyi, 1994; Kilhstrom, 1984; Stern, 1997). How do we get around this? Matthew Erdelyi (1990, 1992, 1994, 2001), a Freud expert, has observed that much of Freud's work suggests that repression includes conscious, willful forgetting and that "Freud—Sigmund, not Anna—used suppression and repression interchangeably, from his earliest writings to his last" (1990, p. 12).

Potential solutions to the problem of knowing and not knowing at the same time would allow that repression could initially be conscious (Erdelyi, 1994). One solution comes from cognitive psychology (Eriksen & Pierce, 1968, cited in Erdelyi, 1990; Kihlstrom, 1984): Repression begins as conscious suppression, but with increasing practice the activity becomes a highly skilled although ultimately unconscious procedure. In this way, conscious defense becomes automatic, and by overlearning, unconscious. This solution does not require inner homunculi because it does not require initial unconsciousness.

Another solution, also resting on the assumption that the later repressed matter is initially conscious is that repression can be understood as reconstruction (Erdelyi, 1994, 2001). Drawing on the understanding that narrative memory is constantly being reconstructed, Erdelyi suggests that repression, understood as reconstruction, makes things more palatable. Along with forgetting, which may partially involve a conscious act, we reconstruct. In both ways, memory of the material we "simply turn . . . away, and keep . . . at a distance," (Freud, 1915, 1957, p. 147) is made inaccessible.

Does Repression Exist?

The concept of repression has had its detractors. David Holmes (1990) analyzed 60 years of experimental studies of repression and concluded that there was no experimental evidence that proved the existence of repression. However, he also acknowledged that this did not disprove the existence of repression. Some have taken the logical problems with repression, along with the difficulty for experimental psychology in proving the existence of repression, as evidence that repression does not exist. It is important to note that among Holmes' criteria for repression was the requirement that "repression is not under voluntary control" (p. 86),[3] in effect, that the process is not conscious.

In contrast with Holmes, George Vaillant (1990) in his study of repression relied on case histories that illustrate a repressive style. For example, when asked about his psychiatrically troubled daughter, one man said, "The details are fuzzy; my mind is blank to things I don't want to remember" (p. 269). Another man compared himself to his wife when problem issues arise: "She wants to talk, I sweep it under the rug . . . I don't want to talk about it" (p. 272).

I am in agreement with Vaillant and others, such as Otto Kernberg (1975), Nancy McWilliams (2011), and Philip Bromberg (1998, 2006, 2011), that repression does exist and is, in a certain way of thinking, a higher level of defense.

Key Differences Between Repression and Dissociation

Repression usually refers to specific forgotten pieces of information that were accessible at one time but not at another. In contrast, dissociated content is generally organized in such a way that one set of material requires the exclusion of other material. It is not just discrete memories that are dissociated, but pieces of living experience. Dissociation refers to competing organizations of experiences, to mental states or self-states that are kept apart, are mutually exclusive, and often dynamically oppose each other. For example, the idea that "my mother is a wonderful person," may be fiercely believed by one self-state, while at the same time another self-state knowingly suffers from memories of years of abuse.

Repressed memories are fully encoded and formulated when repressed. In contrast, dissociation often implies unformulated experience (Stern, 1997). In a similar way, dissociated experiences could not be assimilated and are often encoded neurologically in pieces, in sensorimotor ways, even with different senses: hearing, vision, and smell encoded and remembered separately.

Repression is always both willfully motivated and psychologically defensive. In contrast, dissociation as a process need not be defensive, but it can be. That is, dissociation can arise automatically and without inner motivation, in a moment of terror, but it can also be used defensively to prevent retraumatization. This defensive use can occur in a way that seems automatic after repeated use, but can also be used consciously, or semi-consciously.

Because repressed memories are pushed out of consciousness, they are in large measure independent of context. In contrast, dissociated memories are highly vulnerable to being elicited by context.

Memories that were willfully repressed are not likely to intrude into consciousness. Instead, they most often have to be dug up. In contrast, dissociated experiences do intrude into experience, often in the form of visual, auditory, haptic, or olfactory flashbacks.

Dissociation: Process and Structure

In a broad sense, dissociation refers to aspects of experience that would normally be connected being kept apart. As Frank Putnam (1989) has noted, concepts of dissociation "converge around the idea that dissociation represents a failure of integration of ideas, information, affects, and experience" (p. 19).

Dissociation has many meanings. A basic way of understanding and categorizing the many meanings of dissociation is in terms of a *process* and a *structure* of mind. Dissociative processes include spacing out, going into a trance, psychic numbing, depersonalization, derealization, and even imagining oneself floating above one's body. Dissociative processes may also contribute to dissociative structure. For example, as described in Chapter 2, as I was walking over the Brooklyn Bridge immediately after the 9/11 attacks, I was experiencing a dissociative process in which emotion was largely tuned out. I was in a trance-like and mechanical state, just trying to get to the other side. If I had not had the chance to talk about the experience with other people, I might have developed a chronic PTSD-like psychic structure. This may have included a pronounced avoidance of danger and of extreme grief, coupled with intrusive fears, that is, dissociative self-state that encapsulated and protected me from the terror of the experience.

Dissociative structure is manifested in dissociated self-states, small and large amnesias, intrusive experiences (e.g., flashbacks), and changes or switches in dissociated self-states. Dissociative structure is exemplified in Van der Hart and colleagues' theory (2006) of the structural dissociation of the personality (discussed in Chapter 8) as well as in Ronald Fairbairn's model (1952) of endopsychic structure that includes the split-off parts of libidinal ego, anti-libidinal ego (or internal saboteur), exciting (or libidinal) object and rejecting object (or antilibinal object), along with the central ego. Dissociative structure also includes Harry Stack Sullivan's "not-me" (1953) and Bromberg's descriptions of dissociated self-states (1998, 2006, 2011). It is also manifest in Wilma Bucci's cognitive-psychoanalytic model of dissociation that involves the lack of sufficient referential processes to link symbolic and subsymbolic parts of experience (1997, 2002, 2003).

The dissociatively structured mind (Bromberg, 2006) includes dissociated traumatic experiences, such as fixed ideas, and the segregation of parts of experience, such as dissociated self-states. Janet (1907) described how a frightening, overwhelming event remains active subconsciously as a fixed idea that becomes a subconscious center around which other aspects of psychological experience may cohere: "things happen as if an idea, a partial system of thoughts, emancipated itself, became independent and developed itself on its own account" (p. 42). He explained how fixed ideas belong to a mental system that becomes increasingly extensive in a way that is not subject to conscious will:

> The actual memory of the happening was constituted by a system of psychological and physiological phenomena, of images and movements, of a multiform character. This system, persistent in the mind, soon began to encroach . . . . . Thus enriched . . . it became able to realize itself automatically without passing through the intermediate states of ideation and suggestions, and thus gave rise to actions, dispositions, sufferings, and delusions, of various kinds. (1919/trans. 1925, p. 597)

A Case Vignette of DID

The following case vignette illustrates the extreme form of dissociative personality structure, DID. It also illustrates the usefulness in therapy of working from the inside out rather than inferring motivation from the outside in.

The presence of DID is generally an outcome of a very high magnitude of traumatization (Putnam et al., 1986). To illustrate, we all know that a single rape for an adult can be highly traumatic, often requiring a recovery time of months to years. In such cases *recovery* is often a misnomer, for the person may never be the same afterwards. Now, let's consider a cumulative or multiplication factor: imagine a child raped two or three times a week, *by her father*, for 8 or 9 years or more of her life. This is over 800 rapes, and it is a child (Kluft, 1984). If an adult recovers with great difficulty from a single rape, what happens to a child to whom this is happening many, many times, over a long period of time?

My client, Gloria, who has DID, was frequently raped at night by her father from the age of 5 years until she was 12. Her mother was sleeping upstairs, knocked out on pills. At the time of the following event, Gloria herself had not remembered a number of things, although some of her child parts had started to tell me about them. The things they told me about were horrifying—bloody underwear, extreme pain—and not being able to sit down, something especially painful when she was at school. These child identities had only been able to tell me of the horribly painful and terrifying events a piece at a time because the entirety of this knowledge would have been too destabilizing for Gloria—the part of the self usually in executive control—to bear all at once. One morning I received an alarming phone call from Gloria's husband. He called to tell me that he had had to hospitalize her because of a drug overdose.

Strangely, Gloria did not remember taking any pills. Likewise, she had always insisted that she was not suicidal. In my efforts to discover possible triggers for what seemed from the outside a suicide attempt, I asked to speak to Cheryl, a child identity who often functioned as a somewhat bossy older sister and caretaker for the younger child parts. Cheryl told me that she had become exhausted from hearing the continual wailing of a younger child identity, Fred, whom she experienced as a younger brother. Because she felt she couldn't bear to hear Fred's crying anymore, she decided to give him pills to knock him out and make him stop crying. But she didn't know why he was crying. When I asked Fred why he had been crying so inconsolably, he told me that Gloria was about to take a trip back to the town where she grew up. Fred, who did not have access to Gloria's knowledge of the present, did not know that the father was dead. He thought the father was still alive and could rape him again.

After more exploration, Cheryl could talk about hating to hear Fred's crying (it seemed that Fred, much more than Cheryl, was the part desig-nated to contain most of the pain of the rapes). After talking with each of them I was able to establish better communication between them. Finally Cheryl understood why Fred had been crying. It also became clear that Cheryl, just like Gloria as a child, had always had to fend for herself and take too much responsibility for her young age. She had made a unilateral decision that was inappropriate for her level of matu-rity. To speak of and address Gloria's dissociated identities directly as she experiences them does not reify them. It does not invent a reality for something that did not exist before. The alternate identities, Cheryl and Fred, were already present in her experience as separate and distinct existences or parts of herself, and had been named in her early years. In addition, exploring in detail why Cheryl and Fred felt as they did helped Gloria to become aware of previously unknown aspects of herself, to "put herself together" in a way. In this way, it facilitated the integration of the parts.

As a child, Gloria had had little power to negotiate with her father about his abuse of her. Because her father had told her that if she told her mother it would kill her mother, she couldn't turn to her mother either. She had to bear and figure out everything by herself. Here we see how severe dissociation ensues from traumatic attachment. This reliance on internal grandiosity is a consequence of the absence of a reliable and trustworthy caregiver to turn to when in the vortex of psychological trauma that stems from interpersonal powerlessness. As a result of the failure of attachment figures, there is a failure of the attachment system. Since there was no attachment figure available to help, her overwhelming terror, shame, and pain could not be shared, communicated, or miti-gated. The little girl, Gloria, was completely isolated and captive. Just as

Gloria the child had been isolated, her child parts, Cheryl and Fred, were "isolated subjectivities" (Chefetz & Bromberg, 2004, p. 431).

A view only from outside the system, and initially from Gloria's perspective, did not reveal the motivations for the apparently suicidal behavior. For Gloria's action to be intelligible, I needed to talk to Cheryl and Fred. What emerged was a much more accurate and useful understanding of why Gloria was hospitalized. This included Fred's terror of being raped, and his inconsolable, lonely crying, and, then Cheryl's silencing Fred's unbearable crying, and enacting the solution that she had observed in her mother. This emergent understanding was achieved by my listening to the parts, which linked them separately and together to an outside person. This kind of linkage is what Philip Bromberg (1998) refers to as a *relational bridge*. What is needed to heal and bridge the dissociation of the parts is an *internalization* of the relationship of the separate parts with the outside knower, often the therapist. Once this is accomplished, the parts begin to become less phobic of one another's memories and feelings. For the dissociation in Gloria to begin to be healed, I needed to know more about Cheryl and Fred. Then Gloria had to learn to know what I knew. Thinking in terms of Murray Bowen's family therapy model (1985), Cheryl and Fred became more differentiated as they were able to talk to me and to each other about their different needs and intentions. Becoming differentiated and capable of inter-communication is an important step in healing. When the formerly dissociated self-states become capable of working in harmony, a person's life is happier and more functional.

Although there is a similarity in dissociative structure between dissociative identity disorder and less severe personal problems, DID is unique. In DID, the parts have a "pseudodelusional" (Kluft, 1984) investment in separateness, and the dissociative barriers between self-states are much more extreme and rigid. The presence of DID usually requires significant psychological trauma in childhood, when the capacity for self-hypnosis is high (Maldonado & Spiegel, 1998). People who were so highly traumatized as children that they developed DID are likely to have frequently needed to resort to self-hypnosis to cope. DID may be considered a taxon, a type in itself (Moskowitz, Heinmaa & Van der Hart, 2019; Putnam, 1997).

What does the case just described tell us about the unconscious? Gloria was unconscious of the activities of Cheryl and Fred, and hence, of the reasons for the suicidal behavior for which she was hospitalized. Thinking from the perspective of Gloria's mind, there is not one monolithic unitary unconscious.

The Unconscious

The most fundamental concept to psychodynamic psychotherapy, of whatever persuasion, is the unconscious. Repression and dissociation both result in aspects of experience becoming unconscious. In Freud's repression theory the unconscious is often thought of more as a unity, as a unified place. In trauma–dissociation theory, the dissociated parts of experience are separate, isolated from each other, and potentially numerous—even though there are likely some connections between them. As we know, the idea of an unconscious was in use long before Freud, even as early as the sixteenth century; and that in the nineteenth century and the early part of the twentieth century clinicians, novelists, and philosophers were preoccupied with the problem of dual and split consciousness. Are these the same thing?

Interlinking trauma, dual and split consciousness, dissociation, and hysteria, Pierre Janet outlined a psychodynamics of the personality based on dissociation of psychological phenomena, specifying that overwhelming trauma is dissociated and becomes subconscious. Is this the same as the unconscious? I suggest that there are some important distinctions to be made.

Are the "Unconscious" and Split/Dual Consciousness the Same Thing?

Often people use the terms, *subconscious* and *unconscious* interchangeably. The two constructs are similar in that the mind is divided in a way that creates an unawareness of certain aspects of experience. But, a key difference between the concepts of dual consciousness or fixed ideas (leading to subconscious) and the unconscious is that the *unconscious*, as Freud for the most part described it, refers to what we can infer *from the outside looking in*.

In contrast, Janet—as he was identifying and working with the subjectivities of different parts of the personality that were separate, dual, multiple, and isolated—was largely *looking from the inside out*. Onno van der Hart (2016) tells us that Janet was nicknamed "Dr. Pencil" by his patients because he meticulously wrote down everything they told him, as well as what they did, even awakening them from sleep to hear their dreams (p. 50). Although he was observing, he was also listening from the inside out. Taken together, and observed from the outside, all of these subconscious pieces of the self, from fixed ideas to separate identities, might be considered to constitute an "unconscious." However, I believe that the approach of working from the inside out, one that works with the different subjective aspects of the self, is more specific. It is closer to self-experience, more accurate clinically, and is ultimately more integrative than working with the less specific understanding that there is an unconscious.

Trauma and dissociation theory lends itself better to the Janetian view of fixed ideas and subconscious centers; and repression theory lends itself better to the idea of one unconscious.

The unconscious (as it connotes repression) is an outside view of intricacies of what Janet called doubling of the personality, and of the view of double consciousness that Freud (along with Breuer) initially endorsed in *Studies on Hysteria*. It is like looking at the continents on a globe model of the earth without being aware of all the submerged continents hidden from aerial view: moving tectonic plates, as well as volcanic activity, and ocean currents. Van der Hart (2016) notes that Freud was aware of the second state of consciousness, and used that idea at the same time as the notion of the unconscious early on. He references an 1882 letter by Freud to Breuer, which says: "The memory which forms an hysterical attack is an unconscious one, or more correctly, it is part of the second state of consciousness which is present in a more or less highly organized shape in every hysteria" (p. 31). However, after the publication of *Studies on Hysteria*, he rarely spoke of dissociation and or the second state of consciousness. Rather, he selectively ignored the second consciousness and interpreted his patients' communications in terms of the unconscious and repression (Van der Hart, personal communication, 2019).

Dissociative Unconscious and the Repressed Unconscious

I suggest that the dissociative results of trauma be called the *dissociative unconscious* and that the Freudian unconscious, into which repressed material is theoretically banished, be called the *repressed unconscious*. This does not change the overall meaning that by some means people become unaware of certain aspects of motivation, experience, information, and affect. It does make a differentiation as to how this happens and what it specifically means. The dissociative unconscious refers to a multiplicity of pockets (or realms) of subconscious experience (in Janet's sense). The traumas are still living, undigested fragments of overwhelming experience, even though there are likely some connections between these pockets. Philip Bromberg (1998) has elegantly reformulated the concept of the unconscious in dissociation terms, providing a very usable definition:

> What we call the unconscious might usefully include the suspension or deterioration of linkages between self-states, preventing certain aspects of self—along with their respective constellations of affects, memories,

values, and cognitive capacities—from achieving access to the personality within the same state of consciousness." (p. 182)

From the dissociation perspective, looking at how Gloria experienced herself and her world is very different from thinking in terms of one unified unconscious. Gloria's story exemplifies the dissociative unconscious, in which there are a multiplicity of strands and realms of dissociated experience. In contrast, the idea of a unitary unconscious lumps all of these intricacies of different experiences that are unavailable for conscious inspection into one undifferentiated pot.

Understanding from the Inside Out versus the Outside In

The repressed unconscious (that is, the unitary Freudian unconscious) refers to what we can infer *from the outside looking in.* As people appear to be unaware of their behavior or its meaning, the clinician may infer the meaning. One thing I like about thinking along the lines of the dissociative unconscious is that it approaches the person's mind from the inside out. As mentioned before, one way of thinking of Gloria's dissociative parts is that they were "isolated subjectivities" (Chefetz & Bromberg, 2004). Cheryl and Fred were isolated from each other and from Gloria until they could each talk to me; then I could talk to Gloria.

I believe that the approach of working from the inside out, one that works with the different subjective aspects of the self, is more specific, closer to self-experience, more accurate clinically, and ultimately more integrative than working with the less specific understanding that there is a unitary unconscious. Working from the inside out invites the client's inquiry into what is going on inside the mind and the body—accessing feeling states. This bypasses intellectualization and affords a greater link between mind and body. In contrast, working from the outside in is subject to much more intellectualization and invites inference that could easily be wrong on the part of the therapist. Privileging the client's subjectivity—and subjectivities—by working from the inside out implies empathy and curiosity for the client's different ways of being and feeling.

Is Dissociated Experience an Absence or a Presence?

Are isolated subjectivities, such as Cheryl and Fred, absences or presences? Gloria experienced Cheryl and Fred as both absences and presences, depending on how tenaciously she was holding on to her dissociative structure. Gloria had learned to encapsulate these dissociated experiences in a way that enabled her to manage her ongoing life as a child, by making them absences. However, from their own perspective, Cheryl and Fred were definitely presences. As they became increasingly known—as the dissociative barrier was healed—they became felt as present in Gloria's experience. The increasing acceptance of the presence of formerly exiled parts of the self contributed to the expansion of what was a persona into more of a full person.

The Procedural Unconscious

The repressed unconscious and the dissociative unconscious do not encompass all unconscious phenomena. Lyons-Ruth (1999, 2003ab; Ryle, 1997ab, 2003; Schore, 2003a, 2019) and others have written at length of procedural abilities and ways of being of which we are unaware. Allan Schore (2019) has, as previously noted, described in great detail how people communicate unconsciously, procedurally, and rapidly via the right brain. In particular, literal eye-to-eye communications occur in milliseconds and influence basic mindsets such as trust or fear.

Another aspect of body communication that may be on the border between conscious and unconscious, is *vibes*. A recent (2018) article by Tam Hunt describes how "the hippies were right," with respect to how much interpersonal communication occurs literally in vibrations. This renaissance of interest in vibrations is of great use clinically. As clinicians we respond to vibrations more often than we know. Among many other clinicians, I often feel something in my body such as rage, anger, fear, terror, or love. I then ask the client in one way or another if that is what he or she is feeling, and very often the answer is "yes." Recently, a client was discussing her anxiety about being jilted by a boyfriend. She was talking about anxiety, but I was feeling rage. I told her this, and then we explored rage, which it turned out was what she was feeling. This discussion opened up a new realm of acceptable experience for her. She was pleased that she could be more direct with her feelings toward those who were dismissing her or putting her down.

CHAPTER 6

Disorganized Attachment as Dissociation

The essential experience of trauma (is) an unraveling of the relationship between self and nurturing other, the very fabric of psychic life.
— Laub & Auerhahn (1993, p. 287)

DISORGANIZED ATTACHMENT (DA) AFFECTS about 15% of infants (Van Ijzen-doorn et al., 1999, as cited in Liotti & Gumley, 2008) and has been robustly linked to later dissociative tendencies (Lyons-Ruth, 2003ab, 2006), even more so than known abuse or documented traumas (Carlson, 1998; Lyons-Ruth, 2003b, 2006; Ogawa, Sroufe, Weinfield, Carlson, & Egeland, 1997). DA is the fourth and most recently discovered attachment pattern (Main & Solomon, 1986, 1990) and manifests the effects of a very early kind of developmental trauma. Giovanni Liotti, a world-renowned attachment researcher, viewed disorganized attachment as dissociative in itself (1992, 2004, 2006).

Let's start with a thumbnail sketch of attachment theory. Attachment is an evolutionary blueprint that serves survival. John Bowlby's evolutionary theory of attachment (1969/1983) documented how the baby's physical proximity to the mother is protective against predators and therefore supportive of survival. Thus, initially, physical closeness in situations of threat was understood to be the goal of the attachment system.

The second part of Bowlby's attachment theory was that of internal working models (IWM) that involve mental representations of the self and the attachment figure and concern the infant's expectation of the availability of the attachment figure. IWMs organize a child's feelings, thoughts, and expectations about attachment relationships. Generalizing from past experience with the attachment figure, they predict and regulate the child's behavior with attachment figures.

Even though they were formulated much earlier, attachment theory and trauma theory became widely recognized around the same chronological time, in the 1980s. Notably, attachment theory contradicted both Freudian dual-instinct theory (of libidinal and aggressive drives) and learning theories that viewed attachment in terms of secondary drives. Because of this incompatibility with dominant theories, Bowlby's findings were not immediately accepted. Countering the psychoanalytic emphasis on fantasy as opposed to reality at that time, Bowlby once stood up at a psychoanalytic meeting and emphatically insisted to the audience, "But there *is* such a thing as a *bad* mother" (Mitchell, 2000, p. 84, italics in text).

Attachment: Reducing Fear

Recently, attachment theorists have added to Bowlby's initial observations, stressing how attachment creates enhanced feelings of security and aids in the regulation of affect (Fonagy, 2001, Lyons-Ruth, 2003b). Importantly, attachment "regrounds clinical theory in the developmental dynamics of fear" (Lyons-Ruth, 2001, p. 40). Furthermore, the attachment system is regarded as "preemptive when aroused, since it mobilizes responses to fear or threat" (Lyons-Ruth, 2003b, p. 885). By regulating affect, attachment allows the "developing child's freedom to turn attention away from issues of threat and security toward other developmental achievements, such as exploration, learning and play" (Lyons-Ruth, 2003b, p. 885). Lyons-Ruth noted that this emphasis on reduction of fear significantly differs from an emphasis on libidinal and aggressive drives.

Initially, three attachment patterns were described, based on the behavior of 1-year-olds in the Strange Situation: a procedure devised by Bowbly's colleague, Mary Ainsworth, to evaluate infants' reactions to brief separations from their mothers. These patterns included secure attachment, which accounts for most of the infants studied, and two insecure attachment patterns: anxious avoidant attachment and anxious resistant (also called anxious ambivalent) attachment. Basically, secure babies expect well, avoidant babies expect to be rejected, and resistant ones anxiously expect inconsistency. Avoidantly attached children defend by distracting themselves from knowing about or showing attachment need, and the resistant (ambivalent) child is in your face with heightened attachment bids because the mother has been inconsistent. Despite the attachment difficulties for the two insecure patterns, like secure attachment, they are coherent. They are internally consistent attachment strategies that are adaptive to their particular interpersonal environments.

In contrast to the earlier attachment patterns, DA is not a coherent attachment strategy (Main & Solomon, 1986). Rather, it involves markedly segregated, disconnected, or dissociated models of attachment (Liotti, 1992, 2004, 2006; Lyons-Ruth, 2003b, 2006). DA is associated with maltreatment or gross neglect, and implies a very early kind of developmental trauma. In some way the infant's experience of the attachment figure has been too overwhelming to be assimilated into a consistent strategy of attachment. Although research-measured maltreatment accounts for most of those with DA, DA has also been linked to hidden traumas that are hard to measure, such as neglect, severe misattunement, and overly aggressive play. For example, a mother hissing on all fours, with fingers extended like claws, while playing with her frightened baby (Hesse & Main, 1999) or laughing as she picks up her wailing child (Lyons-Ruth, 1999) have been documented. It is important to recognize that things such as prolonged neglect, parental misattunement, and so on might not be overwhelming to an older child or adult, but are much more likely to be overwhelming to an infant or younger child. Thus, they may be traumatizing.

When a child faces the dilemma of both seeking safety from and fearing a caretaker at the same time, her attachment strategies are not likely to be integrated. Instead, "multiple and dissociated mental structures . . . control the child's actions. These structures may be related to incoherent, simultaneous representations of the self and the attachment figure (Liotti, 1995, p. 348). What is a child to do when the attachment figure, from whom safety is sought, is the one to be feared? In the Strange Situation, disorganized children will often alternatively approach the parent upon return, wanting to be engaged and attached, or flee from the parent. They may reach out toward the mother with their hands, but back up at the same time. They may go in circles or simply collapse on the floor. They may have a facial expression in which one side is eager to greet and another side is terrified. On videotape they often seem to simultaneously approach and withdraw or do both in quick succession. (Jacobvitz, 2000; Lyons-Ruth, 2003ab; Beebe & Lackmann, 2014). This dilemma has been called "fear without a solution" (Hesse & Main, 1999). In effect, one part of the infant wishes to connect with the parent and attach, and another part wants to get away. Here the attachment system has been activated, but so has the fear system, resulting in a repetitive approach-avoidance dilemma: "Caught in this loop, the child will experience such an overwhelming flow of contradictory affects as to exceed his or her capacities for a coherent, or even an ambivalent organization of behavior and attention . . . (and) attachment behavior will become disorganized and disoriented" (Liotti, 1999, p. 764).

Many of the disorganized children exhibit trance-like and stilled behavior, or appear to be staring into space (Jacobvitz, 2000; Lyons-Ruth, 2003ab). Thus, disorganized attachment is phenotypically dissociative (Blizard, 2003). Observing the frequently emotionally shifting, frightening behavior to which these infants are exposed, Liotti suggests that such experiences may be traumatizing if they "exceed the integrative powers of consciousness in this developmental period" (2006, p. 58). On the basis of observations that these babies, like dissociative adults, go into trance-like behaviors, Liotti (2006) stated that these traumatized babies exhibit hypnoid states. In other words, they were exhibiting dissociative symptoms.

This dilemma with which such children must deal often results in the child's difficulty in achieving a coherent sense of self and ways of regulating affect. Disorganized babies and young children have not been able to find coping strategies to regulate their affect. Early schemata that contributed to disorganized attachment are encoded in implicit memory and "are too complex and intrinsically contradictory to be later synthesized in a unitary, cohesive structure of explicit semantic memory. In this sense the IWM [internal working models] of early [disorganized] attachment is intrinsically dissociative" (Liotti, 2004, p. 479). The emotionally shifting, frightening, or violent interpersonal environments to which disorganized infants are exposed simply cannot be assimilated and organized in a coherent way.

In essence, with regard to DA, the basic substrates that may later develop into dissociated parts of the self are sometimes already there in infancy. Without some ameliorative life circumstances, DA is a likely precursor to borderline personality disorder and dissociative disorders, including DID. Even so, someone with DA but no later significant trauma, and who perhaps had accepting and empathic others in their interpersonal environment, may be able to heal the initial internal psychic rifts and avoid later serious psychological problems in living.

Someone with DA and neglectful, inattentive, or noncomforting parents might develop borderline pathology. Someone with DA and continuing severe abuse is likely to develop DID (Liotti, 1992, 2004). As Van der Hart (2018) notes, most of our dissociative clients have had disorganized attachment.

Earned Secure Attachment

Fortunately, attachment style is not set in stone. People can earn secure attachment even if they were not securely attached as infants. The availability of alternative emotional support figures, including psychotherapy, has been found to be associated with earned secure attachment (Saunders, et al., 2011). Earned secure attachment is characterized by metacognitive abilities, including the ability to think about one's own mental states and those of others, to decenter, and to reflect on the meaning of events (Main, 1995). Trauma interrupts and damages metacognitive abilities. Emotional support in thinking about damaging events mitigates the effects of trauma.

Self-Fragmentation Covered Over

Often, as disorganized young children grow older, by 3 to 5 years of age they reorganize their attachment strategies in certain controlling ways: (1) they become either compulsive caretakers of their parents, or (2) they become aggressively bossy and hostile (Liotti, 2006; Lyons-Ruth, 2001, 2006). It appears that they have "given up turning to the parent to help regulate their security and stressful arousal, [instead becoming] immersed in maintaining the parents' attention" (Lyons-Ruth, 2006, p. 608). Liotti (2006) notes these strategies inhibit the attachment system by substituting other motivational systems, such as an inverted caretaking behavioral system or a competitive, hierarchy-based behavioral system. For example, Tracy, age 8 years, had developed a style of seemingly organizing her mother. As a smart if somewhat bratty kid, she appeared well-adjusted and self-assured. Seldom needing reassurance, she would sometimes finish the sentences of her parents' friends. However, this was belied by extreme clinginess if her mother had to leave the home temporarily. In contrast, Sally, who was introduced in Chapter 4, attempted to control her mother from underneath, so to speak. By anticipating her mother's wishes and molding herself to them, she would forget about her own needs and feelings and devote herself to caring for her mother, bringing her tea and massaging her back.

A problem is that these strategies don't work in the long run. In situations in which these seemingly organized but actually disorganized older children (and later, adults) cannot avoid activating the attachment system, they lose their defensive organization that relies on other behavior systems. Exposed to the anxieties of their unresolved attachments, they become highly vulnerable and frightened. In testing situations in which separation anxiety is invoked by such things as the presentation of TAT (Thematic Apperception Test) pictures of a child being left alone, they suddenly become highly anxious, sometimes expressing fantasies of catastrophe at being left alone (Liotti, 2006). As long as the attachment system is not activated, they are relatively anxiety free, but when the attachment system is activated, they become highly symptomatic. The same has been noted of so-called borderline adults (highly traumatized, but organized in ways that overly sidestep attachment deficits and problems) who may become anxious and paranoid in intimate or stressful situations.

The controlling strategies have helped the child to cope with "the unbearable feeling of disorientation and disorganization linked to fright without a solution" (Liotti, 2006, p. 68). Even though the subverted bossy and submissive patterns that were developed in relation to caregivers were ways of coping with unresolved attachment dilemmas, the underlying *dissociative* structure is not defensive (Liotti, 2006). Rather, it is the broken psyche of an overwhelmed child. This brokenness is exposed when the attachment system is activated; when this happens, attachment-related anxieties and catastrophic fantasies emerge.

When the attachment system is activated in people with such dissociatively fragmented psychic organization, separation issues can be extremely painful. The psychotherapy relationship is a key arena in which the attachment system is activated. A frequently emerging issue is that these formerly disorganized children and later unresolved adults (the adult counterpart to DA) *can only regulate themselves by regulating others*. Because they have not been able to develop a coherent strategy for self-regulation, their only way to manage is to control others. When this strategy fails, they become very disorganized. When trauma strikes anew, they do not have a means to self-regulate or recover.

Awareness of this gives us as clinicians a better conceptual sense of how our clients feel when their attachment system is activated in psychotherapy, as it most likely will be. By holding in mind that it is by means of these strategies to manage and regulate the other that such clients have learned to regulate themselves, and that they have not learned other ways, clinicians can mitigate potential problematic countertransferential responses. It can be helpful for the clinician to openly and empathically recognize with such clients that part of the problem was that as a child they were deprived of being able to develop good ways of self-regulation and that dealing with it is part of the work of therapy. For example, Courtney initially said that she wanted to meet for psychotherapy three times a week, and I booked regular times for her. Then she decided that she could not afford that frequency and decided that she wanted to cut back to once a week. I booked a new once-a-week time schedule. Following this, she then frequently called or texted me the day before to say that she "really needed" an extra session the next day. I tried my best to accommodate her, sometimes overaccommodating. Even though she did not want to change the schedule, most of the time we ended up meeting two or three times a week. As we discussed this in the context of her earlier life, it became clear that she had seldom felt she could really have an effect on her mother by telling her how she felt. Instead, she had to do things, such as missing school, to get her mother to notice her. It was not easy for Courtney as we began to notice these things together. It made her anxious, and it was painful for her to face her longing for dependency. She was angry with me for not always having time to see her at the last minute. More and more, it became apparent that a major issue was her terror at not being able to control me—so as to not have to feel anxiously dependent. Bit by bit, she courageously became more vulnerable. She has recognized how hard and painful feeling dependency is for her. Coping anew with such past deprivation requires profound mourning. As Badouk Epstein (2018) notes, "The therapeutic journey thus is a grieving process which involves confronting and eventually accepting the weighty reality that ultimately, one has no control over another person, because we are here not as objects of possession, rather that we are separate beings with separate minds and thoughts" (p. 303).

Multiplicity, Attachment, Relationality, and Dissociation

Another aspect of how dissociation and attachment issues come together is *dissociative multiplicity* (O'Neil, 2009). People grow up embedded in relationships with other people. In accordance with the need to adjust to different attachment figures and relationships, humans are endowed with the capacity for multiplicity. This capacity, which is needed in most social interactions, has fostered the survival of human groups (Slavin & Kreigman, 1992). We all have multiple selves. Multiplicity allows us to enact different roles, such as parent, child, grandparent, student, teacher, victim, rescuer, persecutor, and so on. We have different ways of being and experiencing who we are in different role relationships (Ryle, 1997ab). We are different kinds of people, even different selves, in different relationships (Mitchell, 1993; Sullivan, 1953). Our multiplicity that varies with role and context is healthy. However, such health involves a certain discontinuity of self. As Stephen Mitchell (1991) noted, "because we learn to become a person through interactions with different others and through different interactions with the same other, our experience of self is discontinuous, composed of different configurations, different selves with different others" (p. 128).

In healthy multiplicity, we can flexibly change roles and types of interactions, even as we hold other self-states and role-relationships in an accessible background. Because people have multiple self-states and are more or less dissociative—owing to the inevitability of some relational trauma—none of us is a unity. We shift in our self-states, but what is important while we are in one state of mind is the accessibility of other states of mind. As Philip Bromberg (1993) has said: "Health is the ability to stand in the spaces between realities without losing any of them" (p. 186).

However, in dissociative multiplicity (O'Neil, 2009), one's multiplicity has been hijacked by dissociation, and self-states are not only multiple but dissociated, taking over consciousness without being connected to other states of mind and appearing more or less one at a time. The combined capacities for multiplicity and dissociation can be very helpful to children who find themselves in double-bind situations of contradictory attachment, such as abuse and/or neglect by a parent or caregiver. Here dissociative multiplicity allows a child to remain attached to and, most often, to love abusive or abandoning caregivers. Dissociation of parts of the mind that contain knowledge and feelings about abuse, abandonment, or neglect protects the child's ability to stay attached and to at least partially thrive. The lack of this ability could be psychologically ruinous.

As previously noted, attachment reduces fear. Thus, in a way that may seem counterintuitive, the fear of danger from a frightening caregiver increases the child's attachment need for that caregiver who, simultaneously, is the source of the danger. Dissociative multiplicity allows one dissociated part of the mind, or dissociated self-state, to stay attached, while other dissociated self-states hold the distrust, fear, and rage and remain inaccessible to the part of the self that is attached to the abuser. In this way, dissociative multiplicity protects the traumatized person from unbearable knowledge, preserving sanity.

The riveting memoir *Educated*, by Tara Westover, illustrates both the beneficial and destructive power of dissociative multiplicity. Westover describes an isolated and terrifying childhood and adolescence that was dominated by an authoritarian, exploitative, and highly unpredictable father. One of the beauties of her book is the way that she describes horrifying events from the emotional perspective of herself as a classically eager-to-please dissociated child who does not emotionally comprehend the ruthlessness with which she is being treated (even though Westover does not use the words "dissociated" or "eager to please," from my perspective, the narrative indicates this). For me, the dissociative split in her psyche allowed her to tolerate otherwise unbearable indignities and dangers. As we know, danger increases attachment need. And there was much danger in her life. For example, as a child she worked in her father's junkyard, and at times experienced heavy metal objects being thrown in her direction at high speed, once hitting her full in the stomach and knocking her to the ground. Other times the objects barely missed her body, resulting in her "shaking, but not from cold" (p. 56). Upon leaving home for college and then in graduate school, she had an exceptionally hard time honoring her needs, which were contrary to her father's wishes. Once she was on her own—and forced by her parents to choose between them and her independent life, in which she was a scholar and had friends—she sometimes fell apart. She often found herself unable to function, sometimes even running into the streets at night and screaming in a sleep-trance. Fortunately, she had the benefit of caring friends and advisors, got into therapy, dealt with her dissociative multiplicity, and got her doctorate. Her grit, resilience, persistence, and ultimately her faith in the possibility of goodness in others may have benefitted from her capacity for dissociative multiplicity.

Persistent Dissociative Multiplicity Is Maladaptive

Although the capacity for dissociation is often helpful in the short run, habitual dissociation becomes maladaptive in the long term, especially when the original traumatizing environment is no longer present. A life organized around dissociative avoidance of reminders of trauma makes for a constricted person who selectively inattends (Sullivan, 1953) to evidence that may be contrary to the maintenance of attachment bonds.

A problem for seriously traumatized, dissociated people is that these dissociated pieces of traumatic experience are always living in the present tense, without a sense that *this will be over soon*. Once they are converted into declarative memory, they can be known to be past. Another example of dissociative multiplicity and how dissociation works in the short term but fails in the long term is the story of Marilyn Van Derbur, who was Miss America in 1958. According to her autobiography, *Miss America by Day*, between the ages of 5 and 18, she was sexually abused by her father—every night. Yet, by day, she had no memory of what had happened, and she would go to school as if nothing had. In the daytime, she was a happy, popular, "good girl." She made good grades and was valedictorian of her class, graduating Phi Beta Kappa with honors from college. On the outside she appeared to have a perfect life, with a perfect family, including the wealthy and prominent father (though he secretly abused her). As the daytime persona, Ms. Van Derbur was not aware of the child who was traumatized at night. In my view, it is likely that because these memories of childhood terrors had been dissociated, she was able to excel in the world as a young adult. Yet it did not last: years after her Miss America success, she broke down with extreme anxiety, intruding flashbacks and memories of the abuse, and developed delayed-onset PTSD. She had frequent panic attacks, ulcers, and insomnia. As her experience of herself as the nighttime child abused by her father emerged, she was overwhelmed by the feelings of fear, disgust, and terrible shame that had been dissociated from the good girl with the wonderful family. Fortunately, she was able to find psychotherapeutic ways to heal, is greatly recovered, and is now a sought after motivational speaker.

CHAPTER 7

The Conundrum of Self-Criticism and Self-Attack

In any case, the attack as a rigid external reality ceases to exist and in the traumatic trance the child succeeds in maintaining the previous situation of tenderness.

—Sándor Ferenczi, 1949, p. 162

SHANNON HAS TOLD ME that most of the time she feels suffused with self-revulsion. One can almost see this in her facial expression and her posture. Jonathan constantly criticizes himself for being stupid, yet he is highly intelligent. Maria sometimes says to herself "I hate myself," even out loud, when she becomes anxious about some imagined or real social faux pas. Yet, Maria, who is an ethical and kind human being, doesn't deserve to hate herself. Terry stops herself from receiving promotions, putting herself in a negative light, because she feels she is not good enough—despite the fact that her work is excellent and deserves a promotion. Jenny injures her vagina in a compulsive way when she is in a frightening situation that she feels she cannot control. All she knows is that her husband and earlier abusers have hurt her there. Marty, an ethical, kind person, woke up on the floor in his own bedroom where no one else had been present, to find his body hogtied. Although as a child he had endured being hogtied, he did not know how he did it to himself in his sleep. Jane—a woman of stellar character, received marriage proposals from two kind and wealthy men that she liked—but she chose a man who raped and exploited her; abused her physically and mentally. She said that she did not deserve to marry either of the kind men. Sally continually lets con artists take advantage of her. Why?

What happens? Why is it that some highly competent, intelligent, ethical, essentially kind and loving people undermine themselves, hurt themselves, punish themselves, and feel that they are not good enough to claim many of the simple pleasures and benefits that life can offer?

Different answers have been offered to this question, such as that people seek the familiar, or as is said in Freudian psychoanalytic theory, they have harsh superegos. Beyond providing a sort of theoretical explanation, do these words and phrases tell us anything useful for healing? Other than expressing sympathy or suggesting that the person does not deserve their harsh self-treatment, does it help to tell someone that they have a severe superego or that they are being hard on themselves? Saying this might sometimes even be harmful because it induces the shame of helplessness. What people with such supposed superego problems need is agency, not helplessness. Here, we need to find ways of helping with the self-critical, self-sabotaging, and self-attacking dilemmas. We need to look at the damage done in infancy and childhood by trauma and dissociation, centering on attachment disruptions.

Let's start at the beginning: infancy. Recent attachment research indicates that human beings are hard-wired as infants with the capacity to know and to learn that they are like other humans (Stern, 1995, 2004; Trevarthen, 2009, Beebe & Lachman, 2014, Meltzoff & Moore, 1977). Humans are social animals from birth. Through early interactive, multiple sensory and cross-modal communications, infants can imitate and dialogically communicate within hours of birth. The infant's ability to be aware of others' affects and intentions amounts to a primary intersubjectivity (Trevarthen, 2009a). One learns that one is like other humans by a bidirectional, interregulatory, affective and communicative process in which each influences and is influenced by the other. As Daniel Stern (2004) says: "Intersubjectivity is a condition of humanness" (p. 97).

Biologically designed to respond to other humans and to join in the human conversation, the infant is very sensitive to ruptures in engagement. Let's examine Edward Tronick's famous still-face experiment (Tronick, Als, Adamson, Wise, & Brazelton, 1978). First designed and implemented in the early 1970s, the researcher asks a mother to engage with her baby, playing and responsively interacting, and then to suddenly stop and adopt a still face (videos of this experiment can be found online by searching "still face," or "Tronick"). What does the baby do? First the baby tries to get the mother to reengage by smiling, cooing, gesticulating, pointing, pleadingly reaching out its hands to the mother. Then the baby gives distress calls. Then the baby's body becomes disorganized and appears to fall apart. Finally, the baby gives up, turning its head away sadly and hopelessly. Three minutes later, the mother reengages, and, with a little time, the baby comes back online in a dyadic world of intersubjectivity and interconsciousness. Repair has been achieved. This lab experiment drama ends happily.

What if the kind of parental nonresponsiveness depicted in the Tronick experiment were not an experiment, but occurred in real life frequently or chronically? How would these children feel and behave?

Tronick and his colleagues (1978) compare the final withdrawn behavior of the infant to Bowlby's description of the withdrawn behavior of children who have been separated from their caregivers, and the isolated and frightened behavior of Harlow's monkeys who were separated from their mothers (Harlow & Zimmerman, 1958). The infant's hopeless response is reminiscent of Spitz's cases of "hospitalism" and failure to thrive. Rick Ackerly (2012) writes: "Perhaps the child's distress is the frustration of no longer having an effect on her mother rather than her "loss." Smiling, beguiling faces, pointing, reaching, clapping, whining, even screeching . . . all her tried-and-true methods no longer work. She had power; then she lost it . . . Maybe the baby is experiencing power-lessness." I agree. One very compelling interpretation is that the baby's sense of agency, specifically of being able to have an effect on the mother, is crushed, at least momentarily.

Of course, there are many forms of parental nonresponsiveness and misattunement that do not involve a literal still face and that are psychologically damaging. Sally (introduced in Chapter 4), whose parents thought she was half Indian as a result of her mother's affair, says that her mother never touched her. As a child she would have periods of severe withdrawal and near immobility that doctors diagnosed as failure to thrive and that her parents called weak spells. Asked what this felt like to her, she said, "It's like being swallowed by pain, like drowning." Since childhood, and even into adulthood, Sally has been vulnerable to psychically disappearing "down a rabbit role" when she feels rejected. She says that just before she disappears, she feels like, "I can't take it anymore. I can't fight it . . . it's like throwing in the towel. It feels like going under, like being dead. I've tried to hold up hope, but then the bottom falls out."

How does the young child make sense of the world when the bottom falls out? First, let's examine what happens neurophysiologically.

Posttraumatic Biological States

Sally's severe withdrawals are consistent with the dorsal vagal parasympathetic response of autonomic nervous system, as described by Stephen Porges in his polyvagal theory (2011). The dorsal vagal complex (DVC), which is activated in situations of extreme terror, causes depression of metabolic activity, conserving oxygen and energy.

Porges proposed three phylogenetic substrates of the social nervous system that involve neural regulation of the autonomic nervous system. In humans these are arranged in a hierarchical organization of response patterns. The DVC is the first and earliest of these response patterns. It is characteristic of reptiles and responds to threat by depression of metabolic activity.

The second stage of response is characterized by the sympathetic nervous system (SNS), which can increase metabolic output, thus enabling fight/flight/freeze. It involves increased muscle tension, shutdown of digestion, and rapid heartbeat. A person experiences fear and/or anger, and readiness to move in fight/flight. However, the freeze response is slightly different. The animal is momentarily immobile, but with racing heart and tense musculature—like the deer that resembles a statue as you approach, but is ready to flee the moment you leave. For prey animals freezing on the spot may sometimes be more effective than flight in the open because the motions cues of the latter can activate the predator's strike response (Nijenhuis, et al., 1998). Importantly, the fight/flight/freeze sympathetic system is not socially communicative.

The third stage, the ventral vagal complex (VVC) is unique to mammals and characterized by the social engagement system. This includes social signaling systems for motion, emotion, and communication, as well as the capacity for self-soothing. It enables people to use social communication in service of survival. It also involves the ability to regulate metabolic output. The VVC is the system that the babies in Tronick's experiment were initially engaged in with the mother, before the still face.

Porges proposed that during danger or threat, or when the more advanced systems fail, the organism falls back on the next most recently phylogenetically developed organization. In this way, Tronick's babies went from the ventral vagal social engagement, the VVC, to the sympathetic activation, which is one step lower phylogenetically; when these failed, they reverted to the earliest response, the DVC, the dorsal vagal activation. Perceived imminent threat, threat of impending death, or being rendered immobile can trigger this DVC response in animals. It is characterized by lowered respiration, heartbeat, blood pressure, and muscle tension—even immobility and physiological surrender to the point of looking dead. Although this reversion to earlier phylogenetic forms may be helpful in the short run, when expressed over long periods, according to Porges, it is damaging to the nervous system.

Aspects of this dorsal vagal response have been described variously as a hypoaroused "dissociative" response by Allan Schore (2003ab, 2009, 2019) and by Bruce Perry (1999), as "tonic immobility" (Forsyth, Gallup, Fusé, & Lexington, 2008; Moskowitz, 2004; Sapolsky, 2004), and as "total submission" described by Van der Hart and colleagues (2004).

Discussing the dorsal vagal complex, Schore (2003ab, 2009) pinpoints the infant's two psychophysiological responses to danger: hyperarousal and hypoarousal-dissociation. In terror or trauma, the hyperarousal of the sympathetic component of autonomic nervous system (ANS) is activated first, along with increases in heart rate and blood pressure. There are visible signs of distress. Following this is parasympathetic activation, which results in psychic detachment from unbearable affect. Dorsal vagal activity is like a brake on the sympathetic activity; it decreases heart rate and blood pressure despite the increased stress hormones of noradrenaline and adrenaline. In addition: "The child's dissociation in the midst of terror involves numbing, avoidance, compliance and restricted affect (the same pattern as adult PTSD)" (Schore, 2009, p. 111). Schore adds that in the dissociation response infants seem to be staring off into space with a "glazed look." The dissociative process of this "intensified parasympathetic arousal allows the infant to maintain homeostasis in the face of the internal state of sympathetic hyperarousal" (Schore, 2003a, p. 125).

Bruce Perry (1999), who studied the children of the Waco disaster, has similarly described varied PTSD patterns in children, in particular, posttraumatic neurodevelopmental processes of hypoarousal and hyperarousal. These responses become more pronounced with more severe, chronic, and early trauma. The hypoarousal pattern that Perry also calls *dissociative* involves symptoms such as numbing, analgesia, derealization, depersonalization, catatonia, and fainting, along with low heart rate (bradycardia). The hypoaroused children, especially females, infants, and young children, exhibited robotic compliance, glazed expressions, and passivity. It is adaptive to extreme pain. The other response pattern, hyperarousal, is more characteristic of older boys and men and involves fight/flight reactions, including elevated heart rate, vigilance, behavioral irritability, increased locomotion, and increased startle response. Perry suggests that these patterns were evolutionarily adaptive in that invading tribal warriors would be more likely to kill the men, but capture the women and young children. Thus, fight/flight would be the men's best defense, while being still and quiet would be the best survival behavior for women and young children. Despite the gender differences that Perry found, generally, hypo- and hyperarousal patterns are interactive. Most individuals suffering from this altered neurobiology use combinations of the two patterns.

The Curative Power of Self-Blame

In a world that makes no sense to the abused or neglected child, in which the child feels rejected and alone, self blame makes a disjointed and frightening reality fit into a sense of comprehensibility. It preserves the illusion of personal power, the loss of which can feel devastating. Another serious problem for the neglected or abused child is the intense shame of feeling that one does not matter to the abusing or neglecting caregiver or significant other.

In situations of abuse there is often no way to stop being "bad" in the eyes of the other. The perspective that the child is "bad" has been fixed by the abuser, and is a defining aspect of the interpersonal situation. The child may have been told by the abuser that she or he wants to be abused and that that is the reason for the abuse. Thus, in a convoluted way, being "good," that is, attached to the abuser, depends upon being "bad."

In a seemingly counterintuitive way, self-blame can be a way of coping with the intense shame. In such moments, one is helpless, and the situation can feel unendurable. If one can do something, even if it is with the interpersonal glue of self-devaluation, one can feel better. A self-declaration of personal badness may be preferable to the potentially emotionally overwhelming helplessness of being severely shamed, often unpredictably, by an attachment figure. If one can say something to oneself like, "It's my fault," then the abuse can at least make sense. For example, Sally said that she couldn't figure out (at the time) why her parents hated her. She said, "I loved my parents, but they didn't love me back. The only reason I had to explain this was that I was bad." In situations like this, saying to oneself something like, "I'm useless, stupid, ridiculous" is helping in a kind of way, helping a person not to totally collapse or submit. By marshaling some energy into a schema of the self that makes sense, it helps a person feel continuous and sane and possibly, at least temporarily, prevents dorsal vagal collapse.

The Importance of Attachment

As noted in the previous chapter, John Bowlby observed that human beings are innately wired for attachment (1969), which serves survival. More recent attachment theorists have stressed how attachment aids in affect regulation. Bowlby's theory of internal working models (IWM), involves mental representations of the self and the attachment figure and concerns the infant's expectation of the availability of the attachment figure. Thus, a child such as Sally may internalize the parent's view of herself or himself and view the self as unworthy.

A core dissociative problem originates in a trauma-laden attachment. What happens when the person from whom protection is sought is the same one against whom protection is needed? How does the child handle the danger of attachment loss when the parent or attachment figure is frighteningly punitive, overly neglectful, traumatically shaming, or is predatory—especially since danger intensifies the need for attachment? In such situations, the child's ability to feel safely attached may depend on the dissociative compartmentalization of parts of the self that hold memories, perceptions, cognitions, and affects, including terror and rage, that are contradictory to attachment.

In his concept of *disconnection*, an aspect of his larger concept of *defensive exclusion*, Bowlby (1980) provided an explanation of what happens when the abuser and attachment figure are one and the same. In *disconnection*, information inconsistent with the attachment is disconnected from awareness, so that the child keeps favorable views of the parents in consciousness, while knowledge of their bad or disappointing aspects is excluded from the first information system. In this way, attachment is maintained, but kept in a separate information compartment, so that contradicting feelings and information are kept out of awareness. In the service of attachment, survival, safety, and security, the helpless abused child is more likely to blame the self than the perpetrator.

In her own evolutionary theory developed from her research in cognitive psychology and the study of social contracts, Jennifer Freyd (1996) described how betrayal by a significant attachment figure on whom the child depends, can amount to "betrayal trauma." She states that "betrayal blindness" serves survival in cases of dependence on an abusive caretaker. It follows then, that the betrayal in child abuse, which is a betrayal of attachment trust, often results in the blockage of knowledge about the abuse.

Attachment and the Developmental Dynamics of Fear

The attachment system does not operate only in infancy, but pertains to us throughout the life cycle. As Bowlby (1984) now famously said: "All of us, from the cradle to the grave, are happiest when life is organized as a series of excursions, long or short, from the secure base provided by our attachment figures" (p. 11). Thus, adults, like children in abusive relationships, may also become more attached to the abuser as a result of the abuse. Because of the preemptive power of attachment and the subsequent dissociation of unbearable knowledge and affects that are contradictory to attachment, they often find it hard to leave. This process by which the victim idealizes the abuser while dissociating the abusive aspects has also been called "traumatic bonding" (Dutton & Painter, 1981).

Attachment: Disconnection and Dissociation

Karlen Lyons-Ruth (1999) introduced the concept of "enactive procedural representations of how to do things with others" (p. 585) as an aspect of attachment. These procedural (implicit) enactive models of relationships are often adaptations to the parents' inadequacies, inconsistencies, and defenses (Lyons-Ruth, 1999, 2001). Although not conscious, they are major means of human exchanges and communications, underpinning the interactions of much of our lives. When development has gone fairly well different procedural ways of being with others are interconnected. However, when there is little mutuality or compassionate intersubjective closeness, some implicit ways of being with others may become affectively and cognitively disconnected from each other—as well as from declarative knowledge.

When implicit relational knowledge is contradictory to clear, explicit information of autobiographical memory about the self and others, such incompatibility can evoke conflicting and segregated models of understanding and predicting human relationships. For example, the person may have been told that the abusing parent was a wonderful person or the parent may have represented himself or herself to the world as such. This sets up conflicting ways of understanding and relating to the world. If there is no collaborative relationship within which to work these contradictions out, these patterns of relating remain segregated and unexamined. As a consequence, a person may then be unable to formulate the meaning of painful and traumatic past experiences. A person may consciously believe that the abusing parent was wonderful, yet shrink away when the parent is in the room. For example, one day in a therapy session Sonia told me about the searing pain of being raped by her father

and the desolation of being ignored by her mother. I thought the awareness in her revelation was a good starting point for more intensive work.
The following day she began the session by telling me that her parents
were wonderful parents, and she was a bad daughter. Then I realized
that her tendency to dissociate her terrible memories was the appropriate
focus of our work at that moment in time.

A significant problem is that attitudes and behaviors based on implicit
relational knowledge, for instance, submissiveness or eagerness to please,
may remain unavailable for examination. The person is left with feeling
bad but not knowing why. Feeling bad in the sense of being injured or
humiliated is easily distorted into "being bad, " as Harvey Schwartz has
noted (1994). Self-as- injured becomes self-as-bad. So, the child who is
longing for reciprocation of attachment may be in a constant shame state
of believing oneself is bad. Thus, in a perverse kind of way the security
of attachment rewards the child's shameful "badness."

Identification with the Aggressor

Sándor Ferenczi (1931, 1932, 1949), wrote passionately about what happens to the child in the traumatic moment of being terrified and abused.
In his concept of identification with the aggressor, he wrote of how and
why the child cannot assimilate the events into narrative memory. The
traumatically overwhelmed child goes into a trance-like state:

> These children feel physically and morally helpless . . . for the overpower-
> ing force and authority of the adult makes them dumb and can rob them
> of their senses. The same anxiety, however, if it reaches a certain maximum,
> compels them to subordinate themselves like automata to the will of the
> aggressor, to divine each one of his desires and to gratify these; completely
> oblivious of themselves they identify themselves with the aggressor . . .
> the weak and undeveloped personality reacts to sudden unpleasure not by
> defense, but by anxiety-ridden identification and introjection of the men-

acing person or aggressor . . . .One part of their personalities, possibly the nucleus, got stuck in its development at a level where it was unable to use the alloplastic way of reaction but could only react in an autoplastic way by a kind of mimicry. (1949, pp. 162–163)

Autoplastic means changing the self; alloplastic means having an effect on or modifying the other. While orienting around the abuser's wishes and demands, the child accommodatingly modifies the self. Identifying with the aggressor, for Ferenczi, primarily means identifying with the aggressor's wishes and needs. However, as I read Ferenczi, the child also identifies procedurally and by mimicry with the aggressor's behavior: things like facial expression, posture, and words may be automatically mimicked. This automatic procedural mimicking is in contrast to the purposeful identification with the aggressor's role about which Anna Freud, using the same term, later (1937/1966) wrote.

Infants, even soon after birth, actively engage in mimicry (Meltzoff and Moore, 1977; Trevarthen, 2009), and children spontaneously imitate those around them, in speech, postures, and mannerisms. Today, one would also likely invoke the activity of mirror neurons (Gallese, 2009a, 2009b) in this procedural identification. In their work with monkeys, Gallese, Fadiga, Fogassi, and Rizzolatti (1996) found that the same premotor neurons fire when the monkey performs an action, such as eating a peanut, as when it observes another monkey performing the action. This they call "embodied simulation."

Ferenczi is not describing an identification that involves agency and initiative. Nor is he describing healthy identification in which the process augments and expands the child's developing sense of identity—in which the identification is linked with the rest of the self.

One of the things that Ferenczi's concept of identification with the aggressor helps us to understand is that it is not just that the aggressor has somehow gotten inside the child, causing reenactments of the aggression—usually against the self—but that the psyche has become split so that one part of the self preserves the feeling of tenderness about the relationship, while other parts of the self contain unbearably terrifying memories, and others contain the embodied procedurally mimicked aspects of the aggressor's behavior, often fueled by the person's own rage.

Ferenczi (1949) wrote:

> The aggressor disappears as part of external reality and becomes intra— as opposed to extra-psychic; the intra-psychic is then subjected, in a dream-like state as is the traumatic trance, to the primary process . . . .In any case, the attack as a rigid external reality ceases to exist and in the traumatic trance the child succeeds in maintaining the previous situation of tenderness. (p. 162)

Thus, from the attachment-oriented victim position, a positive attachment relationship with the abuser, a "situation of tenderness" is preserved in consciousness. For example, Sally (mentioned earlier in this chapter), tried her best to mold herself into someone her mother would love. As a consciously loving preadolescent and adolescent, she always came home directly after school so that she could serve her mother tea on a tray. She massaged her mother's body with the fingers that her mother had beaten.

Unfortunately the child's belief in this situation of tenderness is illusory, for in a dissociatively sequestered part of the mind, in the inner world, information and feelings that are unacceptable from an attachment perspective live on.

I (Howell, 2014a) have suggested an expansion of Ferenczi's observations, such that identification with the aggressor can be understood as a two-stage process. The first stage is automatic and initiated by trauma, but the second stage is defensive and purposeful. While identification with the aggressor begins as an automatic organismic process, with repeated activation and use, it gradually becomes a defensive process.

Once established, the development of an inner aggressor part that oversees and preemptively curtails thought and behavior by intuiting and predicting the aggressor's behavior is a great asset to the child in this environment. In a way that is like a preemptive strike, a persecutory, critical part's enacted behavior often mimics the original abuser. That is, identification with the aggressor works predictively and preventively, and this is usually (but not always) directed toward the self, especially the part of the self that interacts with the world.

For example, Nancy, whose psychologically remote mother was often unable to care for her and whose father was absent, was sent from age 6 years until age 16 years to live with her maternal aunt and uncle. Her fundamentally religious aunt and uncle loved and cared for her, and paid for her medical and school needs, including her college, but they also expected extreme obedience. She always felt that she had to "be a good girl." Partly because her aunt and uncle were not her real parents, she always feared deep down that if she was not extremely "good," if she did not bow to every implied injunction, whether she believed in it or not, they wouldn't love her, or at least not as much. Of course, she was never angry or full of her own feelings in relation to them. Possibly unacceptable attitudes or feelings were never discussed; nor did she have any such conscious thoughts at that time. She was too afraid of losing their attachment. Not surprisingly, she now often feels that she is bad for having angry, hateful, or hostile thoughts toward her friends or others. When they occur, such thoughts usher in a self-attack. Recently she even told me that she thought that she was evil for having these bad thoughts.

In our work I have often sympathized with the angry part of Nancy who worked so hard and so continuously and vigilantly to monitor her behavior around her caregivers. I observed what a good job that part of her had done in keeping her safe (from showing negative emotion) in her childhood environment. At the same time I have encouraged self-compassion by enquiring about how she felt about having to be so good. This twin approach has allowed the self-attacking part of her some recognition. By becoming aware of how unthinkable it had been at the time for her to have anything but appreciative thoughts and compliant behavior toward her caregivers, she is beginning to be able to recognize that they were not entirely her saviors. Rather, in many important ways they also restricted her ability to feel like a self, entitled to her own feelings.

Modeled on an abusive caregiver, rageful, persecutory self-states often punish the person because from the perspective of these parts of the mind such punishment is necessary for the person's safety and protection. In the original family environment it was often not safe for the person to express feelings of dissatisfaction or anger. The aggressor-identified part of the self works in a way that is predictive and prevents shock. What looks from the outside to be self-abuse is a defensively learned way to provide safety, preserve attachment, and finally to protect sanity. This has much in common with what Philip Bromberg (1998) called an early warning system, a fail-safe security system that is always hypervigilant for trauma. This dissociative vigilance of being on alert safeguards an ongoing sense of subjectivity and protects against emotional deregulation and annihilation anxiety. Thus, the vigilant intention to avoid current and future trauma ends up contributing to continual internal reenactment of the past traumatic situations.

Better to Be a Sinner in God's World

Ferenczi's thinking anticipated Ronald Fairbairn's (1944/1952) writings about how abused or frightened children preserve the tender aspects of the relationship with the abusive or neglectful caregiver by taking the burden of badness of the aggressor into themselves, thereby maintaining their attachment and tender feelings toward the aggressor. Both Ferenczi and Fairbairn underscored that this internalized aspect of the traumagenic relationship was deeply buried. Fairbairn's (1944/1952) famous statement that:

> It is better to be a sinner in a world ruled by God, than a saint in a world ruled by the Devil. A sinner in a world ruled by God may be bad, but

there is always a sense of security to be derived from the fact that the world around is good . . . In a world ruled by the Devil the individual may escape the badness of being a sinner; but he is bad because the world around him is bad. . . .[with no] sense of security and no hope of redemption. The only prospect is one of death and destruction." (pp. 66–67)

By becoming "a sinner" in God's world, the frightened, neglected, or abused child learns to inhibit knowledge and expression of hatred and emotional longing. This reduces the risk of diminishing the love of the attachment figures, which would make them less "good" in reality. Fairbairn also described a "moral defense" in which the child internalizes some good aspects of the parents, thus providing some internal goodness. As a result, the child can be morally and conditionally bad (and good) in relationship with these internalized good objects.

Fairbairn (1944/1952) also wrote about dissociogenic shame:

The experience is one of shame over needs which are disregarded or belittled. In virtue to these experiences of humiliation and shame, he feels reduced to a state of worthlessness, destitution, or beggardom. His sense of his own value is threatened, and he feels bad in the sense of "inferior" . . . and intensity of need itself increases his sense of badness by contributing to it the quality of "demanding too much." At the same time his sense of badness is further complicated by the sense of impotence which he also experiences. At a still deeper level . . . the child's experience is one of, so to speak, exploding ineffectively . . . It is thus an experience of disintegration and imminent psychic death. (p. 113)

The ultimate result is what Fairbairn (1944/52) called the "schizoid dilemma," in which the self becomes divided, and the person's deepest needs and feelings are hidden from other people.

A small example of how shame can cause a person to keep feelings hidden from others was Jesse's experience at 12 years of age, when her

dog died. She turned to her father with her grief. Instead of sympatheti-
cally understanding, her father criticized her, sternly telling her that she
should not be thinking of her own sadness about her dog's death. Rather,
she should be feeling sorry for and thinking about her dead dog. This
experience was so shaming—especially as it turned on the issue of Jesse's
"goodness," or lack of it, in her father's eyes—that it had an indelible
effect on Jesse's sense of safety in revealing her feelings to others.

The Dissociogenic Power of Shame

Shame encapsulates a person's feelings of unworthiness and personal
badness. In shame, the focus is on the self, while in guilt the focus is on
one's behavior (H. Lewis, 1971; Lynd, 1958). In shame one "is bad." In
contrast, "doing bad" or "did bad," characterizes guilt. Guilt is about an
act, a transgression, and it can often be remedied by an act of penance.
In contrast to guilt, in which one can, as an independent agent, "do
something" to make it go away, shame is often unremitting, and the
person is helpless. As Helen Lewis, a pioneer in work on shame (1990),
put it. "I use the term *shame* to cover a family of feelings: humiliation,
mortification, feeling ridiculous, painful self-consciousness, chagrin,
shyness, and embarrassment. Each of these states differs from the others,
but all have in common that the self is helpless" (p. 249). People blush;
feel self-conscious, worthless, exposed, and powerless; and may feel like
they want to crawl under the table to hide. One of the worst things
about shame is that it begets more shame; one may be ashamed of being
ashamed (H. Lewis, 1990).

A large part of shame's affective power derives from the fear of being
excluded, banished from one's attachment figures and from one's human
context (Lynd, 1958). In intense shame one may feel that one's existence
is held in the eyes of the attachment figure, and shame that is too intense
and unrelieved can be excruciating and immobilizing (H. Lewis, 1971,
1981, 1990; M. Lewis, 1992).

The need for attachment and redemption from shame can be so great that "in the midst of a situation in which one is overwhelmed by shame, one may confess to a crime of which one is innocent, inviting punishment in order to reestablish even through condemnation, communication with others" (Lynd, 1958, p. 66). This preference to feel oneself to be "bad" rather than banished adds texture to Fairbairn's (1944/52) statement that "it is better to be a sinner in a world ruled by God than a saint in a world ruled by the Devil."

The emergence of shame in development is dependent on the capacity for self-consciousness (M. Lewis, 1995). The self reflects upon itself: one is both subject and object simultaneously. When one is shamed, one is acutely and painfully aware of the self. Shame goes to one's core, to the core of the self and of identity. As Sylvan Tompkins, observes: "It does not matter whether the humiliated one has been shamed by derisive laughter or whether he mocks himself. In either event he feels himself naked, defeated, alienated, lacking in dignity or worth" (quoted in Nathanson, 1992, p. 146).

Because shame is potentially so powerful and so noxious, people try to distance themselves from it. Shame that is too severe or too prolonged can be overwhelming. The hallmark of trauma is its capacity to overwhelm. By this definition, overwhelming shame can be traumatic—and therefore dissociogenic. Likening shame to the "severe anxiety" that Sullivan (1953, p. 152) compared to "a blow on the head," Bromberg (1998) states: "Shame signals a traumatic attack upon one's personal identity and typically calls forth dissociative processes to preserve selfhood" (p. 295).

A large part of the traumatic damage of abuse and neglect stems from the unremitting, unendurable, and inescapable shame involved. Writers about the terrors of concentration camps such as Dori Laub and Nanette Auerhahn (1989), Victor Frankl (1959), and Alexandr Solzhenitsyn (1974) assert that the one of the most debilitating aspects of concentration camp experience—an even more powerful threat to survival than physical deprivations and punishments—is the experience of being shamed, being reduced to a nonentity, a nothing, a cipher. Survivors of traumatic abuse often report the same: body injuries don't hurt as much as the emotional pain of feeling so denigrated, so shamed. Often a significant part of the dissociative posttraumatic damage of abuse and neglect stems from the unremitting, unendurable, and inescapable shame involved.

When I asked Maria, mentioned at the beginning of this chapter, if she could trace back in her experience the times she felt compelled to say "I hate myself" out loud or to herself, she began to notice that they all had in common events in which she felt shamed or potentially shamed in the eyes of another person. As we explored some of these different instances in her memory of expressed self-hatred, she was able to catch and momentarily stay with the sense of real emotional terror and anxiety of an intense shame state. It seemed that rather than being able to stay with the anxiety of the shame, her mind split into an attacking and a shamed self, which while extremely unpleasant, seemed to be preferable to being in the grip of the mortifying shame experience.

It seems that the precarious connection to the other in shame can be so traumatic that the self-splitting removes the other from self-experience, making the focus the internal world, so that longing for acceptance and connection and the dread of not having it has been disappeared. For Maria, being able to find this experience was an important beginning for deconstruction of her self-hatred. Re-finding that longing for admission into the human fold is vitally important for healing.

Part of what was healing for Maria was that by being able to tolerate what had previously been overwhelming shame, she turned a compulsive automatic behavior into what could be considered a habit. One cannot conquer a compulsion by will, but it is possible to reflect upon a habit, to realize that some behaviors and reactions are unnecessary, and to change them by choice.

Shame usually depends upon an accepting human relationship for the release from it to occur. One reason that an accepting relationship can provide release is that it shifts the perspective. No longer is the negative self-scrutiny so excruciating: one can see oneself from the perspective of the accepting other. When shame is not too intense, it can also be dissipated or righted by loving humor, empathy, and time.

Compassion and humor can soften the corrosive power of shame. For those old enough to remember, in the late 1980s and early '90s, the network television sitcom, *Family Matters,* had a character named Steven Urkel. Steven was always making silly, shameful mistakes, after which he would innocently look around and say, "Did I do that?" It was funny. We laughed at him, as well as with him and our vicarious selves. The humor of it, which normalized making silly mistakes, was socially curative.

Freud: From Shame to Superego

Curiously, as Freud built his superego construct piece by piece, he first began talking about shame; he eventually came around to talking about fear and terror, exemplified in fears of castration for the boy, or loss of love for the girl, as part of the Oedipus complex. In essence, the superego, like the dissociated structures in the attachment models of Bowlby (1969/83, 1973, 1984), Fairbairn (1944, 1958) and Ferenczi (1949, 1931/80), *is born of traumagenic shame and fear.*

In *Mourning and Melancholia* (1917/1959), Freud notes that in contrast to normal mourning, in melancholia, the person mercilessly berates oneself. However, the castigation is usually not for one's own qualities, but unconsciously for those of an intimate other, where there has been an attachment loss. The melancholic has dealt with this loss, according to Freud, by establishing an "identification of the ego with the abandoned object." How did this come about? Contrasting melancholia to mourning, Freud writes:

An object-choice, an attachment of the libido to a particular person, had at one time existed; *then owing to a real slight or disappointment from this loved person, the object-relationship was shattered.* . . . Thus the shadow of the object fell upon the ego, so that the latter could henceforth be criticized by the special mental faculty like an object, like the forsaken object. In this way . . . the conflict between the ego and the loved person is transformed into a cleavage between the criticizing faculty of the ego and the ego as altered by the identification. (p. 249, italics added)

As I read it, Freud is saying the person who feels inexpressible fury for the loved or needed, but abandoning or departed other is essentially saying, "It's not you, it's me" (that I am angry at). The person has redirected fury at the humiliating or abandoning other into a part of the ego, perhaps saying something like "You are not bad and worthless, I am." That critical voice has been dissociated from the experiencing "I." The way I read this is that Freud is speaking to the power of traumatizing shame, of overwhelming shame to induce a cleavage in the ego, that is, to cause a dissociation of part of ongoing experience.

Freud is speaking about a way of handling loss, of keeping the attachment "in spite of the conflict with the loved person, the love relationship need not be given up" (p. 249).

In 1921, in "Group Psychology and Analysis of the Ego," Freud further described these ideas:

These melancholias . . . show us the ego divided, fallen apart into two pieces, one of which rages against the second. This second piece is the one which has been altered by introjection and which contains the lost object. But the piece which behaves so cruelly is not unknown to us either. It comprises the conscience, a critical agency within the ego, which even in normal times takes up a critical attitude toward the ego, though never so relentlessly and so unjustifiably . . . some such agency develops in our ego which may cut itself off from the rest of the ego and come into conflict with it. We have called it the "ego ideal." (1921/1955, p. 52)

Thus, the *critical agency* (superego, ego-ideal) that has been differentiated out of the ego rages against the ego, which itself has been modified on account of identification. Two years later, in "The Ego and the Id" (1923/1961), Freud develops these ideas about identification further. The child replaces the incestuous and parenticidal feelings that arose in response to the Oedipus complex with identification: "The ego ideal is therefore the heir to the Oedipus complex" (p. 54).

Freud first (1917/1959) described a split self, as a response to overwhelming shame. This split self continues, as a way of maintaining attachment in the face of humiliated fury toward the attachment figures (1917/1959, 1921/1955). These issues dissipated into near obliteration in his Oedipal theory (1923/1961). Although he first described traumatic shame, when he got to his Oedipal theory, his focus changed to the fear of castration. "The male conscience (I believe that to be right and wrong which father believes) is therefore born of fear. 'Conform or be castrated' is the civilizing rule" (Cameron & Rychlak, 1985, p. 71).

It is worth noting that such a threat of violent dismemberment and deprivation of masculinity might well be beyond engendering fear, but actually traumatizing, potentiating dissociation of the part of the self that experiences these feelings, along with the underling rage. Consciousness of such dangerous feelings would be incompatible with attachment; and if dissociated, the intensity of these feelings would account for the forcefulness of the protective prohibition against their expression. Thus, harsh superego structure resembles dissociative structure.

It seems to me that despite Freud's transposition of shame into castration fear, what we still have before us is a split and dissociated self. This is the *dissociative clinical superego* (Howell, 1997) that clinicians often intuitively work with. Once again, as with his discarded seduction theory, I think Freud was right the first time.

The Dissociative Superego

Experiences of overwhelming shame, terror, and fury are held in dissociated aspects of the self. This allows the person to go on living and negotiating a world without feeling shattered to pieces moment by moment. The dissociated, rageful parts (a.k.a., archaic or harsh superego] work to predict the threatening attachment figures' behavior and also serve as a preemptive strike to keep the self in line. But just as importantly it is protective of survival and selfhood while at the same time, affording continuing attachment. *What looks from the outside to be self-abuse is a defensively learned way to provide safety, protect attachment, and finally to protect sanity, the ability to think, and the feeling of having a self.* The person has creatively constructed a model of self and other that works, even though it hurts to navigate the inner and the outer world.

In Sum

I believe that a primary force behind various aspects of self-blame and self-devaluation is the child's striving for attachment in the face of neglectful, abusive, or otherwise inadequate treatment by caregivers that is overwhelming to the mind. The various processes, including dissociative ones, are interactive and cumulative. They result in a shamed person who feels bad and ineffective and who hides from the world because of the feeling that one's own needs and feelings are unacceptable. The child maintains attachment, sanity, and even a continuing sense of selfhood by deeming the self to be bad.

CHAPTER 8

Structural Models of the Psychological Organization of a Traumatized Person

Trauma cannot be made mute. Trauma lives forever.

—Judith Alpert, 2001, p. 275

I PROBABLY WOULD NOT have gone to the National September 11 Memorial and Museum in New York City if colleagues of mine who participated in the design and presentation of the museum had not been leading a tour (Pivnick, 2017; Turkus, Pivnick & Bellinson, 2019). After visiting the museum, I became aware of how much of my emotionally charged experience of that day I had swept under the rug or actually dissociated.

The day of 9/11/2001 was a terrifying day for me, as described in earlier chapters. While in the museum, I saw photos of people's dazed faces and glazed eyes as they looked at the horror, including human beings jumping to their deaths to escape the fire of the burning buildings. These photos mirrored and validated what I had seen; they are probably how my own face looked at that time to others. I was reminded of the constant rain of ashes of human remains and other burned matter that fell on the western part of Brooklyn for days. I remembered the electric- and rubber-like stench from the massive burning of huge structures that stayed in the air in lower Manhattan for weeks. I remembered the joy that the unbereaved living had for the fact that they were living and the loving and considerate way that people interacted for a few days (similar to the way people who were at Pearl Harbor in 1942 described the aftermath of the bombing there) until transportation service was restored, and our attention was diverted by going to war. I remembered how dazed I had been and how I felt as if I had become a version of Coleridge's Ancient Mariner for the several days. I felt a compulsive need to talk to others about my experience. By reexperiencing these memories in a physical structure that was designed to heal, I was at first emotionally activated and at points highly anxious; but afterwards I realized that I felt distinctly more whole. Clearly, much of the 9/11 trauma had become a gap in my memory—of both emotions and facts. During the museum visit and in the aftermath, talking with others who had also taken the tour, I had reactivated and then integrated some subconscious affective contents, as Pierre Janet (1919) would say. I realized also that since 9/11 I had been living to a certain extent as an apparently normal part of the personality (ANP), as Van der Hart, Nijenhuis, and Steele (2006) would say. Having gone almost mythically underground at what was the World Trade Center—now the 9/11 Museum—upon emerging from it I felt markedly more connected to my myself, as one would after a healing psychotherapy session that involved some activation and then some integration. I felt that I had allowed some highly emotionally charged but sequestered mental states into my ordinary experience, as Frank Putnam (1989, 1997, 2016) would say.

For me, the experience of the 9/11 traumas and my subsequent healing in the physical structure of the museum serves as a common ground, a framework for a discussion of trauma-generated structural models of the mind. I will briefly describe several models of dissociative personality structure, along with their explanations of how trauma alters the psyche and how the damage can be healed.

First, let's address the issue of the *why* of a structural model. What good does it do, clinically? Furthermore, what is a structural model? My definition of a structural model is that it is a basically generic version of how the psyche is built—how the parts are arranged together and how they interrelate. Structure in personality also means that it is enduring. We speak of *structural change* in psychotherapy, meaning that the organization of one's view of self and others has changed in a permanent way and has become intrinsic to a person's beliefs and identity. A developmental example is that morals or ethics become an aspect of personality structure when they have become enduring, when they proceed from a system of personally developed beliefs, rather than just how one has been told to behave (Kohlberg, 1966, 1971).

To be clinically helpful a structural model should offer some explanation of the interactions of the parts of the psyche in answering the questions of how people contribute to their own suffering and what helps healing. A psychic structural design should offer clinicians ways of understanding their clients and the best points of intervention.

The Freudian Structural Model: *The* Structural Model

Probably the most often considered structural model is Freud's tripartite model of id, ego, and superego, all in dynamic interaction and conflict. This has been called the "drive-structure" model (Greenberg & Mitchell, 1983). In this model, the drives, or the instincts, the Id, supply the motivation, and, together with ego and superego, personality has a certain enduring form that governs thought and behavior.

Freud's structural model had replaced his earlier topographic model of conscious, preconscious, and unconscious, a model that, while descriptive, lacked an explanatory mechanism of *how* the unconscious affects behavior. The id, ego, and superego structure has been considered a sort of tripartite unity, despite the implicit dissociative split between ego and superego (Cameron & Rychlak, 1985). (See Chapter 7.) Even though dissociation is not explicitly mentioned in the final presentation of the structural model, the dynamic force of the unconscious relies in large measure on the hostile interactions of dissociated, split-off ego and super-ego parts as they strive for control.

The Freudian structural model offers a schematic dynamic explanation of the hidden mysteries of human thought and behavior. Importantly, the structural model is normalizing. Everyone is supposed to have an id, ego, and superego, even if a very few have highly corrupt or deficient superegos (see Howell, 2018; Itzkowitz, 2019; Howell & Itzkowitz, 2018). Finally, a form of personal agency is implicit in the Freudian version of unconscious determinism. Such personal power (e.g., the power of the id and of the ego struggling against it) is the antithesis of the helplessness of the trauma victim.

It is important to remember that despite having been reified in the literature and by many psychoanalysts, superego—like the id and the ego—is a theoretical concept. Even though "formally acknowledged to be a theoretical construct, [superego] was nevertheless treated as an established fact or explanatory system" (H. Lewis, 1990, p. 23). As increasing numbers of studies about human development emerged, it was noticed that the id is not needed to explain affect and motivation. A number of clinicians and theorists turned to the study of ego psychology (Hartmann, 1939/1958) and ego development (Loevinger, 1976) along with an effort to understand superego problems.

A major problem with the superego construct is that it was used to explain both self-punishment and morality. Problematically, such morality, if it is born of fear, and if it is relativistic to culture, can be corrupt. For example, the bombing and destruction of the World Trade Center, the Inquisition, infanticide, stoning of dissenters, and sadistic murders of those of a different religion or gender orientation are valued, even required, as aspects of certain cultural moral codes. The executors of these horrors fully believed that they were doing the right thing. (Kohlberg, 1971; Sagan, 1988). Their actions reflected familial, local, and cultural mores, that is, normative standards that vary with different societies. Furthermore, the fear that comes from harsh parental punishment has not been found to yield healthy, principled morality, but rather the reverse (Kohlberg, 1966; Lewis, 1981).

A model of some inner psychic agency of self-punishment, with which clinicians often work intuitively, can be explained in terms of dissociative outcomes of problematic attachment modes, as noted in Chapter 7. Clinicians aim to soften harsh superego in a way that is quite similar to working with critical, angry, dissociative parts of the self.

Dissociation-Based Structural Models

There are and have been other structural models that are *explicitly* trauma-and-dissociation-based. I believe that the latter better serve the clinician and the client both theoretically and clinically. Some of these fall within the realm of "relational-structural" models (Greenberg & Mitchell, 1983), including interpersonal theories and object relational theories. In my view, most of these theories actually depict a mind that is dissociatively structured. The reason that *bad objects* are introjected or internalized—in the sense of being banished from consciousness—yet being present in other, dissociated parts of the mind (Ferenczi, 1949), is that aspects of the early attachment relationships were too unbearable for the person to assimilate as part of conscious working knowledge. A major outcome of this disappearance from consciousness of the bad objects is often what has been called splitting, in which different affectively toned views of self and other switch back and forth. Splitting is a form of dissociation.

Models of personality organization built around dissociated experiences and systems of dissociated experience that influence thought and behavior stand in sharp contrast to Freud's structural model. I am in agreement with Philip Bromberg's assessment that the mind is dissociatively structured. If this is true, then a true-to-life structural model is a relational-trauma-dissociation model. (As the reader probably surmised from Chapter 7, I argue that the Freudian structural model is actually a trauma–dissociation model.)

In contrast to Freud's structural model, some other notable structural models describe how the mind is structured by trauma. The trauma-generated structure then is a dissociative one, involving sets of psychic contents and affect constellations being kept apart. One goal of psychotherapy is to soften these barriers, to allow an easier flow of information between them so the person becomes internally and emergently organized on the basis of attachment and healthy interchanges with people outside the closed system of the self. The goal is to make the bootstrap organization of a jury-rigged self unnecessary, and to help the person to become more open to relational connections that are sustaining and containing.

All of the models that I will describe share some aspects of what I call the "jury-rigged self" (Howell, 2017), which is my metaphor for dividedness. The term originally referred to improvised repairs on a ship, when the correct tools and materials were unavailable. For example, I have jury-rigged the vertical supports for tomato plants in my garden with broken tree branches as the plants grow beyond their cages and reach for the sunlight. The whole arrangement looks kind of silly, but it works for the moment. Jury-rigging is ideally a temporary construction. If the traumas could be resolved at the time they occurred, this personal kind of structuring and support would not be necessary. However, the traumatized dissociative self is jury-rigged at the time of the trauma so as to allow a person to go on living with optimal functionality in the traumatizing environment, given the constraints of the lopsided arrangements. Only a part of the self is dissociated, as the rest of the self—now only a part of the self—carries on (see discussion of the theory of the structural dissociation of the personality later in this chapter). The jury-rigged self, then, is built only to protect from imminent dangers present at the time of the trauma, not for the long run. When the jury-rigging must remain in place, it dictates a life of navigation around unknown dissociated memories of unbearable experiences.

Of the many models of posttraumatic parts of the personality, one basic model often relied on by trauma therapists is Karpman's drama triangle (1968). This model schematizes how people may feel, behave, and interact with others in roles of Victim, Perpetrator, and Rescuer. Davies and Frawley (1994) have devised a similar but much more comprehensive model involving four matrices of transference and countertransference positions. These are (1) the uninvolved nonabusing parent and the neglected child; (2) the sadistic abuser and the helpless, angry victim; (3) the omnipotent rescuer and the entitled-to-be-rescued child; and (4) the seducer and the seduced. Largely because of the dissociation of traumatic experience, but also because of interpersonal resonance, clients and their therapists can easily switch roles in the transference and countertransference. For example, the therapist may at one moment experience herself as a rescuer, only to find that in the flash of an eye she is now being perceived as and is enacting the role of the persecutor. In the ensuing enactments, a major part of the work for both parties is to disentangle and learn from these enactments. It is very important for trauma therapists to be alert to the roles and reciprocal role interactions in which they find themselves. Davies and Frawley emphasize how the therapist's finding herself in unfamiliar feeling states and role positions often gives her firsthand information of how the client may have felt growing up. This can be immeasurably helpful when empathically conveyed to the client.

Another major model of psychic structure that is often posttraumatic is Richard Schwartz's (1997) internal family systems model (IFS). This model posits a central Self, with three major subparts. The subparts are: Aliens, usually child parts whose shame, terror, and trauma have been sequestered from normal daily experience; Firefighters, who distract from and try to put out the disturbing emotional fire experiences of the Aliens—often with addictions; and Managers, whose job it is to protectively manage interactions in the world and within the self. Although this model does not assume psychopathology, its structure is certainly applicable to posttraumatic dissociative structuring. Schwartz started out as a family therapist who specialized in working with eating-disordered clients. He found that by asking certain family members to step aside into another room, he could enable the actual patient who was vulnerable to the influence of the family members to articulate her real feelings. He then realized that this *outside* family system existed in an internalized version within the client. Working with these *inside* parts yielded much success, and Schwartz proceeded to schematize the typical roles and interactions that are normally hidden within the person. Schwartz's model of internal family systems (IFS) has become popular. He frequently gives lectures and workshops around the world. In one such workshop I witnessed how, by asking audience members to represent a client's internal family system parts, he was able to create on stage a three-dimensional illustration of the system and to work with it successfully. The person acting as the client was a member of the audience who had been willing to self-reveal. Schwartz's model is normalizing and applicable to virtually everyone.

As detailed in Chapters 2 and 7, Sándor Ferenczi described how the mind becomes structured by the split induced by trauma in the service of the maintenance of attachment. Ferenczi's concept of "identification with the aggressor" (1949) explains how the child splits off conscious knowledge of the aggressor's damaging behavior and orients the self around the aggressor's needs, so as to maintain a feeling of tenderness. This becomes a very basic split in the personality, in which the person consciously proceeds as if all is well and believes that early relationships are tender, while at the same time, terrifying memories of childhood abuse are held in dissociated child states of mind. As Ferenczi (1949) said, the aggressor has become "intra- instead of extra-psychic," and in effect the person's mind "consists only of the Id and Super-Ego" (p. 228). Furthermore, in saying that "there is neither shock nor fright without some trace of splitting of personality" (p. 229), Ferenczi implicitly laid out a model of the structure of dissociative identity disorder and how it works.

Ronald Fairbairn's (1944/1952) endopsychic model is an elegant and comprehensive model of the schizoid, dissociative psyche. Fairbairn posited a central ego, an ideal object, the internalized bad object, and four different split-off parts. Split off from the main core of the repressed internal bad object are the exciting object and the rejecting object. The first represents the yearned-for promise of love, and the second holds fears of rejection. Then there are repressed and split parts of the ego: "libidinal ego" and the "anti-libidinal ego" (earlier called the "internal saboteur"). The internal saboteur is attached to the rejecting object, and aggressively rejects any longings for tenderness. This gets to be a rather complicated design, but the upshot is that because of the persistent attacks of the internal saboteur (basically protecting against the potential of the traumatizing shame of rejection), the child develops a persistent self-hatred and resistance to feelings of dependence and the need for love. Many people who have studied Fairbairn have found the term internal saboteur to be highly evocative of their own feelings about their inner dynamics. It is remarkably similar in its controlling function to superego.

John Bowlby (1969, 1973, 1980, 1984) wrote of his concept of defensive exclusion, which divides the psyche by cordoning off information antithetical to attachment needs into a separate compartment. Perhaps even more importantly, Bowlby's attachment models of IWMs describe not only various forms of attachment, but also a structuring within the individual of differing IWMs in different relationships and in different versions of the same relationship. For example, a simple IWM of a child with secure attachment might be of the self as lovable, protected, and valued, while an IWM of an insecure attachment might be unlovable, unprotected, and unvalued. Bowlby's work on attachment led to advances in understanding attachment styles, specifically disorganized attachment (Main & Solomon, 1986), which involves two competing behavioral systems: the attachment system and the fear system, resulting in the child's simultaneous desire to approach for attachment and to run away because of fear (Liotti, 2006). Since attachment is the solution to fear, this results in "fear without a solution" (Hesse & Main, 1999). The result is segregated IWMs that are contradictory to each other. This then becomes a template for the underlying splits that characterize borderline personality disorder (BPD) and dissociative identity disorder (DID) (Liotti, 1992, 2006).

Harry Stack Sullivan (1953) wrote of the compelling power of dissociation in keeping experiences that are too overwhelmingly anxiety-ridden out of consciousness. He postulated what he called personifications of a "good me," a "bad me," and a "not-me." Both the "good me" and the "bad me" can be held in consciousness. However, the "not-me" cannot be contained in consciousness. It is filled with dread, awe, and overwhelming terror. The "not-me" is very important for therapists to be aware of, for this is the part of the person most filled with anxiety and shame—and most shunned by the conscious self.

Philip Bromberg (1998, 2006, 2011), who was highly influenced by Sullivan, has written voluminously of dissociated self-states that are avoided by the person because they hold reminders of trauma or overwhelming affects. Although he has not schematized his insights into a formal structural model, the reader can identify with how his patients are enacting dissociated parts of themselves. The reader can appreciate how Bromberg has been able, in the therapeutic collaboration, to help his patients wake up to more alive vistas of who they are and can be.

Frank Putnam (1997, 2016) has created a complex and comprehensive model of how isomorphic states of brain/mind/body are optimally linked but can be unlinked from each other by trauma—and how trauma prevents linking. Putnam's State Dependent Learning and Memory (SDLM) model emphasizes the great extent to which our lives are state-dependent. (I discuss Putnam's work in more detail in Chapter 10.) Along with Janet's model, it explains gaps in memory due to trauma.

Pierre Janet presented a very basic, if not *the* basic, model of how trauma divides the mind, but subsequent clinicians have not adequately heeded his elaborate formulations of the personality. Janet wrote voluminously about the dissociative consequences of traumatic experiences. He described how vehement emotions brought on by overwhelming, traumatic experiences caused a disruption in memory, such that these experiences became unavailable to consciousness. He specified how dissociated traumatic experiences were present in a subconscious state (and thus not known to the individual) but that nonetheless powerfully influenced behavior and experience. Because of the isolation from ordinary consciousness and ordinary will, they operated autonomously and could be stimulated or triggered by external or internal emotional events.

A common aspect of these models is that the posttraumatic personality is structured around dissociated traumatic experiences. They have a common emphasis on the exile of the traumatic experience and the protection of attachment. They differ in the precise form of the sequestration and in the contents of what each author considers to be the most traumatic and potentially traumatizing experiences to be avoided. Yet an important commonality is that major parts of the self, even though differently described by the different theorists, have their own autobiographical sense of "I."

Dissociative Structure in Different Personality Organizations

So far, I have been discussing different models that in their own terms describe the personality structure of a traumatized person. However, dissociative structure, that is, the structure of dissociated self-states, can vary with different personality organizations and diagnoses (Howell, 1996, 2002, 2003, 2018).

Otto Kernberg (1980) highlights "primitive dissociation or splitting" (p. 13) as a defense that keeps apart libidinal and aggressive object relational units. I view splitting more specifically as an outcome of relational trauma, with an etiological core of identification with the aggressor, as described by Ferenczi (1949) (see Chapters 2 and 7; Howell, 2002, 2005, 2014). In my view, the result of this process is at least two highly incompatible self-states involving the child's relationship to the caregiver: two dominant internal relational positions of victim and abuser. The configurations of these relational positions can vary in different personality disorders.

In so-called borderline personality disorder, this fragmentation of the psyche is predominantly reflected in two distinct self-states (or groups of self-states), one attachment-oriented and one aggressive. The alternation between these self-states is the basis of the characteristic *stable instability* of BPD. The splitting found in BPD may be quite similar to state switches in dissociative identity disorder. However, as primarily an affective switch, it is a partial dissociation. The alternation of these self-states contributes to the hallmark stable instability.

In many other personality configurations, the organization is stable. For example, in so-called masochism, attachment-oriented self-states are generally executive, ascendant, and conscious, whereas aggressive and rageful self-states are usually dissociated, with the exception of when such people do become angry. In psychopathy and more aggressive and malignant narcissism, I suggest that attachment-oriented and needy self-states are dissociated from the usually conscious aspects of self, which are aggression and power oriented. The psychopath's dominant self-state is omnipotent, grandiose, devaluing, and aggressor-identified, a state that must be continually maintained by devaluing others.

This way of thinking is consistent with other defenses that Kernberg sees as related to splitting. Kernberg (1975, 1980, 1984) has described five typical defenses of Borderline Personality Organization that are all related to splitting: projective identification, denial, primitive idealization, omnipotence, and devaluation. Primitive idealization is felt from, and only from, the perspective of the victim-identified state. Omnipotence, which defends against helplessness and dependency, and devaluation, which in turn defends against envy (Kernberg, 1975), both characterize the abuser-identified state and are usually attitudes with which the abuser treats the victim.

The Theory of the Structural Dissociation of the Personality

Of the various models, I will focus in most detail on Van der Hart, Nijenhuis, and Steele's (2006) theory of the structural model of the dissociation of the personality. This model has gained popularity worldwide, and many clinicians are using the terms specified in the model in their work.

Drawing on Janet's work, Van der Hart, Nijenhuis, and Steele have together created a model of the dissociative structure of the personality that has wide applicability. Although partially based on Janet's theories, it also draws on multiple sources and is highly comprehensive.

My first initiation to what would become the theory of the structural dissociation of the personality was a compelling lecture on PTSD delivered by Onno van der Hart, a Janetian scholar, in 2000. In this lecture Van der Hart explained how PTSD is inherently and necessarily dissociative. He reconceptualized posttraumatic intrusions, such as flashbacks—which had not previously been considered dissociative—as an illustration of lack of integration of the personality. He described the personality constriction of PTSD as the result of the avoided reexperience of the trauma and how the combination and alternation of constriction and intrusions characterizes PTSD. This made eminent sense to me since I always thought that PTSD should not be classified simply descriptively under the rubric of anxiety disorders; that classification under dissociative disorders made more sense dynamically. I had not spelled out to myself exactly how this was so.

Soon after, Van der Hart and Ellert Nijenhuis, an expert on somatoform dissociation, and Kathy Steele collaborated in the creation of the Structural Model of the Dissociation of the Personality, later more succinctly described in the title of their 2006 book, *The Haunted Self*. The authors incorporated into their developing theory the concepts of Charles Myers, a World War I physician and psychologist who treated acutely traumatized solders. Myers observed that the traumatized soldiers would at times, sometimes in sleep, suddenly change their body postures, mental states, and words, often as if ready to do battle even though they were in fact for the moment safe in sick bay. Myers developed a conceptualization of the posttraumatic psychic structure of these traumatized soldiers, describing the suddenly enacted agitated behavior as the emotional personality (EP). The seemingly normal part of the person, who may however suffer constrictions of posture, speech, and other behavior, he called the apparently normal personality (ANP). Myers wrote that:

> The "emotional" personality may also return during sleep, the "functional" disorders of mutism, paralysis, contracture, etc., being then usually in abeyance. On waking, however, the "apparently normal" personality may have no recollection of the dream state and will at once resume his mutism, paralysis, etc. (Myers, 1940, pp. 66–67, quoted by Van der Hart, Van Dijke, Van Son & Steele, 2000, p. 40)

The EP is the part of the personality that is stuck in and reenacts the trauma. What remains in ordinary consciousness is the ANP, the constricted, avoidant, often numb posttraumatic personality that we frequently see in trauma patients. Symptoms may also include inhibition, amnesia, anesthesia, paralysis, blindness, mutism, and so on.

The fact that the experiences of the EP are dissociated from the ANP enables the ANP to avoid the affect and information held by the EP. This is successful only up to a certain extent: the fact that the ANP is only *apparently* normal is demonstrated by periodic intrusions of agitated emotional states and somatic symptoms.

So, we have one person but two different parts of the person that are dissociated. Now, too, we have the rudiments of a dynamic psychology— for these two parts are phobic of each other. The ANP part does not want to know about the trauma and avoids the EP. In turn, the rejected and avoided EP intrudes into the experience of the ANP in the form of flashbacks, nightmares, upsetting memories, and unwanted bodily experiences. The constriction and the numbing of the ANP is designed to avoid these intrusive memories and experiences. Yet when traumatic memories are triggered, an ANP may be quickly succeeded by an EP.

The important thing to recognize is that we are already talking in a language of parts. The authors have retained Myers' basic terminology for the sake of clarity and historical accuracy, but they specify that for them, EP means *the emotional part of the personality*, and ANP means the *apparently normal part of the personality*. As Van der Hart and colleagues (2006) clarify, the constricted ANP is not just a ravaged version of the former presenting self. It is only a part of a person, not the whole person. Even though the ANP may often appear to have a larger scope and greater functionality, once there is an EP, the ANP can only be a part of the personality. In addition, these ANPs and EPs have at least a rudimentary sense of self that is accompanied by distinct differences in psychobiological function.

It is very important for the clinician to be alert to the probability that our PTSD clients had a very different premorbid presentation from what we see in the person who walks in the door. For example, John, who entered treatment because of immense posttraumatic distress, called himself "a changed person." The person I met was a friendly but anxious, cautious, and stiff person who was troubled by persistent terrifying nightmares. One might conclude that except for the nightmares, this was just the way he was. However, his description of himself only one year before was strikingly different. As a taxi driver in Manhattan he had had a terrifying car accident (that involved no malfeasance of his own) in which he was injured and one person died. After intensive discussion of the minutiae of the situation, followed by EMDR, he became much better able to confront and handle his terrors, as well as his enormous guilt, sorrow, and loss. With the significant diminution of his nightmares and excessive anxiety, he was able to reclaim much of his former version of himself. Over time, he became able to convert most of his somatic and visual intrusions into narrative memory—although of course, one can never change the lasting impact of these kinds of experiences. It was a good thing for him that he had the opportunity to get psychotherapy, for his ANP presentation could have become chronic and automatic, for: "Apparent normality can evolve into a detached lifestyle that relies on avoidance of intimacy and emotion" (Nijenjuis & Van der Hart, 1999, p. 43).

In the further development of their theory, Van der Hart and colleagues (2004, 2006) have noted the remarkable correspondences between these the parts of the personality, the ANP and the EP, and two sets of psychobiological action systems, relating to daily life and defense, respectively. Although the ANP may often be chronically depersonalized and has low body awareness, it is focused on performing functions of daily life, such as those concerning reproduction, child rearing, attachment, sociability, exploration, and play. In contrast, the emotional part of the personality (EP) is focused on response to physical defense to threat, involving defensive action systems and subsystems that are devoted to the survival of the individual in conditions of threat. These latter defensive action systems include hypervigilance, fight/flight, freeze, and total submission.

Under the impact of trauma, especially chronic trauma, these two types of psychobiological action systems, those devoted to daily life and those devoted to defense, become segregated and divided against each other. As Van der Hart and colleagues (2004) have noted:

> The essential and primary form of trauma-related dissociation of the personality is a lack of integration between parts of the personality that are mediated by daily life action systems and defensive action systems as a result of threat to bodily integrity and threat to life. The action tendencies involved in these two sets of action systems tend to inhibit each other once they are strongly evoked, hence are not easily integrated in circumstances of major threat, particularly chronic threat. (p. 909)

In yet another important aspect of their theory, Van der Hart and colleagues delineate primary, secondary, and tertiary dissociation. The best examples of primary dissociation are simple PTSD and simple somatoform disorders. Primary dissociation involves one ANP and one EP. In contrast, secondary dissociation is characterized by the existence of one ANP and two or more EPs, i.e., two or more defensive subsystems, such as those devoted to flight, fight, submission, and so on. Examples of secondary dissociation are complex PTSD, borderline personality disorder, complex somatoform disorders, and some forms of acute stress disorder.

In tertiary dissociation, of which the prime example is dissociative identity disorder (DID), there are two or more ANPs, in addition to two or more EPs. Different ANPs may perform aspects of daily living, such as child rearing, work in the workplace, and playing. My client, Sally, mentioned in Chapters 4 and 7, exemplifies tertiary dissociation. In Sally's personality structure, there are many ANPs, including several mother parts, a driver part (who can always be counted on to drive safely), one who cooks, and others who perform daily living functional tasks. There are also many EPs, including frightened child parts and some previously suicidal ones, who have been hurt and traumatized.

Regarding the use of ANP/ EP language in DID, I have heard a number of clinicians refer to "The ANP," as if there is only one, in their work with DID clients. The term "ANP" is more respectful and accurate than a term such as "host" to refer to a primary part of the self that is currently taking executive function or who is most frequently interacting with the outside world. However, for DID, it is important to remember that by definition in this theory there must be more than one ANP in tertiary dissociation.

The theory of the structural model of the dissociation of the personality is more than just a theory. It has been operationalized in a number of studies. In a series of ingenious brain and body scan studies, the existence of EP and ANP as *one brain, two selves* has been demonstrated.

One Brain: Two Selves

Two remarkable studies by Reinders and colleagues (2003) and Reinders and other colleagues (2006) demonstrate how DID clients' brains and bodies showed remarkable correspondences with their differing phenomenological states of mind (EP and ANP). The research participants in both the first and second study were 11 persons with DID who were able to switch at will between a traumatic state (EP) and a neutral one (ANP). There were four conditions: the participants were asked to listen to an autobiographical trauma script and an autobiographical neutral script while in both EP and ANP states.

In the first study, titled "One Brain, Two Selves" Reinders and colleagues (2003) document the cerebral and body correlates of two markedly different autobiographical selves. Using functional neuroimaging (PET scan) the authors demonstrated certain changes in localized brain activity—two different cerebral blood flow patterns—that occurred in a traumatized EP state responding to the trauma script, versus a neutral ANP state responding to the trauma script, and both ANP and EP reading the neutral script. Among the four conditions, only reading the trauma script in the EP state created a different blood flow pattern. No significant differences were found between the two personality states in response to the neutral script. In the ANP neutral personality state the participants responded to the trauma script similarly to how they responded to the neutral script because in this state the trauma script was not personally, emotionally relevant for them.

The PET scans showed, patterns in the ANP states of disturbances in the parietal and occipital blood flow that were indicative of an inability to integrate visual and somatosensory information. The study's results suggest that when DID patients are in the ANP states, they are neurologically protected against trauma-related information in a way that prevents further emotional processing. As a result, similar to Miss America, Marilyn Van Derbur, as described in Chapter 6, and many others, they are able to carry on in daily life despite being somewhat depersonalized, until or unless they are triggered into symptomatology or decompensation. In sum, Reinders and colleagues (2003) state: "We have shown that these patients have state-dependent access to autobiographical affective memories and thus different autobiographical selves" (p. 2124). Furthermore; "Our results indicate the possibility of one human brain to generate at least two distinct states of self-awareness, each with its own access to autobiographical trauma-related memory, with explicit roles for the MPFC [medial prefrontal cortex] and the posterior associative cortices in the representation of these different states of consciousness" (p. 2124).

In the 2006 study, Reinders and colleagues found a parallel pattern— that in response to listening to a trauma script, only the EPs (or Traumatized Identity States), showed increased heart rates and blood pressure. The EPs also reported strong emotions and sensory experiences reminiscent of the traumatic event. In contrast, in response to the neutral script, neither EP nor ANP displayed elevated heart rate or blood pressure. The EPs showed more activity in the amygdala and other areas relevant to defensive motor activity, as well as reduced activity in prefrontal areas. In contrast, the ANPs showed more activity in the anterior cingulate cortex (the ACC), which is involved in inhibitions of emotional responses, as well as more activity in other frontal areas involved in self-awareness and planning.

Subsequent to the Reinders studies just described, there have been a number of studies that demonstrate markedly different blood flow patterns in the brain, as well as different heart rate and blood pressure patterns, in DID alters. One such study, using a similar basic design, found that EP and ANP differed markedly in heart rate and facial expression when exposed to a small object that was moved in the direction of the face (Nijenhuis & Den Boer, 2007).

In addition, some of these studies also demonstrate the neurological and physiological differences between true DID subjects and controls who were instructed "to switch" (Palermo & Brand, 2019; Putnam, 2016), clearly showing that one cannot neurologically fake having DID.

An important issue for the clinician's work with EPs, ANPs, and other fully or partially dissociated parts of a person is how to help the client connect these parts in experience. For example, my client, Fiona had a sudden depersonalization response during an EMDR session right after she had recalled an incident in which her father had viciously scratched her face, just barely missing her eyeball. All of a sudden she felt nothing, just as she had felt nothing at the time of the attack. It took a while, and required some grounding work and talking, for her to exit her depersonalized state and return to her usual self. Extreme states of mind such as being in the grip of an overwhelming traumatic memory or being in a depersonalized state that defends against recognition of the trauma, need to be identified and connected to more usual ways of being. In brief, a significant part of the therapist's job is to help make the extreme emotional states accessible to reflection, to help a person convert both dissociated traumatic experiences and the defenses against them into the changing narrative language of ordinary experience.

Often this task requires finding an entry into the closed system. As Van der Hart and colleagues say in *The Haunted Self* (2006), the first

phobia to be overcome is the phobia of attachment and then, more specifically, of attachment to the therapist. Therapeutic transformation
requires that the therapist be able to forge an attachment that breaks
through the self-sufficiency of the closed system (addressed in the following chapter, Chapter 9).

CHAPTER 9

Exit from the Closed System as the Therapist Becomes Real

I have come to regard as the greatest source of all resistance—viz.
the maintenance of the patient's inner world as a closed system . . . It
becomes [an] aim of psychoanalytic treatment to effect breaches in the
closed system which constitutes the patient's inner world, and thus to
make this world accessible to the influence of outer reality
—Ronald Fairburn, 1958/1994, p. 84

JORGE WAS TRYING TO make a very important decision: whether or not to tell his adoptive parents how severely his biological parents had physically and emotionally abused him. Even though his adoptive parents were good and caring people who loved him and had already gone through a lot with him, they liked to hear good things. It had not always been easy for them to comprehend the extent of the abuses that he had suffered. As far as they knew, things had been bad for Jorge, but not overwhelmingly so. In his time with his adoptive parents and since leaving his former home, he had tried hard to be "good." In fact, it had been difficult for him three years ago to tell his adoptive parents how depressed he was. When he did, they arranged for his psychotherapy. Jorge, now 20 years of age, adopted when he was 12, was afraid that his adoptive parents would reject even shun him for the terrible ways he felt about herself. He felt very alone.

Jorge had told me horrifying stories of sadistic sexual and physical abuse in his early years. Initially he had felt ashamed and shocked by the information his flashbacks gave him, and he had a strong tendency to refuse entry into his consciousness knowledge of the terrible physical and emotional abuse he had suffered at the hands of his biological parents. But, he had worked hard in therapy to face his memories. As he integrated more of these memories into his experience he realized that he wanted the people closest to him, his adoptive parents, to be able to do so as well.

Even though he wanted them to know, he was frightened to tell them. When I asked him what he was afraid of, he said that he was afraid that even though they knew a lot already about how he had been mistreated, they would not believe him about the extent of the sadistic abuse and would accuse him of making it up. These terrifying experiences had been sequestered away in exiled parts of himself. He had not wanted to know about them, had not wanted to allow the possibility that his biological parents had done these horrible things to him. He had not wanted to know that they had actually happened to him. I wondered aloud if he was worried that like himself, his parents would reject knowing about the terrible things he experienced. I was wondering aloud about possibilities in his mental process. Was he worried that just as he had not wanted to hear from the brutalized and then banished parts of his own experience, his parents might also would find such news hard to hear and bear? I wasn't predicting how his parents would respond (I did not know), but I was helping him to know in a more formulated fashion what he already knew, and in this way, supporting him to be more self-reflective.

Over time, Jorge had become able to accept these terrified, banished self-states containing extreme pain, shame, and misery because of the safety and closeness that we had been able to achieve in our psychotherapy relationship. Now we were working on his understanding of his own mind and that of others, including his parents.

One thing that had been happening for Jorge was that in becoming aware of the dividedness of his own experience, he had (in a way that might seem paradoxical) been brought closer to his own experience. Being aware of one's own dividedness, while listening to the exiled parts of oneself, holds the potential to open a vista of understanding one's interpersonal expectations and engagements.

Intrapersonal and Interpersonal Dividedness

For me, closeness to experience versus dissociative dividedness of experience is a more apt polarity than unity versus dividedness. I think that the popular concept of unity versus dividedness of the self has impeded a probably more meaningful juxtaposition, which would be closeness to experience versus dividedness. That is, being able to stay close to experience, another's or one's own, allows pieces of our lives to cohere in context, to make internal sense. This construct of dividedness versus closeness works both between people (interpersonally) and within the self (intrapersonally). What creates dividedness is the lack of close engagement, the lack of intersubjectivity. This lack necessitates the creation of a closed system. Real, perceived compassion is de-shaming, facilitates mourning, and is integrative; it helps clients feel compassion for themselves. It is compassionate intersubjective closeness that is the opposite of dividedness. By dividedness, I'm not talking about intrapsychic conflict, but about shutting off one set of experience from another or not connecting these experiences. Also, I'm talking about the closed system of the psyche, which derives from interpersonal dividedness.

Even though dividedness versus unity has been the usual juxtaposition, it is problematic to me to speak of the self as a unity, as a unit, or as unified. First of all, if we're all multiple selves depending on context both external and internal, the result seems rather limitless; it would be hard to say what is the whole self. In addition, any unit is part of supra units and is also composed of subunits, and sub-subunits, and so on (Erdelyi, 1990). Finally, from the perspective of contextualism, things must be understood in relationship to their environments. For example, as Winnicott (1960) observed, there really is no such thing as a baby, in isolation. The baby must be understood in relationship to the mother. Often, we patch over our lapses of awareness and changes in self-states in ways that generate a conscious illusion of unity (Bromberg, 1998).

I wonder if part of what is being implied or grasped at with the notion of a unified self is that the dynamic pieces of experience and agency are somehow operating consistently in a way that one might identify as "me." That is, they cohere, and they fit together with each other in a way that works and that might be called harmonious. Even though I have used the word, integration often in this book, it is a word of multiple meanings. Even in the sense of repair of dissociation, the ideal is much more than simply blending, which the word, integration can imply— even though that is usually not what is explicitly meant. Pathological dissociation involves intense internal warfare; it is about a complex organization of antagonisms. The idea of simply making one whole out of many parts—of simply knitting together parts without dealing with inner antagonisms—does not work.

Open and Closed Systems

The psychotherapy dyad, like the infant-mother dyad and other intimate relationships, is ideally characterized by mutual regulation and is an open system. All living organisms are open systems. As such, they require continuous exchanges with the environment to maintain their complex forms and functions. An open system assumes interaction with and influence from the outside. One reason that the whole is more than the aggregate of its parts is that the whole is in constant interaction with, nourished by, and thereby transformed by, the environment. This is particularly applicable to the psychotherapy dyad in which relationality and connection are implicit. Part of the therapist's job is to keep the dyadic system as open as possible, even though this may at times be uncomfortable for the therapist.

The brilliant mathematician Kurt Gödel (Nagel & Newman, 1958) proved that an arithmetical system cannot be both complete and consistent: if a system is complete it cannot be consistent, and if it is consistent it cannot be complete. What happens with early, repeated trauma is that without benign and meaningful interchanges with others, the mind attempts to be consistent and complete within itself. When affect is overwhelming and there is no outside source of safe support, then the psyche will of necessity become more and more self-referential and closed. Then open self-expression and vulnerability to the possibility of the helpfulness of real others are foreclosed.

Psychopathology that is not inherited usually represents the attempt to self-regulate alone. When things go very wrong, whether by overt trauma, massive neglect, or overwhelming misattunement by the attachment figure, the child must become precociously self-reliant. In severely problematic development, although it was initially a form of resilience, people had to both pull themselves up by their own bootstraps and become intensely hypervigilent to the twin dangers of outer threat and inner overwhelm.

As noted in Chapter 6 the attachment system works as a buffer against fearful arousal; it combats stress. However, in traumatic attachments in which the attachment figure fails to provide a protective shield against perceived danger or threat, or is herself or himself dangerous and frightening, the attachment system becomes distorted in significant ways, causing the self to become increasingly self-sufficient (ironically, so as to be able to maintain an affectional bond with the attachment figure). For example, Brianna's biological mother accused her of lying when she relayed that her father's friend had raped her. This double betrayal forced her into premature self-reliance, resulting in severe depression and complex PTSD. This would be in contrast to a situation in which a mother would have been horrified and helped the daughter process her experience of being terribly violated and at the same time making it knowable in the mother-daughter relationship.

When a child must dissociate or disown parts of the self in order to maintain attachment to such a caretaker, the self becomes more and more a self-contained system, in which attachments then occur on the inside to *internal objects*. The true vulnerability of a real relationship has been replaced by the internal object that predicts and in a way provides a defensive buffer against the psychic impact of the behavior of the frightening attachment figure. When this happens, genuine responsiveness to others (originally, the attachment figure) is replaced by a set of expectations and behaviors that reflexively and self-protectively attempt to manage the other person. What remains in consciousness is a set of beliefs and strategies that mitigate fear and work interpersonally.

In dissociative psychopathology, the mutuality of relationships, both interpersonal and intrapersonal, has collapsed in significant ways. The closed system precludes interpersonal intersubjectivity, the mutual recognition of separate others who have their own experiences and agency. Coinciding with hypervigilant fears of being impacted by others, there is often a lack of awareness of one's impact on others.

For example, Brianna had a habit of cancelling sessions at the last minute. Despite cancellation policies in place, these behaviors felt necessary to her. When I brought up how her other commitments interfered with our scheduled sessions and work and that it mattered to me, she was surprised. At first she told me that since she was paying me for my time it shouldn't bother me. When she understood that the continuity of our work mattered to me, that began to make sense to her, and her attendance became more regular. I think that Brianna had been insufficiently aware that her behavior had an impact on me—and others. I do not believe that she was unconsciously or manipulatively trying to derail her therapy. In contrast, she may have been trying to preserve the therapy by keeping her dependent feelings at bay. Even if there had been an element of that, I don't think it would be the best or the primary issue to bring up, for it could easily suggest that she was doing something wrong and blame or shame her. As she began to feel safer in the therapy, she was better able to allow the dependent aspects of herself to come in. Once she could recognize her dependent aspects, she could regulate herself better. As our interaction around this issue evolved and increasingly resolved, and as she began to understand that as a separate person I had feelings about her dismissive treatment of our work—and of me—it began to matter to her that our treatment collaboration mattered to me.

Donald Kalsched (1996), a Jungian psychoanalyst, has called this kind of dissociative self-sufficiency "the self-care system." The self-care system is compensatory and self-protective, functioning protectively to prevent retraumatization. The self-care system provides hope. By replacing missing aspects of the needed attachment relationships with created parts of the self who function in hoped-for ways, it provides an illusion of self-parenting. The child may invent illusionary sources of protection, such as inner caregivers, defenders, and helpers (Beahrs, 1982). For example, one highly dissociative client who had been severely abused, neglected, and psychologically tortured by her parents, had imagined when she was young that the rocks, bushes, and trees were her friends and that they would take care of her. This human tendency to invent a caring other is also exemplified in the movie *Cast Away*. The main character, played by Tom Hanks, upon realizing that he is completely alone, begins to talk to a volleyball that has washed up on the shore; he names it Wilson, the name of the brand printed on the ball.

The self-care system is not relational and as such it resists transformation. Because the self-care on the inside is only an illusion, without some kind of benign connection to the real interpersonal world, hope cannot last. This is one of the most difficult challenges of trauma psychotherapy. Recognizing that the therapist is a potential attachment figure to be connected with in an interpersonal world is a double-edged sword. Such recognition heightens the failure and inadequacy of the initial caregivers—while at the same time framing in bold how the closed system of self that was developed to cope with this is more illusory than real. The therapy space must become a secure base that is safe and predicable. As Orit Badouk Epstein (2018) has said,

> The process of finessing trust is an ongoing one. The secure base built in therapy will provide a safe, empathic, predictable and transparent relationship [that helps] the client realize the impoverishment of their relational past . . . .Only this time, the shared space between client and therapist is free of the real fear the client had to endure all those years, and the possibility of being with another person becomes viable and authentic. In this safe shared reality, the client slowly begins to develop a capacity to explore, to mentalize and recognize her impact on the other and to see that the locus of control is an internal one. (p. 303)

Interpersonal and Intrapersonal Intersubjectivity

Intersubjective failure in primary interpersonal relationships is at the root of intrapersonal dissociation. Likewise, when severe dissociation severs internal links, interpersonal ones are blunted as well. Intrapersonal communication is closed off just as interpersonal connection is. In intrapersonal dissociation each dissociated self-state excludes information that is not consistent with its unique organizational structure. Because there is such a massive partitioning of information, memory, and affect, the ability to contextualize is poor; each dissociated self-state fallaciously claims to possess the real and whole truth. The person is closed off to the influence of others. Unfortunately, the lack of early interpersonal intersubjectivity precludes intrapersonal intersubjectivity in the psyche. This makes for the struggles for control by different self-states that characterizes highly dissociative people.

Once a person has gone inside, so to speak, the inner protectors may end up as inner persecutors. If there has been more persecution than protection in the early interpersonal environment, the problem is that without better models from the outside, an internalized copy cannot be better than what one experienced in reality. The protector becomes a persecutor, in part because persecution and attack were what the child knew. Initially, the rescuer-protector is created in omnipotent fantasy, and this often works to a certain extent. However, protector-persecutor parts often then replace the capacity for trust of another person—in essence, defending the person against memories of trauma and the experience of helplessness. Just as helpless-feeling individuals may attach themselves to those they think are more powerful and can protect them, so do the inner helpless self-states attach to those seemingly more powerful, blustery, inner aggressive states. Herbert Rosenfeld (1971), a Kleinian psychoanalyst, noted that the helpless, dependent parts of the person are more sane than the omnipotent, aggressive internal parts. The ability of the therapist to rescue the dependent, sane part requires that the client become aware of the omnipotent, destructive part(s).

However, it is the very interrelationship and intense attachment between these self-states that makes it hard to break into the closed system. For instance, a dominant, aggressive self-state may keep the person in a subordinate or harmful external relationship, often labeled masochistic, that matches the internal structure of dissociated self-states. That is, the helpless, frightened self-states or parts are controlled by the harsh, aggressive ones, in an old tried-and-true way of protecting attachment to an abusive caregiver. This is a key reason that current interpersonal abusive relationships tend to replicate past ones. It is not that the person wants to be abused or mistreated. She doesn't. The problem is that her harsh internal protector-persecutor parts in a closed, self-sufficient system make her afraid to protest or break away. She is too wrapped up on the inside, so that inside and outside representations are not always distinguished, and the dearly held illusions on the inside temper adequate, deep-down recognition of the bad things happening in reality. Thus, the therapist needs to make contact with both the omnipotent parts and the dependent parts inside the system.

Because so much is on the inside, it is often hard for the person to distinguish in a deep emotional way between the guiding inside parts and the reality of outside ones. In work with highly traumatized and dissociative clients, partially or fully dissociated self-states may come forth, sometimes such that the client sees the therapist as if the therapist were the original traumatic figure. Resolving these dilemmas in the work often results in deeply moving recognitions and insights.

In contrast to the traumatic attachment that breeds the closed system, what I call *generative attachment* can facilitate the healing of the closed system. What contributes to generative attachment? Two important factors are: (1) experiencing oneself as capable of having an effect on the other, and (2) what Constance Dalenberg (2000), a prominent traumatologist, calls "anger in connection." In a substantial study of trauma patients' responses to the expression of anger in the psychotherapy relationship, Dalenberg found that the therapists whom the patients found the most helpful were those who could accept their client's anger and who were emotionally disclosing of some of their own, without blaming the client. What the clients learned was that they could be angry and stay in the relationship. This is a very different kind of relationship from the early survival-oriented one; this is a relationship that can endure the expression of intense affect. In this relationship the expression of anger means neither abandonment nor imminent physical danger. The therapists who rarely expressed anger were distressingly more likely to express it vehemently and explosively at some point. The therapists that trauma patients found the least helpful were the *blank screen* psychoanalysts: those who, while the patient is on the couch and cannot see them, rarely interact, theoretically in the service of abstinence and the developing transference. Thankfully, most psychoanalysts and psychodynamically oriented clinicians do not practice as blank screens.

In an illuminating recent paper, Donald Kalsched (2015) recounts a dramatic enactment between himself and a patient, in which his own aggression and his patient's aggression each became tolerable to the other. The patient, Mike, was a man who, despite having a vulnerable, loving side, had been developmentally forced into an impulsive aggressive style of dealing with fears and disappointments as a child. His knee-jerk aggressive reactions continually got him into serious trouble. One day, after much previous work on the problem, Mike entered the session and 'superciliously,' but with a guilty grin on his face, confessed to another incident of road rage in which he had seriously hurt the other man. He displayed "no guilt or remorse . . . only the pumped up hyperarousal of this addictive violence" (p. 488). When Mike was unable or refused to be reflective, Kalsched said, "something snapped in me, and I lost my mind—at least my analytic mind . . . I heard myself say to him,

> 'Look, you are threatening everything you've created in your life—your profession, your family, your relationship with your wife, the boys, your relationship with me, and that new friendship with that little boy inside you—all for the temporary high of your little shit-fit rages. You think you're getting even or administering some kind of sick justice but the fact is you're simply indulging yourself like a two-year-old. You're just emotionally incontinent! That's your problem. You can't hold it! When are you . . . gonna learn to hold it? [Silence] [ibid.]'

Mike lurched away, saying he was "outta here," but instead locked himself in the bathroom. Kalsched followed and apologized, saying, "Let's not let this wreck our connection. Let me in so we can process this together. We've got too much going for us." Mike then let him in. After a few minutes, Mike's eyes began to fill with tears, and then he began to sob, and said:

Nobody ever cared! I had to take care of it all by myself . . . I was always crying out for help in my acting out, but nobody got it . . . Six felonies before I was 18 and my father never spoke to me about it! All they could do was make me bad. You're not making me bad. [p. 489].

In his retrospective analysis of the event, Kalsched states:

I had really hated him for a moment and it hadn't destroyed him. And it hadn't destroyed us. Both love and hate, the good and the bad, were held together in this moment for each of us but love was stronger, and hence the relationship was both preserved and deepened. Mike took my hand and we just sat looking at each other in this wet beautiful moment. It was like the Balm of Gilead—healing and reconciliation poured down on us both. Trauma repeated, acted out, but repaired, right there in the session . . . the little boy and the murderous protector (in both of us) present and getting to know each other [p. 489].

Both anger in the relationship and the experience of having an effect, are relevant to Donald Winnicott's concept of "object usage." Winnicott (1971) described how the client's experience and expression of aggression toward the therapist, who in turn does not retaliate, then enables her to experience the therapist as "real in the sense of being part of shared reality and not just a bundle of projections" (Winnicott, 1971, p. 88). This transformation involves a very important psychological shift away from being an isolated closed system. The therapist (or another person) becomes real by virtue of having been killed in fantasy, surviving, and not retaliating, withdrawing, or submitting. That is, the therapist becomes real when it is okay for the client to think about and have feelings of being needy, angry, furious, and even murderous toward her therapist. The experience of unfettered and unpunished aggressive feelings toward an attachment figure has often been absent in people who were subjected to traumatic attachments and whose internal world is a relatively closed system.

In essence, the parts—both the sane, dependent ones, and the angry, aggressive ones—that have been sequestered on the inside need to be invited into the treatment relationship. In Winnicott's language, the therapist has to become "real," not someone just to be managed.

A recent interaction with my client, Sophia, illustrates how I became real to her. When she was growing up, Sophia's mother had been too wrapped up in her own issues to pay much attention to Sophia or adequately care for her. Sophia's father's narcissism verged on cruelty at times, especially in her adolescence when he refused to pay for most of her school expenses or her clothes, despite the fact that he could easily afford to. Sophia was mostly left to figure things out for herself and she learned that she had to be both psychologically and economically self-sufficient. It was hard for Sophia to even imagine that someone else might do something for her. She had even said that she felt that it was as if some force within her wouldn't let her even long for caring.

Sophia always came to session well prepared. She brought her own Kleenex even though she knew that my office had Kleenex on the table in front of her on also on the end table beside her. She always brought checks already made out. Thus, she never even had to ask to borrow a pen. She never needed anything from me. Yet, on one particular day, her cell phone was strangely not charged, and she hadn't brought a charger either. In a very unusual behavior, she asked if she could charge her phone in the office during the session. I didn't have a charger cord, but I realized that I could take the one off my computer, and I offered this to her. It worked, and we plugged her phone into the charger.

As it happened, both of us forgot that she was charging her phone, and she left the session without her phone. I began my next session. Then about 15 minutes into that session, I saw a text on my phone, saying that she had forgotten her phone. She came back to get her phone, and

I interrupted my session for a moment to smilingly return her phone to her at the outside door.

In the next session, she told me how extremely upset she had been about forgetting her phone. She had feared that I would be furious with her for bothering me. She even imagined that I would have a scowl on my face, a scowl that looked to her in her mind's eye just like her mother's scowl. She said that when she saw my smile and my relaxed face, that she became not only relieved of her worry, but that she had felt transformed in a way. She said that I had become more real to her. As she looked at me, she said, "You *are* real, in some ways I felt you weren't real. In my imagination I was afraid of you."

CHAPTER 10

Conclusion:
Toward Psychological Healing

The mind-nourishing "bread" of culture is its meaning—the stories we share about "what" happens, "when" and "where" it happened, and "who" were involved.

—Colwyn Trevarthen, 2009b, p. 87

Ask not what you can do for the world. Instead ask what makes you feel alive, because the world needs alive people.

—Lynn Preston, personal communication, 2019

IN THIS BOOK, I have advocated for close attention to dissociative processes in our clinical work. Processing the events, affects, and meaning inherent in what was dissociated requires mourning. An emotionally difficult part of the therapist's work is to hear and bear witness, thereby offering support for facing and processing the traumas and adverse experiences that the client had to endure. The therapist as well as the client must mourn. Participating as a human being, the therapist helps the client to reconnect dissociated parts of experience. Endorsing this approach requires a new metaphor. The Freudian metaphor of Oedipus, instinctually motivated to lust for his mother and murder his father, no longer fits.

Osiris and Isis

Trauma treatment has arrived at a new metaphor, the Osiris Complex (C. Ross, 1989). Colin Ross (1989) has proposed that the myth of Osiris is the best model for the damage done by trauma and for the healing of dissociation. Osiris was the revered Egyptian god of the Nile who provided for the rebirth of crops with the life-source of water when the Nile flooded every spring. However, Osiris was overcome and cut up by his brother, the evil god, Set, who threw the pieces of his body all over Egypt. Osiris's grieving and distraught wife-sister, Isis, found the pieces and sewed them back together again and resuscitated him with her tears of mourning.[4] Eventually, Osiris became the god of the underworld, of the afterlife, and of rebirth in ancient Egyptian religions.

The story of the split up, fragmented Osiris is apt for traumatized and dissociative clients. As therapists we facilitate our clients' becoming able to knit together the dissociated pieces of their lives that have been scattered within the mind in pockets of subconscious life. This happens in many different ways, including being able to listen intently, even to hear about unconscionable acts of perpetration that our clients had to endure, and to mourn with them. It also includes active interventions such as helping parts of a person become more aware of and sympathetic to each other, resulting in greater self-compassion, via somatic therapy, EMDR, dreamwork, and other modalities.

Despite being a god, Osiris cannot resurrect himself. It is only with the help of a loving empathic other—Isis—that he is brought back together into wholeness. Isis's devotion can be likened to that of a nurturing parent whose sympathy for a child's emotional scratches, cuts, and bruises actually helps them to heal. The parent's empathy helps heal the emotional bruising by helping the child feel recognized and less alone in pain. Similarly, a therapist helps the client put the trauma into words, thus making it knowable. Isis's tears symbolize how mourning is necessary for psychological healing from trauma. Mourning and searching occur together, for the process of mourning metacognitively casts the mind to past experiences and actions, allowing lost pieces of self to begin to cohere.

The idea that Osiris is not in the long run overcome by the evil Set, but that life has a will of its own and regenerates, can take various forms. As a novice gardener, I once cut up what I thought was a dead fig tree; merely to add ballast and mass to the soil, I put the pieces in a pot in which to grow something new. To my great surprise and pleasure, the following spring, these seemingly dead branches that I had cut up and buried began to sprout new stems and leaves. They became a new fig tree! In my mind, this has become a metaphor for people's inherent and resilient will to life and to potentiality of rebirth of the self even after it has been ruthlessly cut up, as I did to my fig tree.

Denial of Trauma

A significant problem in the mental health field is that severe relational trauma has too long been unthinkable. the unconscionable has been unthinkable. When a person is in denial of something horrible, it is hard to think about the possibilities of healing that would emanate from accepting those horrors. If Isis in the Egyptian myth had ignored the dismemberment of Osiris, he would never have been healed; the meaning of the myth that the continuity of life depends on mourning and the difficult task of putting the pieces together of a person's life would have been lost. The condition for the healing of the damage done by horrors is their acceptance by the client, the therapist, and society.

Oedipus

Freud's Oedipal theory might be considered the ultimate denial of the unconscionable. In my view, the idea of the dismembered psyche was present all along in the dominant psychoanalytic metaphor of the Oedipus myth. As I noted in Chapter 1, when Freud disavowed his seduction theory, he also disavowed trauma and dissociation as realities, plunging much of psychological theory into a kind of intellectual dark ages for about a century. When we examine the Oedipus myth that Freud made the centerpiece of his new psychoanalytic theory, we find marked signs of the impact of trauma and dissociation that Freud apparently did not notice.

The primary meaning that Freud took from the ancient Greek play by Sophocles, *Oedipus Rex,* coalesced on the fate of the tragic hero, Oedipus, who unknowingly committed parricide and maternal incest. In his exposition of the story, Freud (1924) adapted this Oedipal motif to support his view that boys universally wish to sexually possess their mothers and are rivalrous, even murderously so, with their fathers and that similarly, girls generally arrive at the Oedipal position of wanting sexual involvement with their fathers. Freud began developing this position within months after abandoning his seduction theory. In September 1897, he wrote to his friend, Fliess, saying, "I no longer believe in my Neurotica" (Gay, 1988, p. 88); and in October 1897, he wrote again to say that the Oedipal relationship of the child to its parents was a "general event in early childhood" (Gay, p. 100).

In the Sophocles play, Oedipus, the crown prince of Corinth, had been told by the Oracle that he was destined to murder his father and marry his mother. Consequently, he left home to avoid this fate. On his travels away from home on the outskirts of Thebes he happened to quarrel with and slay another traveler, who unbeknownst to him was his biological father, Laius, the king of Thebes. Soon thereafter, he solved the riddles of the Sphinx, and thereby released the kingdom of Thebes from her tyranny. As a result, Oedipus was proclaimed the new king of Thebes and he married the widowed queen, Jocasta. Oedipus had not known that the man he killed was his biological father, Laius, or that the Corinthian king and queen whom he left had been his adoptive parents. Oedipus only discovered these things when the occurrence of a plague, seemingly in retribution for the murder of Laius, required that he consult the Oracle again. This time the Oracle informed him of his own, previously unwitting, guilt. Upon hearing the news, Jocasta, Oedipus's wife-mother, hanged herself in shame; upon finding her, in grief and despair Oedipus blinded himself with the pins from her garment.

Amazingly, Freud ignored the reason behind Oedipus's disastrous fate: a curse that had been placed on his biological father, Laius, the king of Thebes, for the abduction and rape of the son of a neighboring king. The retributive curse, as repeated by an Oracle (Fromm, 1980; J. Ross, 1982) was that Laius would be murdered by his son, and that his son would marry his (Laius's) wife, Jocasta. To avoid this curse, Laius and Jocasta attempted to murder their own son by instructing a servant to abandon the child in the forest with his feet bound and pinned together, thus ensuring that he would die. (The name *Oedipus*, means "swollen foot.") However, the servant was not as heartless as he had been instructed to be, and he gave the child to a man who worked for the neighboring king of Corinth. The king then adopted him. Thus, Freud's famous rendition of the heroic but tragic Oedipus story is trenchantly embedded in themes of child rape and attempted infanticide.

Freud did not observe that the underlying meaning of the Oedipus myth centers on child abuse and attempted infanticide (Devereux, 1953; Fromm, 1980; Pines, 1989; J. Ross, 1982), along with the implied retribution that the perpetrator will be punished for these crimes. The not- infrequent origins of human psychopathology in child sexual abuse are exactly what Freud first reported on in his 1896 (1962) paper, "The Aetiology of Hysteria." Child sexual abuse at that time for Freud was the origin of hysteria. As we know, Freud soon denied his findings and rephrased the issue as the child's guilty wishes. Freud, in effect, blinded himself to what he had omitted—as Oedipus blinded himself for what he committed. The message of *Oedipus Rex* is not that boys want to sexually possess their mothers and girls their fathers. The message is that pederasty is a crime, a crime that if it is not stopped at its source will poison generations. The answer to Oedipus is simply this: to stop the curse, we as cultures and societies need to stop child abuse, notably child sexual abuse. Not even kings have immunity to the dictates of universal law. Such heinous acts destroy the lives of their offspring for generations to come. Thus, the Oedipus story is about the intergenerational transmission of trauma.

Although trauma treatment usually cannot restore justice for crimes of the past, it can reduce intergenerational repetition of the same crimes—by confronting the unconscionable in a given person's experience, thereby connecting the severed, dissociated pieces of experience, and stopping or mitigating the re-infliction of damage against the self or others.

Connection, Disconnection, and Reconnection

As we know, poor psychological integration follows from family environments characterized by combinations of abuse, trauma, deprivation, and neglect (Allen, 2001; Putnam, 1997, 2016). When too much has been disconnected and too much dissociated, a person is likely to experience life events one at a time, without contextualization and connection to other events. For example, some may be blind to dangerous others because they have dissociated harmful outcomes from such dangerous relationships in the past. The memories of too many unbearable experiences have been scattered within the mind and remain unlinked to the rest of experience. It is then hard for a person to learn from experience. The result is that the same kinds of life problems occur over and over again, but that each reoccurrence is experienced as if it is the first time.

Discrete Behavior States and Lack of Association

Dividedness is the way we are. Multiple and shifting states of mind and behavior characterize human life. Not only is the self divided by trauma;

people start out life in disconnected behavior states. In his groundbreaking books, *The Way We Are: How States of Mind Influence Our Identities, Personality and Potential for Change* (2016) and *Dissociation in Children and Adolescents* (1997), Frank Putnam has shown that rather than beginning as a unity, a person begins life as discrete behavioral states that must become integrated over time. An important developmental task, then, is to link these discrete states so that we can predict and make sense of the world. Notably, trauma also impedes this process.

Discrete Behavioral States: Linked and Not Linked

Early on, in his research on behavioral-mental states of being, Putnam was struck by the accumulated knowledge of scientific "baby-watchers" (Putnam, 1997, 2016) who observed and coded the infant's body and brain transitions between different behavioral states. The baby-watchers identified the discrete states of sleep and waking by noting the concurrence of certain measured behaviors of the infant's body: motor activity, muscle tone, facial expressions, skin perfusion, heart rate, and respiration. They found five distinctly different behavioral states of sleep, waking, and crying in infants that they were able to map onto a multi-dimensional state-space. These states are self-organizing, functioning as *strange attractors* in state space as described by dynamical systems theory, or chaos theory. Chaos theory is deterministic, but nonlinear, often exemplified by the idea that the air displacement caused by a butterfly's flapping wings could contribute to the occurrence of a much larger weather event somewhere else and later on. Many different states—such as moods, states of sleep, or cognitive states—function as strange attractors, and there can be jumps (state switches or reorganizations) from one basin of attraction to another.

Putnam successfully applied measurements of states to older children's and adults' behavior and found that discrete states of being are isomorphic across different measures of brain, body, and phenomenally reported self-experience. Discrete states are mind, brain, and body variables that influence a person's thoughts, behavior, and emotions. For example, shifting body states correlate with shifting mental and emotional states. Putnam notes that these coding systems have revealed that child and adult complex behaviors "are composed of a limited set of distinct states flowing from one to another in a roughly predictable, repeating sequence. Brain imaging revealed that discrete states exist on multiple time and dimensional scales from microstates lasting a fraction of a second reflecting activation in specific neural networks to global brain states such as depression lasting months" (pp. 86–87).

Learning Self-Regulation

These self-organizing states inevitably end and switch into other self-organized states. In time, other affective or biological states are added, and the transitions between them become regularly linked. As these linkages become more complex, the child gains greater control and ability to self-regulate.

In a facilitating environment, caregivers assist in emotional regulation, such as by minimizing negative affect, down-regulating hyperarousal, and assisting the child to transition from negative to positive states (Tronick, 1989; Putnam, 2016), thereby promoting the child's reflective functioning (Fonagy, Gergely, Jurist & Target, 2002). Matching of emotional states (Schore, 2019; Stern, 1985) and attunement between caregivers and young children leads to healthy, or at least organized, attachments; together these are key for the child's learning affect regulation. Internalization of the caregiver's reading back of their emotional states (Siegel, 1999) helps children develop metacognitive skills of understanding their own and others' minds.

In contrast, trauma and neglect impair the linking of associative pathways among states. Neglect, deprivation, and rejection tend to co-occur with abuse (Gold, 2000). Such interpersonal environments have failed to provide the infant and the child with the requisite resources to nourish the acquisition of fundamental skills in living. In environments of abuse and neglect a child's affect states may not be labeled and linked by the attachment figures—such that people who have grown up in these environments may not know when they are angry, or sad, or frightened, or they may not have learned the experiential meaning of the word compassion.

State Dependence

Putnam's state-dependent learning and memory (SDLM) model emphasizes the great extent to which our lives (even lives framed by healthy attachments), are state-dependent. For example, the associative aspect of ordinary recall is influenced by one's current state of mind and its link to earlier states of mind; emotionally charged autobiographical memories are not easily recalled in ordinary states of consciousness and may depend on special ways to access them, whether being in a similar situation again, or in dreams, or by such methods as EMDR or somatic processing. According to this model, "identity and emotional states are behaviorally present or psychologically activated in varying degrees depending on life experiences. They may be largely insulated from each other by SDLM, permitting people to behave in contradictory ways across different settings and not be troubled by their inconsistency" (Putnam, 2016, p.17). But this more or less normal state dependence is highly exacerbated for those who have been traumatized:

> Children exposed to repeated ACEs (Adverse Childhood Experiences) recurrently experience these extreme states of being. They are frightened, panicked, helpless, depressed, horrified, abused, neglected, troubled, and isolated—over and over and over again. Because ACEs tend to occur together . . . these children will accumulate a history of having repetitively experienced many types of extreme states of being. This

cumulative history becomes a growing vulnerability because each time you experience an extreme state it becomes easier to re-experience it or something like it in the future. A pathway is being formed in state-space. Thus, it becomes easier to switch into an extreme state of being when confronted with situations reminiscent of the initial trauma. (Putnam, 2016, pp. 218–219)

Putnam explains that the repeated experiences of these extreme states interrupt what would otherwise be the normal flow and sequences of states of mind/body in waking experience and sleep cycles. For example, flashbacks or nightmares intrude into and interrupt ongoing being. A significant problem for people is state dependence; at times of being pulled into a traumatic reexperience, a person can feel extremely agitated and lack recourse to ways of calming down.

We begin life as unlinked states, and to varying degrees, we as human beings, often remain inadequately linked in our states. Putnam noted that: "Our global personality is comprised of many identity states. Its public expression reflects the dynamic interactions among these identity states, each with their state-dependent knowledge, skills, values, etc." He adds: "As a result of the demands of modern life we have many identities, which are typically activated in specific contexts or interpersonal situations" (Putnam, 2017). Indeed, "the idea of a unitary, continuous 'self' is actually an illusion our minds attempt to create . . . We have multiple and varied 'selves' which are needed to carry out the many and diverse activities of our lives" (Siegel, 1999, p. 231). The degree to which we can feel "unified" or continuous in time and memory (even though we may not be aware of our shifting states) is the degree to which we have achieved internal intersubjectivity across mental states, that is, that our states of mind can be aware of and can access connection to each other. This allows the retrieval of knowledge from different states and generalization of information across them. Trauma disrupts this linkage and continuity of different mood and cognitive states.

Tying the Pieces Together: Isis's Thread of Self-Reflection

Functioning well, while feeling, but not necessarily being unified or continuous requires the glue of self-observing metacognitive abilities that were ideally learned via parental attunement but can be earned in psychotherapy. Experiences of *interpersonal intersubjectivity* promote internal, *intrapersonal intersubjectivity*. Psychotherapy helps clients learn about and learn to tolerate their dissociated feelings and thereby connect formerly separated states of mind. In therapy people can learn to keep an eye on themselves, which results in a better connected "I," variously termed "observing ego," the observing "I" (Ryle, 1997a, 1997b) "reflective functioning," "executive functions," or "mentalizing" (Fonagy, 2000, 2001). These are the ways that people hold themselves together; they are the glue—or better, the thread of Isis's sewing—that hold states of mind together and help to keep highly charged emotional states from spinning out of control. The increasing interconnections of self-knowledge held in different states, contributes to a greater accessibility of an autobiographical "I." A more accessible autobiographical "I" helps bring highly charged state-dependencies back into orbit.

Psychotherapy can help a person reclaim all the bits and pieces of autobiographical memories and the feelings that go with them that may be scattered across different self states, so that the fragments knit together under a widening umbrella of remembered and reflective self.

Dreamwork

This book has described different listening stances, both theoretical and spontaneously authentic, as well as different practical technical approaches for working with trauma. One modality that I have found especially productive for working with disconnected self-states is dreamwork.

In contrast to ordinary conscious thinking, dreams reveal secrets, hidden truths, or hidden-in-plain-sight aspects of a person's life. Dreams speak to us in a different language that accords importance to different information than that of daytime thought in which our minds are connected to the "real" world and act upon it. Dreams have the capacity to be healing, because they place before us the elements of our lives that need to be connected or integrated.

Dream perceptions, thoughts, and images are often overlaid. They may express wish-fulfillment, solve a problem, state a message to the dreamer, or frame a point of view. Dreams also tell us our own stories, although in their own special language of symbols, metaphor, substitutions, and collapsed time/place.

Dreams provide a way for dissociated parts of the self to be noticed. That is, the inhibitory power of waking life combined with the contextual demands of conscious life keeps other parts of ourselves that hold important knowledge out of awareness—for reasons ranging from past trauma to current expedience. In our dreams, these more usually sequestered parts of the mind can express themselves. The ghosts of the neglected or dissociated self-states come out at night in dreams, and they can teach us about ourselves. Dreams allow us to notice elements of our lives that have been anomalous to our usual way of thinking about ourselves.

Dreams of highly dissociative people often show in bold relief a correspondence between dream characters and alters, or identities, that emerge in the real, non-dreaming world. These vividly illustrate how parts of the self can take on a character and a voice, stating their perceptions, beliefs, fears, and desires in dreams. In her research on dreams of people with DID, Dierdre Barrett (1996) found that over half of her sample reported that their alters actually appeared as dream characters. Notably, one person who dreamt of fighting with cats, awoke the next morning to find cat hairs on her clothing.

I have proposed (Howell, 2014b) that dreams of people who are to varying degrees less dissociative also express something similar, that dream characters may correspond to certain self-states. Often different self-states take center stage in dreams, communicating various concerns, not necessarily held by all parts of the personality system. The interrelationships of dream characters that often represent dissociated self-states reveal the psychodynamics of the self-states in the personality system.

In Chapter 7, I described a common psychic split brought on by traumatizing attachment dilemmas in which clients feel they are bad or punish themselves so as to protect the attachment to the parent. The following vignette explores a way to work with this dilemma using dreams.

Case Vignette

The dream is about how the client felt she was bad because her mother often treated her as if she wasn't worth bothering with. In the dreamwork, an injured child state was contacted and then emerged at the end of the session with the realization that she wasn't bad. Subsequently, the client was able to absorb this message and realize that it was her childhood circumstances that had been bad, not herself.

> *I was a teenager in the home I grew up in, except that it was much nicer, bigger, with big sparkling windows, cleaner and more attractive than the actual house. My mother had picked up my friend and taken her to the movies, so that she could deliver her to me at home at exactly the time I wished to see my friend.*

In telling the dream the client realized that this was highly different in many ways from what her home life had really been like. In contrast to her dream, her home was often disorganized, chaotic, and dirty, certainly not sparkling. Her mother was frequently neglectful and felt harassed. The client's mother often left her to fend for herself and became enraged and critical if she asked for something.

Suddenly the dream shifted to a different scene:

I was sitting in the back seat of my car, which was parked on the road, read-
ing. A gang of kids approached me in the car and began mildly harassing me.
I ignored their harassment and went on reading. Then the surrounding gang
became mostly older adolescents, boys and girls. One of the adolescent girls
remarked to me, "Nice breasts." I ignored it and went on reading. Then sud-
denly, two big, adult men got in the front seat and turned on the ignition—
with the car keys that had been left there. I asked where we were going but
they did not answer. Suddenly I became panicked, but also with a sense of
inevitability. I realized they were taking me some place, probably to rape me
and kill me.

In discussing the dream, the client remembered how much she had
relied upon reading in her home to insulate herself from the chaos. She
remembered how very hurt and rejected she had felt when her mother
became angry and critical of her for needing something. She remembered feeling like a very bad girl for needing things from her mother, for
being a bother to her mother. She realized that she often felt that she was
a bother and bad around people. It then became clear to her that she had
reversed the view of her mother and herself in the first dream. In the first
dream, her mother was treating her like a princess and she was acting
like one, almost the opposite of her real life.

THERAPIST: *Hmm, so you were bad because you were needing . . . ? Perhaps*
you really didn't want to face how neglectful she was to you, how alone
and helpless her rejection made you feel. So you just tried to tune every-
thing out by reading. And, as you mention, could you have been protect-
ing your mother by making things the opposite of how they were?

CLIENT: *Oh, my God! And I'm still tuning everything out, not noticing that*
things are bad when they are bad. That's what I have been doing recently.
The dream was a warning . . .

THERAPIST: *. . . to wake up. Not noticing that things are bad when they are* *bad, because you are in some way avoiding thinking about the feeling of your being bad? Is that what you are saying? Something like that?*

The rest of the session was spent examining her feeling of her badness. She felt it in the center of her chest, "like a big hole," she said. It was a kind of squiggly, smudgy blackness. She felt alone with it, unacceptable to the world because of this badness. She recalled that she had tried hard to help her mother, but was rejected even for that. She remembered her murderous rage, which I normalized by reminding her that all human beings have murderous feelings at times, even children. And the work continued.

When we met for the next session, she reported that as she was leaving the office building, she found herself saying to herself, *"I'm not bad. I'm just a little kid."*

Note her use of the present tense. That bad-little-girl state had been contacted in the session. She has reported feeling highly relieved of this sense of badness since that session.

This dream may have elements of wish-fulfillment in it, but the fact that it not only makes the mother good, but also makes the child bad, suggests to me that it is showing the dreamer a particular perspective on the organization and defenses of her psyche. The dream dramatically shows the client how she is covering up for her mother and making herself the bad one. We have a denial of mistreatment and the child's idealization of her mother along with harsh disparagement of herself for being such a demanding child (she is a selfish princess who abuses her caring mother). In the second part of the dream, we have the client's dream insight that her methods of coping with her childhood mistreatment (including having been inappropriately shamed)—such as tuning out and transforming herself into the bad one—are potentially dangerous to her in the present time.

This inside-out way of working invites hidden, dissociated states of mind to enter the precious, protected therapy space and recount their own autobiographical history. Once talked about in a safe interpersonal context, formerly dissociated voices can become part of the conversation. In this way, the defensive psychic structure begins to be gradually deconstructed, and certain strands of dissociated experience become untangled and conscious.

Thomas Kuhn's proposition (1962) says scientific revolutions occur not by gradual, orderly accretion of new information, but rather when enough anomalous information is accepted into the official knowledge system that a paradigm shift occurs and transforms the system. This is also apt for psychotherapy. Thus, psychotherapy not only yields anamnesis, additively restoring what was forgotten, but is potentially reorganizing and transformative, enabling the discovery of potent strands of joy and innocence.

ENDNOTES

1. There is controversy over the *extent* to which Freud continued to acknowledge that child sexual abuse does occur and is pathogenic. Some Freudian theorists (e.g., Blum, 2008; Hanly, 1986) have noted that Masson's treatise conveyed the false impression that Freud *completely* renounced his earlier observation that seduction (or sexual abuse) of young children occurs and that its results are pathogenic. For example, to his paper, "Further Remarks on the Neuro-Psychoses of Defense" (1894/1962), Freud added a footnote in 1924 stating his recognition of the reality that seductions occur, saying that although he had been mistaken to believe that all neuroses were caused by early seduction, that does not mean that none are. Referring to his error (1924), he says:

   > At that time [1896] I was not yet able to distinguish between my patients' phantasies about their childhood years and their real recollections. As a result, I attributed to the aetiological factor of seduction a significance and universality which it does not possess . . . Nevertheless, we need not reject everything written in the text above. Seduction retains a certain aetiological importance, and even today I think some of these psychological comments are to the point. (1894, p. 168)

   Again, in 1905, in "Three Essays on the Theory of Sexuality," he remarks in reference to his earlier emphasis on the pathogenic influence of sexual abuse in the 1896 paper: "I cannot admit that . . . I exaggerated the frequency or importance of that influence, though I did not then know that persons who remain normal may have had the same experiences in their childhood (pp. 190–191).

2. A recent study (Greulich & Cherniack (2019) that simulated EMDR in rats found that fear extinction was successful, using alternating bilateral stimulation (ABS), which is the core method in EMDR when a person self-exposed to a traumatic memory. The author's hypothetical conclusion is that the ABS shifts the balance between competing brain circuits, so that fear extinction can occur.

3. Noting the confusing uses and criteria of repression, Holmes specified that "(1) repression is selective forgetting of materials that cause an individual pain, (2) repression is not under voluntary control; and that (3) repressed material is not lost, but instead is stored in the unconscious and can be returned to consciousness if the anxiety that is associated with the memory is removed (Freud, [1915] 1957)." p. 86.

4. According to Erich Neuman (1955/1963), a Jungian iconographer, the character of Isis, along with the Greek Demeter (or Ceres in the Roman), the Virgin Mary, and other nurturing and healing goddesses, is a manifestation of the Positive Element of the larger archetype of the Great Mother, who gives life but also takes it away. The Positive Element only gives and nurtures life.

REFERENCES

Ackerly, R. (2012, March 14). Still face experiments are more about power than attachment parenting [Blog post]. Retrieved from http://rickackerly.com/2012/03/14/still-face-experiments-are-more-about-power-than-attachment-parenting/

Allen, J. G. (2001). *Traumatic relationships and serious mental disorders.* New York, NY: John Wiley.

Ahbel-Rappe (2006). "I no longer believe": Did Freud abandon the seduction theory? *American Psychoanalytic Association, 54,* 171–199.

Allen, J. G. (2001). *Traumatic relationships and serious mental disorders.* New York: Wiley.

American Psychological Association (2013). *The diagnostic and statistical manual of mental disorders: DSM-5.* BookpointUS.

Badouk Epstein, O. (2018). From proximity seeking to relationship seeking: Toward separation from the "scaregivers." *Frontiers in the Psychotherapy of Trauma and Dissociation,* 1(2), 290–306 .

Barrett, D.L. (1996). Dreams in multiple personality disorder. In: *Trauma and Dreams,* Ed. D. Barrett. Cambridge, MA: Harvard University Press, pp. 68–81.

Barnett, J. (1966). A structural analysis of theories in psychoanalysis. *Psychoanalytic Review,*53(1), 85–98.

Beebe, B. & Lachmann, F. M. (2014). *The origins of attachment: infant research and adult treatment.* New York: Routledge.

Benjamin, J. (1990). Recognition and destruction: An outline of intersubjectivity. In S. A. Mitchell & L. Aron (Eds.), *Relational psychoanalysis: The emergence of a tradition* (pp. 181–210). Hillsdale, NJ: Analytic Press, 1999.

Betcher, W., & Pollack, W. S. (1993). *In a time of fallen heroes.* New York: Guilford Press.

Birtles & Scharff, *From instinct to self: Selected papers of W.R. D. Fairbairn, vol. II: Applications and early contributions.* Northvale, New Jersey: Jason Aronson.

Blizard, R. A. (2003). Disorganized attachment, development of dissociated self-states, and a relational approach to treatment. *Journal of Trauma & Dissociation, 4*(3), 27–50.

Blum, H.P. (2008). A further excavation of seduction, seduction trauma, and the seduction theory. *Psychoanalytic Study of the Child, 63,* 254–269.

Boon, S., Steele, K., & Van der Hart, O. (2010). *Coping with trauma-related dissociation: Skills training for clients and therapists.* New York: Norton.

Boadella, D. (2011). Psycho-physical synthesis of the foundations of body psychotherapy: The 100-year legacy of Pierre Janet (1859–1947). In: C. Young (Ed.), *The Historical Basis of Body Psychotherapy* (pp. 49–66). Stow, UK: Body Psychotherapy Publications.

Boulanger, G. (2007). *Wounded by reality: Understanding and treating adult onset trauma.* New York: Analytic Press.

Bowen, M. (1985). *Family therapy in clinical practice.* Northdale, NJ: Jason Aronson, Inc.

Bowlby, J. (1969/1983). *Attachment and loss: Vol. 1. Attachment.* New York: Basic Books.

Bowlby, J. (1973). *Attachment and loss: Vol. 2. Separation.* New York: Basic Books.

Bowlby, J. (1980), *Attachment and Loss, Vol. 3: Loss: Sadness and Depression.* New York: Basic Books.

Bowlby, J. (1984). Psychoanalysis as a natural science. *Psychoanalytic Psychology, 1,* 7–22.

Brand, B. L., Classen, C. C., McNary, S. W., & Zaveri, P. (2009). A review of dissociative disorders treatment studies. *Journal of Nervous and Mental Disease, 197*(9), 646–654.

Brand, B. L., McNary, S. W., Myrick, A. C., Classen, C. C., Lanius, R., Loewenstein, R. J., . . . Putnam, F. W. (2013). A longitudinal naturalistic study of patients with dissociative disorders treated by community clinicians. *Psychological Trauma: Theory, Research, Practice, and Policy, 5*, 301–308. doi:10.1037/a0027654

Brand, B. L., Myrick, A. C., Loewenstein, R. J., Classen, C. C., Lanius, R., McNary, S. W., . . . Putnam, F. W. (2012). A survey of practices and recommended treatment interventions among expert therapists treating patients with dissociative identity disorder and dissociative disorder not otherwise specified. *Psychological Trauma: Theory, Research, Practice, and Policy, 4*, 490–500. doi:10.1037/a0026487

Brand, B. L., Şar, V., Stavropoulos, P., Kruger, C., Korzekwa, M., Martínez-Taboas, A., & Middleton, W. (2016). Separating fact from fiction: An empirical examination of common myths about dissociative identity disorder. *Harvard Review of Psychiatry, 24*(4), 257–270. doi:10.1097/HRP.0000000000000100

Brand, B., Shielke, H., Putnam, K., Putnam, F., Loewenstein, R., Myrick, A., Jepson, E., Langeland, W., Steele, K., Classen, C., Lanius, R. (2019). An online educational program for individuals with dissociative disorders and their clinicians: 1-year and 2-year follow-up *Journal of Traumatic Stress, 32*(1), 156 166. doi:10.1002/jts.22370.

Breger, L. (2000). *Freud: Darkness in the midst of vision*. New York: Wiley.

Breger. L. (2011). *A dream of undying fame: How Freud betrayed his mentor and invented psychoanalysis*. New York: Basic Books.

Bremner, J.D. & Vermetten, E. (2007). Psychiatric approaches to dissociation: Integrating history, biology, and clinical assessment. In: Eric Vermetten, Martin Dorahy & David Spiegel (Eds.), *Traumatic dissociation: Neurobiology and treatment* (pp. 239–258). Washington D.C.: American Psychiatric Publishing.

Breuer, J., & Freud, S. (1893–95). On the psychical mechanism of hysterical phenomena: Preliminary communication from studies on hysteria. In J. Strachey (Ed. & Trans.), *The standard edition of the complete psychological works of Sigmund Freud* (Vol. 4, pp. 1–17). London: Hogarth Press, 1955.

Breuer, J. & Freud, S. (1893–95). *Studies on hysteria* (J. Strachey, Trans.). London: Hogarth Press, 1955.

Bromberg, P. (1998). *Standing in the spaces: Essays on clinical process trauma and dissociation*. New York: Routledge.

Bromberg, P. (2006). *Awakening the dreamer: Clinical journeys.* Mahwah, NJ: Analytic Press.

Bromberg, P.M. (2008). Shrinking the tsunami: Affect regulation, dissociation, and the shadow of the flood. *Contemporary Psychoanalysis, 44,* 329–350.

Bromberg, P. M. (2011). *In the shadow of the tsunami.* New York: Taylor and Francis.

Brothers, D. (1995). *Falling backwards: An exploration of trust and self experience.* New York: Norton.

Brown, E. M., Laub, D., Loew, C., Richman, S., Itzkowitz, S., Sussillo, M. V., Behm, A., Itzkowitz, S., and Sussillo, M. V. (2007). Last witnesses: Child survivors of the Holocaust; Pt. 1. *Psychoanalytic Perspectives, 4*(2), 1–50.

Brown, L. S. (1991). Not outside the range: One feminist perspective on psychic trauma. *American Imago, 48,* 119–133.

Bucci, W. (1997). *Psychoanalysis and cognitive science.* New York, NY: Guilford Press.

Bucci, W. (2002). The referential process, consciousness, and the sense of self. *Psychoanalytic Inquiry, 22,* 766–793.

Bucci, W. (2003). Varieties of dissociative experiences: A multiple code account and a discussion of Bromberg's case of "William." *Psychoanalytic Psychoanalysis, 20,* 542–557.

Buck, R. (1993). Emotional communication, emotional competence, and physical illness: A developmental-interactionist view. In: J. Pennebaker & H Treve, Eds: *Emotional expressiveness, inhibition and health.* Seattle, Washington: Hogrefe and Huber.

Cameron, N., & Rychlak, J. F. (1985). *Personality development and psychopathology: A dynamic approach.* Boston: Houghton Mifflin.

Carlson, E. A. (1998). A prospective longitudinal study of attachment disorganization/disorientation. *Child Development, 69,* 1107–1128.

Chefetz, RA. (1997) Special case transference and countertransference in the treatment of dissociative identity disorder. *Dissociation, 10*(4), 255–265.

Chefetz, R. A. (2000a). Affect dysregulation as a way of life. *Journal of the American Academy of Psychoanalysis, 28,* 289–303.

Chefetz, R.A. (2015). *Intensive psychotherapy for persistent dissociative processes: The fear of feeling real.* New York: Norton.

Chefetz, R. A., & Bromberg, P. M. (2004), Talking with "me" and "not-me": A dialogue. *Contemporary Psychoanalysis, 40,* 409–464.

Chu, J. A. (1998), *Rebuilding shattered lives.* New York: Wiley.

Cloitre, M., Garvert, D. W., Brewin, C. R., Bryant, R. A., & Maercker, A. (2013). Evidence for proposed ICD-11 PTSD and complex PTSD: A latent profile analysis. *European Journal of Psychotraumatology, 4*, 20706.

Courtois, C. A. (1999). *Recollections of sexual abuse: Treatment principles and guidelines.* New York, NY: Norton.

Courtois, C. A. (2004). Complex trauma, complex reactions: Assessment and treatment. *Psychotherapy: Theory, Research, Practice, & Training, 41,* 412–425.

Courtois, C. A., & Ford, J. D. (2009). *Treating complex traumatic stress disorders: An evidence-based guide.* New York, NY: Guilford Press.

Dalenberg, C. (2000). *Countertransference and the treatment of trauma.* Washington, DC: American Psychological Association.

Dalenberg, C. J. (2004). Maintaining the safe and effective therapeutic relationship in the context of distrust and anger: Countertransference and complex trauma. *Psychotherapy: Theory, research, practice, training, 41*(4), 438–447.

Davies, J. M. (1996), Linking the "pre-analytic" with the postclassical: Integration, dissociation, and the multiplicity of unconscious process. *Contemporary Psychoanaysis, 32,* 553–576.

Davies, J. M., & Frawley, M. G. (1994). *Treating the adult survivor of childhood sexual abuse: A psychoanalytic perspective.* New York: Basic Books.

Dell, P. F. (2009). Understanding dissociation. In P. F. Dell & J. A. O'Neil (Eds.), *Dissociation and the dissociative disorders: DSM–V and beyond* (pp. 709–825). New York: Routledge.

Devereux, G. (1953). Why Oedipus killed Laius: A note on the complementary Oedipus complex in Greek drama. *International Journal of Psycho-Analysis, 32,* 132.

Dutton, D. C., & Painter, S. L. (1981). Traumatic bonding: The development of emotional attachments in battered women and other relationships of intermittent abuse. *Victimology, 6,* 139–155.

Ehling, T., Nijenhuis, E. R. S. & Krikke, A. P. (2003). Volume of discrete brain structures in florid and recovered DID, DDNOS and healthy controls. Presented at 20th Annual Conference of the International Society for the Study of Dissociation, Chicago, November 4, 2003.

Ellenberger, H. (1970). *The discovery of the unconscious: The history and evolution of dynamic psychiatry.* New York: Basic Books.

Erdelyi, M. H. (1990). Repression, reconstruction, and defense: History and integration of the psychoanalytic and experimental frameworks. In J. L. Singer (Ed.), *Repression and dissociation: Implications for personality theory, psychopathology, and health* (pp. 1–32). Chicago: University of Chicago Press.

Erdelyi, M. H. (1992). Psychodynamics and the unconscious. *American Psychologist, 47,* 784–787.

Erdelyi, M. H. (1994). Dissociation, defense, and the unconscious. In D. Spiegel (Ed.), *Dissociation, culture, mind and body* (pp. 3–20). Washington, DC: American Psychiatric Press.

Erdelyi, M. H. (2001). Defense processes can be conscious or unconscious. *Amer. Psychol., 56,* 761–762.

Fairbairn, R. (1944/1952). *Psychoanalytic Studies of the Personality.* Boston: Routledge & Kegan Paul.

Fairbairn, W. R. D. (1929). Dissociation and repression. In: E. D. Scharff & E. F. Birtles (Eds.), *From Instinct to Self. Selected Papers of* W. R. D. *Fairbairn. Volumes II* (pp. 13–79). Northvale (NJ) / London: Jason Aronson 1994.

Fairbairn, W. R. D. (1929/1994). Dissociation and repression. In E. F. Birtles & D. E. Scharff (Eds.), *From instinct to self: Selected papers of W. R. D. Fairbairn* (Vol. 2, pp. 13–73). Northvale, NJ: Aronson.

Fairbairn, W. R. D. (1958/1994). On the nature and aims of psychoanalytical treatment. In E. F. Birtles & D. E. Scharff (Eds.), *From instinct to self: Selected papers of* W. R. D. *Fairbairn* (Vol. 1, pp. 74–92). Northvale, NJ: Aronson.

Felitti, V. J., Anda, R. F., Nordenberg, D., Williamson, D. F., Spitz, A. M., Edwards, V., Koss, M. P., Marks, J. S. (1998). Relationship of childhood abuse and household dysfunction to many of the leading causes of death in adults. The Adverse Childhood Experiences (ACE) Study. *American Journal of Preventative Medicine, 14*(4), 245–258.

Ferenczi, S. (1931/1980). Notes and fragments: Relaxation and education. In M. Balint (Ed.) (E. Mosbacher, Trans.), *Final contributions to the problems and methods of psycho-analysis* (pp. 236–238). London, England: Karnac Books.

Ferenczi, S. (1949). Confusion of the tongues between the adults and the child—(The language of tenderness and of passion). *International Journal of Psycho-Analysis, 30,* 225–230.

Fine, C. G. (1993). A tactical integrationalist perspective on the treatment of multiple personality disorder. In R. P. Kluft & C. G. Fine (Eds.), *Clinical perspectives on multiple personality disorder* (pp. 135–153). Washington, DC: American Psychiatric Press.

Fitzgerald, M. (2017). Why did Sigmund Freud refuse to see Pierre Janet? Origins of psychoanalysis: Janet, Freud or both? *History of Psychiatry, 28*(3), 358–364.

Fonagy, P. (2000). Attachment and borderline personality disorder. *American Psychoanalytical Association, 48,* 1129–1146.

Fonagy, P. (2001). *Attachment theory and psychoanalysis.* New York: Other Press.

Fonagy, P., Gergely, G., Jurist, E. L., & Target, M. (2002). *Affect regulation, mentalization, and the development of the self.* New York: Other Press.

Frankl, V. (1959). *Man's search for meaning: An introduction to logotherapy.* New York, NY: Pocket Books.

Freud, S. (1893/1962). Obituary for Charcot. In J. Strachey (Ed. & Trans.), *The standard edition of the complete psychological works of Sigmund Freud* (Vol. 3, pp. 11-33). London: Hogarth Press.

Freud, S. (1894/1962). Further remarks on the neuropsychoses of defense. In J Strachey (Ed. & Trans.), *The standard edition of the complete psychological works of Sigmund Freud* (Vol. 3, pp. 45–61). London: Hogarth Press.

Freud, S. (1896/1962). The aetiology of hysteria. In J. Strachey (Ed. & Trans.), *The standard edition of the complete psychological works of Sigmund Freud* (Vol. 3, pp. 187–221). London: Hogarth Press.

Freud, S. (1905/1953). Three essays on the theory of sexuality. In J. Strachey (Ed. & Trans.), *The standard edition of the complete psychological works of Sigmund Freud* (Vol. 7, pp. 125–248). London: Hogarth Press.

Freud, S. (1910/1957). Five lectures on psychoanalysis. In J. Strachey (Ed. & Trans.), *The standard edition of the complete psychological works of Sigmund Freud* (Vol. 11, pp. 26-27). London: Hogarth Press.

Freud, S. (1915/1957). Repression. In J. Strachey (Ed. & Trans.), *The standard edition of the complete psychological works of Sigmund Freud* (Vol. 14, pp.146–158). London: Hogarth Press.

Freud, S. (1917/1959). Mourning and melancholia. In J. Strachey (Ed. &

Trans.), *The standard edition of the complete psychological works of Sigmund Freud* (Vol. 14, pp. 237–260). London: Hogarth Press.

Freud, S. (1921/1955). Group psychology and analysis of the ego. In J. Strachey (Ed. & Trans.), *The standard edition of the complete psychological works of Sigmund Freud* (Vol. 18, pp. 65–143). London: Hogarth Press.

Freud, S. (1923/1961). The ego and the id. In J. Strachey (Ed. & Trans.), *The standard edition of the complete psychological works of Sigmund Freud* (Vol. 19, pp. 1–16). London: Hogarth Press.

Freud, S. (1924). The dissolution of the Oedipus complex. In J. Strachey (Ed. & Trans.), *The standard edition of the complete psychological works of Sigmund Freud* (Vol. 19, pp. 172–179. London: Hogarth Press.

Freyd, J. (1996). *Betrayal trauma: The logic of forgetting childhood abuse.* Cambridge, MA: Harvard University Press.

Fromm, E. (1980). *Greatness and limitations of Freud's thought.* New York: Signet.

Fromm, E. (1987). Significant developments in clinical hypnosis during the past 25 years. *International Journal of Clinical and Experimental Hypnosis, 35*(4), 215–230.

Gabbard, G. O., & Lester, E. P. (1995). Boundaries and boundary violations in psychoanalysis. New York: Basic Books.

Gallese, V. (2009a). Mirror neurons, embodied simulations, and the neural basis of social identifications. Psychoanalytic Dialogues, 19(5), 519–536.

Gallese, V. (2009b). Mirror neurons and the neural exploitation hypothesis: From embodied simulation to social cognition. In J. A. Pineda (Ed.) *Mirror neuron systems: The role of mirroring processes in social cognition* (pp. 163–190). New York: Springer.

Gallese, V., Fadiga, L., Fogassi, L. & Rizzolatti, G. (1996). Action recognition in the premotor cortex. *Brain,* 119(7), 593–609.

Gartner, R. (1999). *Betrayed as boys.* New York: Basic Books.

Gartner, R. B. (2014). Trauma and countertrauma, resilience and counterresilience. *Contemporary Psychoanalysis, 50*(4), 609–626.

Gay, P. (1988). *Freud: A life for our time.* New York: Norton.

Gilligan, C. (1982). *In a different voice.* Cambridge, MA: Harvard University Press.

Gold, S. N. (2000). *Not trauma alone: Therapy for child abuse survivors in family and social context.* Philadelphia: Brunner/Routledge.

Greenberg, J., & Mitchell, S. (1983). *Object relations in psychoanalytic theory.* Cambridge, MA: Harvard University Press.

Greulich, H., & Cernicack, A. (2019). Brains that learn not to fear. *Nature, 566,* 335–336.

Grotstein, J. S. (1999), The alter ego and déjà vu phenomena. In: *The Plural Self: Multiplicity in Everyday Life,* ed. J. Rowan & M. Cooper. Thousand Oaks, CA: Sage, pp. 28–50.

Gunderson, J. G., & Chu, J. A. (1993). Treatment implications of past trauma in borderline personality disorder. *Harvard Review of Psychiatry, 1,* 75–81.

Gunderson, J. G., & Sabo, A. N. (1993). The phenomenological and conceptual interface between borderline personality disorder and PTSD. *American Journal of Psychiatry, 150,* 19–27.

Hanly, C. (1986). The assault on truth: Freud's suppression of the seduction theory (book review). *International Journal of Psycho-Analysis, 67:* 517–519.

Harlow, H. & Zimmerman (1958) *Proceedings of the American Philosophical Society 102* (5), 501–509.

Harris, N. (2018). *The deepest well: Healing the long-term effects of childhood adversity.* New York: Houghton Mifflin Harcourt.

Hartmann, H. (1939/1958). *Ego psychology and the problem of adaptation.* (David Rapaport, Trans.). New York: International Universities Press.

Herman, J. L. (1992). *Trauma and recovery: The aftermath of violence from domestic abuse to political terror.* New York: Basic Books.

Hesse, E., & Main, M. (1999). Second generation effects of unresolved trauma in non-maltreating parenting: Dissociated, frightened and threatening parental behavior. *Psychoanalytic Inquiry, 19*(48), 1–540.

Hilgard, E. (1977). *Divided consciousness: Multiple controls in human thought and action.* New York: Wiley.

Holmes, D. (1990). The evidence of repression: An examination of sixty years of research. In J. L. Singer (Ed.), *Repression and dissociation: Implications for personality theory, psychopathology, and health* (pp. 85–119). Chicago: University of Chicago Press.

Hopenwasser, K. (2008). Being in rhythm: Dissociative attunement in therapeutic process. *Journal of Trauma & Dissociation, 9*(3), 349–367.

Howell, E. F. (1981). Women: From Freud to the present. In E. F. Howell & M. Bayes (Eds.), *Women and mental health* (pp. 3–25). New York: Basic Books.

Howell, E. F. (1996). Dissociation in masochism and psychopathic sadism. *Contemporary Psychoanalysis, 32*(3), 427–453.

Howell, E. F. (1997). Desperately seeking attachment: A psychoanalytic reframing of harsh superego. *Dissociation, 10,* 230–239.

Howell, E. F. (1999). Back to the States: Victim Identity and Abuser Identification in Borderline Personality Disorder. Presented at the Sixteenth Annual Conference of the International Society for the Study of Dissociation, November 12, 1999, Miami.

Howell, E. F. (2002). Back to the "states": Victim and abuser states in borderline personality disorder, *Psychoanalytic Dialogues, 12*(6), 921–957.

Howell, E. F. (2003). Narcissism: A relational aspect of dissociation, *Journal of Trauma And Dissociation, 4*(3), 51–71.

Howell, E. F. (2005). *The dissociative mind.* Hillsdale, NJ: Analytic Press.

Howell, E. F. (2008). Inside and outside: "Trauma/dissociation/relationality" as a framework for understanding psychic structure and problems in living. *Psychoanalytic Perspectives, 5* (1), 47–67.

Howell, E. F. (2014a). Ferenczi's concept of identification with the aggressor: Implications for understanding the dissociative structure of mind involving interacting victim and abuser self-states. *American Journal of Psychoanalysis, 74*(1), 48–59.

Howell, E. F. (2014b). Dreaming Dissociative Multiplicity. Presented at the European Society for the Study of Trauma and Dissociation (ESTD), March 28, 2014, Copenhagen, Denmark.

Howell, E. F. (2016). Models of dissociation in Freud's work: Outcomes of dissociation of trauma in theory. Chapter 6. In E. F. Howell & S. Itzkowitz (Eds.), *The dissociative mind in psychoanalysis: Understanding and working with trauma* (pp. 73–84). New York: Routledge.

Howell, E. F. (2017). Speaking to and validating emotional truth in the jury-built self: On therapeutic action in the psychoanalytic treatment of trauma. In Richard Gartner (Ed.), *Trauma and countertrauma, resilience and counter-resilience: Insights from psychoanalysts and trauma experts* (pp. 97–111). New York: Routledge.

Howell, E. F. (2018). Regressing to reality: Finding and listening to the inner world of the traumatized child. In Aleksandar Dimitrijevic, Gabriele Cassullo, & Jay Frankel (Eds.), *In the tradition of Sándor Ferenczi* (pp. 147–152), New York: Karnac.

Howell, E.F. (2018). Outsiders to love: The character and dilemma of the psychopath. *Contemporary Psychoanalysis, 54* (1), 17–39.

Howell, E. F. (2019). From hysteria to chronic relational trauma disorder: The history of borderline personality disorder and its connection to trauma, dissociation, and psychosis. In Andrew Moskowitz, Martin Dorahy & Ingo Schafer (Eds.): *Dissociation and psychosis: Evolving perspectives on severe psychopathology* (pp. 83–96). New York: Wiley.

Howell, E. F., & Blizard, R. A. (2009). Chronic relational trauma: A new diagnostic scheme for borderline personality and the spectrum of dissociative disorders. In P. F. Dell & J. A. O'Neil (Eds.), *Dissociation and the dissociative disorders: DSM–V and beyond* (pp. 599–624). New York, NY: Routledge.

Howell, E. F., & Itzkowitz, S. (2016a). Is trauma-analysis psycho-analysis? Chapter 1. In E. F. Howell & S. Itzkowitz (Eds.), *The dissociative mind in psychoanalysis*: *Understanding and working with trauma.* 7–19. New York: Routledge.

Howell, E. F., & Itzkowitz, S. (2016b). From trauma-analysis to psycho-analysis and back again. Chapter 2. In E. F. Howell & S. Itzkowitz (Eds.), *The dissociative mind in psychoanalysis*: *Understanding and working with trauma.* 20–32. New York: Routledge.

Howell, E. F. & Itzkowitz, S. (2016c) The everywhereness of trauma and the dissociative structuring of the mind. Chapter 3. In E. F. Howell & S. Itzkowitz (Eds.), *The dissociative mind in psychoanalysis*: *Understanding and working with trauma* (pp. 33–43). New York: Routledge.

Howell, E.F. & Itzkowitz, S. (2018). Introduction to special issue on human evil and psychopathy. *Contemporary Psychoanalysis, 54* (1), 5–16.

Itzkowitz, S. (2019). Psychopathy and human evil: An overview. In: Sheldon Itzkowitz & Elizabeth Howell, *Psychoanalysts, psychologists, and psychiatrists discuss psychopathy and human evil* (pp. 13–37). New York, NY: Routledge.

Hunt, T. (2018, December). The hippies were right: It's all about vibrations, man! *Scientific American.*

James, W. (1902/1958). *Varieties of religious experience.* New York, NY: New American Library.

Jacobvitz, D. (2000, November). *Disorganized mental processes in mothers, frightening caregiving, and disorganized and disoriented attachment behavior in infants.* Presented at 17th International Fall Conference of the International Society for the Study of Dissociation, San Antonio, TX.

Janet, P. (1885). Note sur quelques phénomènes de somnambulisme. *Bulletin de la Société de Psychologie Physiologique, 1:* 24-32. Also in: *Revue Philosophique,* 1886, *21,1:* 190–198.

Janet, P. (1886a). Les actes inconscients et le dédoublement de la personnalité pendant l'état somnambulisme provoqué. *Revue Philosophique 22, II:* 577–792.

Janet, P. (1886b). Deuxième note sur le sommeil provoque à distance et la suggestion mental pendant l'état somnambulique. *Bulletin de la Société de Psychologie Physiologique, 2,* 70–80. Also in: *Revue Philosophique,* 1886, *22, II:* 212–223.

Janet, P. (1887). L'anesthésie systematisée et la dissociation des phénomènes psychologiques. *Revue Philosophique, 23(1),* 449–472.

Janet, P. (1888). Les actes inconscients et la mémoire pendant le somnambulisme. *Revue Philosophique, 25(1),* 238–279.

Janet, P. (1889). *L'Automatisme Psychologique: Essai de Psychologie Expérimentale sur les Formes Inférieures de l'Activité Humaine.* Paris: Félix Alcan. Reprint: Paris: Société Pierre Janet, 1973. (Italian edition: *L'Automatismo Psicologico.* Milano: Raffaello Cortina, 2013.)

Janet, P. (1907). *The major symptoms of hysteria: Fifteen lectures given in the medical school of Harvard University.* New York/London: Macmillan. doi:10.1037/10923-000

Janet, P. (1919). *Les Médications Psychologiques.* Paris: Félix Alcan. (English edition: *Psychological Healing* (1925). New York: Macmillan).

Janet, P. (1925/1976), *Psychological healing, Vol. 1.* New York: Macmillan (Reprint: Arno Press).

Kalsched, D. E. (1996). *The inner world of trauma: Archetypal defenses of the personal spirit.* New York: Routledge.

Karpman, S. (1968). Fairy tales and script drama analysis. *Transactional Analysis Bulletin, 26(7),* 39–43.

Kernberg, O. (1975). *Borderline conditions and pathological narcissism.* New York: Jason Aronson.

Kernberg, O. F. (1980). *Internal world and external reality.* New York: Aronson.

Kernberg, O. F. (1984). *Severe personality disorders.* New Haven, CT: Yale University Press.

Kilpatrick, D., Resnick, H., Milanack, M., Miller, M., Keyes, K., & Friedman,

M. (2013). National estimates of exposure to traumatic events and PTSD prevalence using DSM-IV and DSM-5 criteria, *Journal of Traumatic Stress, 5,* 537–547.

Kihlstrom, J. F. (1984). Conscious, subconscious, unconscious: A cognitive perspective. In , K. S. Bowers & D. Meichenbaum (Eds.), *The unconscious reconsidered.* New York: Wiley, pp. 149–210.

Kluft, R. (1984). Treatment of multiple personality disorder. *Psychiatric Clinics of North America, 7,* 9–29.

Kluft, R. P. (1987). First rank symptoms as diagnostic indicators of multiple personality disorder. *American Journal of Psychiatry, 144,* 293–298.

Kluft, R. P. (1999). Current issues in dissociative identity disorder. *Practical Psychiatry and Behavioral Health, 5,* 3–19.

Kluft, R. P. (1993). Treatment of dissociative disorder patients: An overview of discoveries, successes, and failures. *Dissociation, 6,* 87–101.

Kluft, R. P. (2013). *Shelter from the storm: Processing the traumatic memories of DID/DDNOS patients with the fractionated abreaction technique.* North Charleston, SC: CreateSpace Publishing Platform.

Kohut, H. (1959). Introspection, empathy, and psychoanalysis: An examination of the relation between mode of observation and theory. In P. H. Ornstein (Ed.), *The search for the self* (Vol. 1, pp. 205–232). New York: International Universities Press.

Kohut, H. (1971). *The analysis of the self.* New York: International University Press.

Kohut, H. (1984). *How does analysis cure?* Chicago: University of Chicago Press.

Kohlberg, L. (1966). A cognitive-development anaysis of children's sex-role concepts and attitudes. In E. E. Maccoby. (Ed.), *The development of sex differences,* pp. 82–173. Stanford, CA: Stanford University Press.

Kohlberg, L. (1971). From is to ought: How to commit the naturalistic fallacy and get away with it in the study of moral development. In T. Mischel. (Ed.), *Cognitive Development and Epistemology,* pp. 151–235. New York: Academic Press,.

Kroll, J. (1993). *PTSD/borderlines in therapy.* New York, NY: Norton.

Kuhn, P. (2002). "Romancing with a wealth of detail": Narratives of Ernest Jones's 1906 trial for indecent assault. *Studies in gender and sexuality, 3,* 344–379.

Kuhn, TS. (1962). *The structure of scientific revolutions*. Chicago, IL: University of Chicago Press.

Kupersmid, J. (1993). Freud's rationale for abandoning the seduction theory. *Psychoanalytic Psychology, 10*, 275–290.

Kuriloff, E. (2013). *Contemporary psychoanalysis and the legacy of the Third Reich: History, memory, tradition*. New York: Routledge.

Laplanche, J., & Pontalis, J.-B. (1973). *The language of psycho-analysis*. New York: Norton.

Laub, D. (2015). Listening to my mother's testimony. *Contemporary Psychoanalysis. 51*(2), pp. 151–235.

Laub, D., & Auerhahn, N. C. (1989). Failed empathy—A central theme in the survivor's Holocaust experience. *Psychoanalytic Psychology, 6*(4), 377–400.

Laub, D., & Auerhahn, N. C. (1993). Knowing and not knowing massive psychic trauma: Forms of traumatic memory. *International Journal of Psycho-Analysis, 74*, 287–302.

Leighton, J. (2016). Precarious places: Intersubjectivity in traumatized states. In E. F. Howell & S. Itzkowitz (Eds.). *The dissociative mind in psychoanalysis: Understanding and working with trauma* (pp. 127–137). New York: Routledge.

Levine, P. A. (2015). *Trauma and memory: Brain and body in a search for the living past*. Berkeley, CA: North Atlantic Books.

Levine, P. A. (1997). *Waking the tiger: Healing trauma*. Berkeley, CA: North Atlantic Books.

Lewis, H. B. (1971). *Shame and guilt in neurosis*. New York: International Universities Press.

Lewis, H. B. (1981), *Freud and modern psychology, Vol. 1: The emotional basis of mental illness*. New York: Plenum Press.

Lewis, H. B. (1990), Shame, repression, field dependence and psychopathology. In J. Singer (Ed.), *Repression and dissociation: Implications for personality theory, psychopathology and health* (pp. 233–258). Chicago: University of Chicago Press.

Lewis, M. (1992), *Shame: The exposed self*. New York: Free Press.

Liotti, G. (1992). Disorganized/disoriented attachment in the etiology of the dissociative disorders. *Dissociation, 5*, 196–204.

Liotti, G. (1995). Disorganized/disoriented attachment in the psychotherapy of the dissociative disorders. In S. Goldberg, R. Moiré, & J. Kerr (Eds.) *Attach-*

ment theory: Social, developmental and clinical Perspectives (pp. 343–363). Hillsdale, NJ: Analytic Press.

Liotti, G. (1999). Understanding the dissociative processes: The contribution of attachment theory. *Psychoanalytic Inquiry, 19*(5), 757–783.

Liotti, G. (2004). Trauma, dissociation and disorganized attachment: Three strands of a single braid. *Psychotherapy: Theory, Research, Practice, Training, 41*, 472–486.

Liotti, G. (2006). A model of dissociation based on attachment theory and research. *Trauma & Dissociation, 7*, 55–74.

Liotti, L., & Gumley, A. (2008). An attachment perspective on schizophrenia: The role of disorganized attachment, dissociation and mentalization. In A. Moskowitz, I. Schafer, & M. J. Dorahy (Eds.), *Psychosis, trauma, and dissociation: Emerging perspectives on severe psychopathology* (pp. 117–133). London, England: John Wiley.

Loeveninger, J. (1976). *Ego development: Conceptions and theo*ries. New York: Jossey-Bass.

Loewenstein, R. J. (1993). Posttraumatic and dissociative aspects of transference and counter-transference in the treatment of multiple personality disorder. In R. P. Kluft & C. G. Fine (Eds.), *Clinical perspectives on multiple personality disorder* (pp. 51–85).Washington, DC: American Psychiatric Press,

Luxenberg, T., Spinazzola, J., & Van der Kolk, B. A. (2001). Complex trauma and disorders of extreme stress (DESNOS) diagnosis, Part 1: Assessment. *New Directions in Psychiatry, 21*(25), 373–394.

Lynd, H. (1958). *On shame and the search for identity.* New York: Harcourt Brace.

Lyons-Ruth, K. (1999). Two-person unconscious: Intersubjective dialogue, enactive relational representation, and the emergence of new forms of relational organization. *Psychoanalytic Inquiry, 19*, 576–617.

Lyons-Ruth, K. (2001). The two-person construction of defenses: Disorganized attachment strategies, unintegrated mental states and hostile/helpless relational processes. *Psychologist-Psychoanalyst, 21*(1), 40–45.

Lyons-Ruth, K. (2003a, November 1). Disorganized attachment and the relational context of dissociation. Presented at 19th Annual Meeting of the International Society for Traumatic Stress Studies, Chicago, IL.

Lyons-Ruth, K. (2003b). Dissociation and the parent–infant dialogue: A longitudinal perspective from attachment research. *American Psychoanalytic Association, 51*, 883–911.

Lyons-Ruth, K. (2006). The interface between attachment and intersubjectivity: Perspective from the longitudinal study of disorganized attachment. *Psychanalytic Inquiry, 26*, 595–616.

Main, M. (1995). Recent studies in attachment: Overview, with selected implications for clinical work. In S. Goldberg, R. Muir, & J. Kerr (Eds.), *Attachment theory: Social, developmental, and clinical perspectives* (pp. 407–474). Hillsdale, NJ: Analytic Press, Inc.

Main, M., & Solomon, J. (1986). Discovery of a new, insecure-disorganized/disoriented attachment pattern. In M. Yogman & T. B. Brazelton (Eds.), *Affective development in infancy* (pp. 95–124). Norwood, NY: Ablex Press.

Main, M., & Solomon, J. (1990). Procedures for identifying infants as disorganized/disoriented during the Ainsworth Strange Situation. In M. T. Greenberg, D. Cicchetti, & E. M. Cummings (Eds.), *Attachment in the preschool years* (pp. 121–160). Chicago: University of Chicago Press.

Maldonado, J. R. & Spiegel, D. (1998), Trauma, dissociation, and hypnotizability. In J. D. Bremner & C. R Marmar (Eds.), *Trauma, memory, and dissociation*.

Marx, B. P., Forsyth, J. P., Gallup, G. G., Fusé, T., & Lexington, J. M. (2008). Tonic immobility as an evolved predator defense: Implications for sexual assault survivors. *Clinical Psychology: Science and Practice, 15*, 74–90.

Masson, J. M. (1984). *The assault on truth.* New York: Signet.

Masson, J. M. (Ed.). (1985). *The complete letters of Sigmund Freud to Wilhelm Fliess.* Cambridge, MA: Harvard University Press.

Maté, G. (2003). *When the body says NO: Exploring the stress-disease connection.* Hoboken, NJ: Wiley.

McWilliams, N. (2011). *Psychoanalytic diagnosis: Understanding personality structure in the clinical process* (2nd ed.). New York, NY: Guilford.

Meltzoff, A. N. & Moore, M. K. (1977). Imitation of facial and manual gestures by human neonates. *Science, 198*(4312), 75–78.

Mitchell, S. (1988). *Relational concepts in psychoanalysis.* Cambridge, MA: Harvard University Press.

Middleton, W., Dorahy, M. J., & Moskowitz, A. (2008). Historical conceptions of dissociation and psychosis: Nineteenth and early twentieth century perspectives on psychopathology. In A. Moskowitz, I. Schafer, & M. J. Dorahy

(Eds.), *Psychosis, trauma, and dissociation: Emerging perspectives on severe psychopathology* (pp. 9–20). London, England: John Wiley.

Mitchell, S. (1991). Contemporary perspectives on self: Toward an integration. *Psychoanalytic Dialogues, 1,* 121–147.

Mitchell, S. (1993), *Hope and dread in psychoanalysis.* New York: Basic Books.

Moskowitz, A. (2004). Scared stiff: Catatonia as an evolutionary-based fear response. *Psychological Review, 111,* 984–1002.

Moskowitz, A. (2008). Association and dissociation in the historical concept of schizophrenia. In A. Moskowitz, I. Schäfer, & M. J. Dorahy (Eds.). *Psychosis, trauma, and dissociation: Emerging perspectives on severe psychopathology* (pp. 35–50). London: Wiley.

Moskowitz, A., Heinimaa, M., & Van der Hart, O. (2019). Defining psychosis, trauma, and dissociation: Historical and contemporary conceptions. In A. Moskowitz, I. Schäfer, and M. Dorahy (Eds.), *Psychosis, trauma, and dissociation: Evolving perspectives on severe psychopathology* (pp. 9–29). New York: Wiley.

Myers, C. S. (1940). *Shell shock in France: 1914-18.* Cambridge: Cambridge University Press.

Nagel E., & Newman, J. (1958). *Godel's proof.* New York: New York University Press.

Nathanson, D. (Ed.) (1987). *The many faces of shame.* New York: Guilford

Neumann, E. (1955/1963). *The great mother: An analysis of an archetype.* Bollington/Princeton University Press.

Newton, P.M. (1973). Social structure and process in psychotherapy: A socio-psychological approach to transference, resistance and change. *International Journal of Psychiatry.* 2: 480–512.

Nijenhuis, E. R. S. (2000). Somatoform dissociation: Major symptoms of dissociative disorders. *Journal of Trauma & Dissociation, 1*(4), 7–32.

Nijenhuis, E. R. S. (2003), Looking into the brains of patients with dissociative disorders. *Internat. Soc. Study Dissoc. News, 21*(2), 6–9.

Nijenhuis, E.R. S. & Den Boer, J.A. (2007). Psychobiology of traumatization and trauma-related structural dissociation of the personality. In Eric Vermetten, Martin Dorahy & David Spiegel (Eds), *Traumatic dissociation: Neurobiology and treatment* (pp. 219–236). Washington D.C.: American Psychiatric Publishing.

Nijenhuis, E. R. S., Spinhoven, P., Vanderlinden, J., Van Dyck, R., & Van der Hart, O. (1998). Somatoform dissociative symptoms as related to animal defensive reactions to predatory imminence and injury. *Abnormal Psychology, 107,* 63–73.

Nijenhuis, E. R. S., & van der Hart, O. (1999). Forgetting and reexperiencing trauma. In J. M. Goodwin & R. Attias (Eds.), *Splintered reflections: Images of the body in trauma* (pp. 39–65). New York: Basic Books.

Nijenhuis, E. R. S., Vanderlinden, J., & Spinhoven, P. (1998). Animal defensive reactions as a model for trauma-induced dissociative reaction. *Journal of Traumatic Stress, 11*(2), 243–260.

Ogden, P. (2019). Acts of triumph: An interpretation of Pierre Janet and the role of the body in trauma treatment. In: G. Craparo, F. Ortu, and O. van der Hart (Eds.), *Rediscovering Pierre Janet: Trauma, dissociation, and a new context for psychoanalysis* (pp. 200–209). London and New York: Routledge.

Ogden, P., Minton, K. & Pain, C. (2006). *Trauma and the body: A sensorimotor approach to psychotherapy.* New York, NY: Norton.

O'Neil, J. (2009). Dissociative multiplicity and psychoanalysis. In P. F. Dell & J. F. O'Neil (Eds.), *Dissociation and the dissociative disorders: DSM–V and beyond* (pp. 287–325). New York: Routledge.

Ogawa, J. R., Sroufe, L. A., Weinfeld, N. S., Carlson, E. A., & Egeland, B. (1997). Development and the fragmented self: Longitudinal study of dissociative symptomology in nonclinical sample. *Development and Psychopathy, 9,* 855–879.

Palermo, C. A., & Brand, B. L. (2019). Can the Trauma Symptom Inventory-2 distinguish coached simulators from dissociative disorder patients? *Psychological Trauma: Theory, Research, Practice, & Policy.* doi:10.1037/tra0000382

Pearlman, L. A., & Saakvitne, K. W. (1995). Countertransference responses to dissociative processes in psychotherapy. In L. A. Pearlman & K. W. Saakvitne (Eds.), *Trauma and the therapist* (pp. 120–146). New York, NY: W. W. Norton.

Perlman, S. (2014). Who dissociates? Incest survivor or therapist? *Progress in Self Psychology,* 20, 95–108

Perry, B. (1999). The memory of states: How the brain stores and retrieves traumatic experience. In J. Goodwin and R. Attias (Eds.), *Splintered reflections: Images of the body in treatment* (pp. 9–38). New York: Basic Books.

Pines, M. (1989). On history and psychoanalysis. *Psychoanalytic Psychology, 6,* 121–136.

Pivnick, B.A. (2017). Transforming collapse: Applying clinical psychoanalysis to the relational design of the National September 11 Memorial Museum. *International Forum of Psychoanalysis: Violence, Terror and Terrorism Today: Psychoanalytic Perspectives, Part II, 26*(4), 248–257.

Porges, S. (2011). *The polyvagal theory: Neurophysiological foundations of emotions, attachment, communication, and self-regulation*. New York: Norton.

Putnam, F. W. (1989). *The diagnosis and treatment of multiple personality disorder*. New York, NY: Guilford Press.

Putnam, F. W. (1997). *Dissociation in children and adolescents: A developmental perspective*. New York: Guilford Press.

Putnam, F. W. (2016). *The way we are: How states of mind influence our identities, personality, and potential for change*. New York: IP Books.

Putnam, F. W. (2017). International Society for the Study of Trauma and Dissociation, virtual book club, March 1, 2017.

Putnam, F. W., Guroff, J. J., Silberman, E. K., Barban, L., & Post, R. M. (1986). The clinical phenomenology of multiple personality disorder. *Journal of Clinical Psychiatry, 47,* 285–293.

Reinders, A. A. T. S., Nijenhuis, E. R. S., Paans, A. M., Korf, J., Willemsen, A. T., den Boer, J. A. (2003). One brain, two selves. *NeuroImage, 20,* 2119–2125.

Reinders, A. A. T. S., Nijenhuis, E. R. S., Quak, J., Korf, J., Haaksma, J., Paans, A. M., Willemsen, A. T., den Boer, J. A. (2006). Psychobiological characteristics of dissociative identity disorder: A symptom provocation study. *Biological Psychiatry, 60,* 730–740.

Rosenfeld, H. (1971). A psychoanalytic approach to the theory of the life and death instincts: An investigation into the aggressive aspects of narcissism. *International Journal of Psycho-Analysis, 52,* 169–178.

Ross, C. A. (1989). *Multiple personality disorder*. New York: Wiley.

Ross, C. A. (2009, May). Members' clinical corner: Expert commentary: *How the dissociative structural model integrates DID and PTSD, plus a wide range of comorbidity*. McLean, VA: International Society for the Study of Trauma and Dissociation. Retrieved from http://www.isst-d.org/

Ross, J. (1982). Oedipus revisited—Laius and the "Laius complex." *Psychoanalytic Study of the Child, 37,* 169–174. New Haven, CT: Yale University Press.

Rothschild, B. (2000). *The body remembers: The psychophysiology of trauma and trauma treatment*. New York: Norton.

Ryle, A. (1997a). The structure and development of borderline personality disorder: A proposed model. *British Journal of Psychiatry, 170,* 82–87.

Ryle, A. (1997b). *Cognitive analytic therapy and borderline personality disorder: The model and the method.* New York: Wiley.

Ryle, A. (2003). Something more than the "something more than interpretation" is needed: A comment on the paper by the Process of Change Study Group. *International Journal of Psycho Analysis, 84*(Part 1), 109–118.

Sagan, E. (1988). *Freud, Women and Morality: The Psychology of Good and Evil.* New York: Basic Books.

Salter, A. (2003). *Predators: Pedophiles, rapists and other sex offenders.* New York: Basic Books.

Salyard, A. (1988). Freud as Pegasus yoked to the plough. *Psychoanal. Psychol., 5,* 403–429.

Sapolsky, R. M. (2004). *Why zebras don't get ulcers.* New York: Henry Holt.

Şar, V. (2011). Epidemiology of dissociative disorders: An overview. *Epidemiology Research International,* 1–8. doi:10.1155/2011/404538

Saunders R., Jacobvitz D, Zaccagnino M, Beverung LM, Hazen N. (2011). Pathways to earned security: the role of alternative support figures. *Attach Hum Dev. 4,* 403–20. doi: 10.1080/14616734.2011.584405.

Scaer, R. C. (2001). *The body bears the burden: Trauma, dissociation, and disease.* Binghamton, NY: Haworth Medical Press.

Schneider, K. (1939/1959). *Psychisher befund and psychiatrische diagnose [Clinical psychopathology* (5th ed)]. New York, NY: Grune and Stratton.

Salter, A. (2003). *Predators: Pedophiles, rapists and other sex offenders.* New York: Basic Books.

Schore, A. N. (1997). *Affect regulation and the origin of the self.* Mahwah, NJ: Lawrence Erlbaum Associates.

Schore, A. N. (2003a), *Affect dysregulation and disorders of the self.* New York: Norton.

Schore, A. N. (2003b). *Affect regulation and the repair of the self.* New York: Norton.

Schore, A. N. (2009). Attachment trauma and the developing right brain: Origins of pathological dissociation. In P. F. Dell & J. F. O'Neil (Eds.), *Dissociation and the dissociative disorders: DSM–V and beyond* (pp. 107–141). New York: Routledge.

Schore, A. N. (2019). The growth-promoting role of right brain mutual regressions in long term psychotherapy of relational trauma. Presented at the ISSTD 36th Annual Conference: The World Conference on Complex Trauma, April 1, 2019, New York City.

Schwartz, H. L. (1994). From dissociation to negotiation: A relational psychoanalytic perspective on multiple personality disorder. *Psychoanalytic Psychology*, 11, 189–231.

Schwartz, R. (1995). *Internal family systems therapy*. New York: Guilford Press.

Shapiro, F. (2001). *Eye movement desensitization and reprocessing: Basic principles, protocols and procedures* (2nd ed.). New York: Guilford Press.

Shonkoff, J. P., Garner, A. S.; American Academy of Pediatrics Committee on Psychosocial Aspects of Child and Family Health; Committee on Early Childhood, Adoption, and Dependent Care; Section on Developmental and Behavioral Pediatrics. (2012). The lifelong effects of early childhood adversity and toxic stress. *Pediatrics, 129*(1), e232–e246. Retrieved from http:// pediatrics.aappublications.org/content/129/1/e232.full.

Simeon, D & Abugel, J. (2006). *Feeling unreal: Depersonalization disorder and the loss of self*. New York, NY: Oxford University Press.

Siegel, D. (1999). *The developing mind: Toward a neurobiology of interpersonal experience*. New York: Guilford Press.

Slavin, M. O., & Kreigman, D. (1992). *The adaptive design of the human psyche: Psychoanalysis, evolutionary biology, and the therapeutic process*. New York: Guilford Press.

Solzhenitsyn, A. (1974). *The gulag archipelago*. New York: Harper and Row.

Somer, E. (2004). Trance possession disorder in Judaism: Sixteenth-century dybbuks in the Near East. *Journal of Trauma & Dissociation, 5*(2), 131–146.

Spiegel, D. (1990). Trauma, dissociation, and hypnosis. In R. Kluft (Ed.), *Incest-related syndromes of adult psychopathology* (pp. 247–262). Washington, DC: American Psychiatric Press.

Spiegel, D., Loewenstein, R. J., Lewis-Fernández, R., Şar, V., Simeon, D., Vermetten, E., Cardeña, E., Dell, P. F. (2011). Dissociative disorders in *DSM-5*. *Depression & Anxiety, 28,* 824–852. doi:10.1002/da.20874

Spitz, R.A. (1945). Hospitalism—An Inquiry Into the Genesis of Psychiatric Conditions in Early Childhood. Psychoanalytic Study of the Child, 1, 53-74.

Stern, D. B. (1997). *Unformulated experience: From dissociation to imagination in psychoanalysis.* Hillsdale, NJ: Analytic Press.

Stern, D. N. (1985). *The interpersonal world of the infant.* New York: Basic Books.

Stern, D. N. (2004). *The present moment in psychotherapy and in life.* New York: Norton.

Stolorow, R., Atwood, G., & Orange, D. (2002). *Worlds of experience: Interweaving philosophical and clinical dimensions in psychoanalysis.* New York: Basic Books.

Sullivan, H. S. (1953). *The interpersonal theory Of psychiatry.* New York: Norton.

———(1954). *The psychiatric interview.* New York: Norton.

———(1956). *Clinical studies in psychiatry.* New York: Norton.

———(1962). *Schizophrenia as a human process.* New York: Norton.

Sulloway, F. J. (1979). *Freud: Biologist of the mind.* New York: Basic Books.

Sutherland, J. D. (2000), Fairbairn's achievement. In J. S. Grotstein, & D. B. Rinsley (Eds.), *Fairbairn and the Origin of Object Relations,* pp. 17–33. New York: Other Press.

Tabin, J. (1993). Freud's shift from the seduction theory: Some overlooked reality factors. *Psychoanalytic Psychology, 10,* 291–298.

Terr, L. (1990) *Too scared to cry: How trauma affects children and ultimately us all.* New York: Basic Books.

Terr, L. C. (1994). *Unchained memories: True stories of traumatic memories, lost and found.* New York: Basic Books

Trevarthen, C. (2009a). The function of emotion in infancy: The regulation and communication of rhythm, sympathy, and meaning in human development. In D. Fosha, D. Siegel, & M. Soloman (Eds.), *The healing power of emotion: Affective neuroscience, development, & clinical process* (pp. 55–85). New York: Norton.

Trevarthen, C. (2009b). The intersubjective psychobiology of human meaning: learning of culture depends on interest for co-operative practical work-and affection for the joyful art of good company, *Psychoanalytic Dialogues. 19*(5), 507–518.

Trevarthen, C., & Aitken, K. J. (2001). Infant intersubjectivity: Research, theory and clinical applications. *Annual Research Review, Journal of Child Psychology and Psychiatry, 42*(1), 3–48.

Tronick, E. Z. (1989). Emotions and emotional communication in infants. *American Psychologist, 44*(2), 112–119.

Tronick, E. Z., Als, H., Adamson, L., Wise, S., Brazelton, T. B. (1978). The infant's response to entrapment between contradictory messages in face-to-face interaction. *American Academy of Child Psychiatry.* 17, 1–13.

Turkus, J., Pivnick, B., & Bellinson (2019, March 28). Remembering the vanishing forms of 9/11: ruptures, ripples, and reflections. Preconference workshop presented at the World Congress on Complex Trauma, International Society of the Study of Trauma and Dissociation, New York, NY.

Vaillant, G. E. (1990). Repression in college men followed for half a century. In J. L. Singer (Ed.), *Repression and dissociation: Implications for personality theory, psychopathology, and health* (pp. 85–119, pp. 259–273). Chicago: University of Chicago Press.

Van Derbur, M. (2003). *Miss America by day.* Denver, CO: Oak Hill Ridge Press.

Van der Hart, O. (2000, November). *Dissociation: Toward a resolution of 150 years of confusion.* Presented at 17th International Fall Conference of the International Society of Dissociation, San Antonio, TX.

Van der Hart, O. (2016). Pierre Janet, Sigmund Freud, and dissociation of the personality: The first codification of a psychodynamic depth psychology. In E. Howell & S. Itzkowitz (Eds.), *The dissociative mind in psychoanalyis: Understanding and treating trauma* (pp. 44–55). New York: Routledge.

Van der Hart, O. (2018). Understanding trauma-generated dissociation and disorganized attachment: Giovanni Liotti's lasting contributions. *Attachment: New directions in psychotherapy and relational psychoanalysis,* 101–109.

Van der Hart, O., & Friedman, B. (1989). A reader's guide to Pierre Janet on dissociation: A neglected intellectual heritage. *Dissociation, 2,* 3–15.

Van der Hart, O., & Friedman, B. (2019). A reader's guide to Pierre Janet on dissociation: A neglected intellectual heritage. In G. Craparo, F. Ortu, and O. van der Hart (Eds.), *Rediscovering Pierre Janet: Trauma, dissociation, and a new context for psychoanalysis.* London: Routledge. pp. 4–27.

Van der Hart, O., Nijenhuis, E. R. S., & Steele, K. (2006). *The haunted self: Structural dissociation and the treatment of chronic traumatization.* New York: Norton.

Van der Hart, O., Nijenhuis, E. R. S., Steele, K., & Brown, D. (2004). Trauma-related dissociation: Conceptual clarity, lost and found. *Australia & New Zealand Journal of Psychiatry, 38,* 906–914.

Van der Hart, O., Van der Kolk, B. A., & Boon, S. (1998). Treatment of dissociative disorders. In J. D. Bremner & C. R. Marmar (Eds.), *Trauma, memory, and dissociation* (pp. 253–283). Washington, DC: American Psychiatric Press.

Van der Hart, O., Van Dijke, A., Van Son, M., & Steele, K. (2000). Somatoform dissociation in traumatized World War I combat soldiers: A neglected clinical heritage. *Journal of Trauma & Dissociation, 1*(4), 33–66.

Van der Kolk, B. A. (1996), Trauma and memory. In B. A. van der Kolk, A. McFarlane, & L. Weisaeth (Eds.), *Traumatic stress: The effects of overwhelming experience on mind, body, and society* (pp. 279–302). New York: Guilford Press.

Van der Kolk, B. A. (2002). Posttraumatic therapy in the age of neuroscience. *Psychoanalytic Dialogues, 12,* 381–392.

Van der Kolk, B. A. (2014). *The body keeps the score: Brain, mind, and body in the healing of trauma.* New York: Penguin.

Van der Kolk, B. A. (2015). Forward. In P. Levine, *Trauma and memory: Brain and Body in a search for the living past* (pp. 11–18). Berkeley, CA: North Atlantic Books.

Van der Kolk, B. A., & Van der Hart, O. (1989). Pierre Janet and the breakdown of adaptation in psychological trauma. *American Journal of Psychiatry, 146*(12), 1530–1540.

Vermetten, E., Schmal, C. Lindner, S., Lowewenstein, R.J. & Brember, J.D. (2006). Hippocampal and amygdalar volumes in dissociative identity disorder. *American Journal of Psychiatry,* 163, 630–636.

Westover, T. (2018). *Educated: A memoir.* New York: Random House.

Winnicott, D. W. (1960).*The maturational processes and the facilitating environment.* New York: International Universities Press.

Winnicott, D.W. (1971). Use of the object and relating through identifications. In *Playing and Reality,* pp. 86–94. New York: Tavistock.

Wolff, P. H. (1987). *The development of behavioral states and the expressions of emotions inearly infancy: New proposals for investigation.* Chicago: University of Chicago Press.

Yehuda, N. (2016). *Communicating trauma: Clinical presentations and interventions with traumatized children.* New York: Routledge.

Yehuda, R. (2000). Cortisol alterations in PTSD. In A. Y. Shalev, R. Yehuda,

& A. C. McFarlane (Eds.), *International handbook of human response to trauma* (pp. 265–284). New York, NY: Kluwer Academic/Plenum Publishers.

Zanarini, M. C. (1997). Evolving perspectives on the etiology of borderline personality disorder. In M. C. Zanarini (Ed.), *The role of sexual abuse in the etiology of borderline personality disorder* (pp. 1–14). Washington, DC: American Psychiatric Press.

Zimbardo, P. (2007). *The Lucifer effect: Understanding how good people turn evil.* NY: Random House.

INDEX

abreaction
  remembrance and, 9
ABS. *see* alternating bilateral stimulation
    (ABS)
absence
  dissociated experiences as, 95
abuse
  attachment-based defenses against
    acknowledging, 18–19
  child sexual *see* child sexual abuse
  deprivation related to, 178–79
  neglect related to, 178–79
  rejection related to, 178–79
  trauma resulting from, 27
  traumatic, 129
abuser(s)
  in Oedipal theory, 19–20
ACEs. *see* adverse childhood experiences
    (ACEs)
Ackerly, R., 113
adverse childhood experiences (ACEs),
    51–55
  physical health effects of, 51–55
  trauma and dissociation–related, xxi
affect(s)
  conveying of, 67

isolation of, xiv
  reducing and controlling intensity of,
    41–42
  regulation of, 98–99
  "strangulated," 9
affective arousal, 33
agency
  critical, 132
  Freudian model and, xviii
  personal, 138
  in repressed unconscious, 82
aggressor(s)
  case example, 124–25
  identification with, xv, 121–25
Ainsworth, M., 99
alloplastic
  defined, 122
Alpert, J., 32, 135
Al Qaeda terrorists
  WTC attack by, 36–37
alternating bilateral stimulation (ABS)
  in fear extinction, 188
America by Day, 108
amnesia, 4, 33
amygdala, 33
Anda, R.F., 51

"anger in connection," 166
Anna O. *see* Pappenheim, B.
ANP. *see* apparently normal personality
    (ANP)
ANS. *see* autonomic nervous system (ANS)
"anti-libidinal ego," 143
anxious ambivalent attachment, 99
anxious avoidant attachment, 99
anxious resistant attachment, 99
apparently normal personality (ANP), 21,
    136
    described, 148–52
    in DID, 151–54
arousal
    affective, 33
    emotional, 33
Assault on the Truth, 13
association
    lack of, 176–77
attachment
    anxious ambivalent, 99
    anxious avoidant, 99
    anxious resistant, 99
    Bowlby's theory of, 97–98
    described, 97–99
    developmental dynamics of fear and,
        119–20
    disconnection and, 120–21
    disorganized *see* disorganized attach-
        ment (DA)
    dissociation and, 120–21
    earned secure, 102
    generative, 166
    importance of, 118–19
    insecure, 99
    learning theories on, 98
    need for, xix, 128
    in reducing fear, 98–102, 106–7
    secure, 99
attachment-based defense(s)
    against acknowledging abuse, 18–19
attachment-based dissociation, 120–21
    neurosis *vs.,* xviii
attachment dilemmas
    in criticizing oneself, xxii–xxiii

attachment patterns
    types of, 99
attachment system, 161–63
    case example, 161–63
    described, 98–99
attachment theory
    Bowlby's, 97–98
    described, 97–98
    IWMs in, 98, 101
    trauma theory and, 98
attack(s)
    self- *see* self-attack
attractor(s)
    in state space, 177
attunement
    "dissociative," 73
Auerhahn, N.C., 97, 128
authority roles
    in psychotherapy, 61–63
authority structure, 61–63
autobiographical memory, 32
autonomic nervous system (ANS), 116
    dorsal vagal parasympathetic response
        of, 114
autoplastic
    defined, 122

"baby-watchers"
    scientific, 177–78
"bad me," 144
Barrett, D.L., 182
battle fatigue, 22
behavior(s)
    DA–related, 100–1
behavioral-mental states of being,
    177–78
behavior state(s)
    discrete, 176–77
"betrayal blindness," 119
"betrayal trauma," 119
"better to be a sinner in God's world,"
    125–28
biological states
    posttraumatic, 114–17
blame-other patterns of thinking, xix

blame-self patterns of thinking, xix
blank screen psychoanalysts, 166
blindness
  "betrayal," 119
body(ies)
  dissociation effects on, 45–57
  trauma effects on, 25, 45–57
body psychotherapy
  Janet and, 7
body rhythms
  affects conveyed by, 67
bonding
  "traumatic," 120
Boon, S., 41, 42
borderline
  defined, 56
borderline personality disorder (BPD), 56
  DA as precursor to, 101–2
  fragmentation of psyche in, 146
  PTSD and, 56
  splitting associated with, 56–57, 146
  stable instability of, 146
borderline personality organization
  defenses of, 146–47
bottom-up processing, 49–51
  described, 49
Boulanger, G., 82
Bowen, M., 90
Bowlby, J., 97–99, 113, 118–19, 130,
  143–44
  attachment theory of, 97–98
  IWMs of, 98, 101, 118–19, 143–44
BPD. see borderline personality disorder
  (BPD)
brain
  MRI of, 54
  traumatic experiences processed in,
  32–33
brain stem, 33
Brand, B.L., 39, 42–43
Breger, L., 3, 10, 13–14
Breuer, J., 8–11, 20, 23, 93
Bromberg, P., xiv, xv, 39, 46, 74, 77–79,
  84, 86–87, 90, 93–94, 106, 125, 128,
  139, 144

Brown, E.M., 16
Brown, L.S., 22
Bucci, W., 87
Buck, R., 49

"caput Nili", 11
Cast Away, 163
chaos theory, 177
Charcot, J.M., 5–6, 9, 20–21
Chefetz, R.A., 28, 29, 67–68
children
  Waco disaster–related PTSD in, 116–17
child's egocentric beliefs
  ratification of, 17–18
child sexual abuse
  hysteria due to, 11–12, 17
"chimney sweeping of the mind," 9–10
"chronic relational trauma disorder," 56
chronic stress
  effects of, 54
Chu, J.A., 41
client(s)
  awareness of therapists' murky psyches,
    67–68
  being triggered by, 65
  healing of, xviii
  self-blame of, 17
  therapists becoming real to, 168–70
  what they know about therapists, 66–75
clinical dyad
  as wounded dyad, xxi–xxii, 59–75
closed system(s), 160–64
  exit from, xxiii, 157–70
Clytemnestra, 19
cognitive-psychoanalytic model of dissociation, 87
Communicating Trauma, 36
communication
  facial expression in, 67
  vibes in, 95–96
compassion
  in softening shame, 130
competence
  "emotional," 49
complex PTSD, 40

complex trauma
    treatment of, 40–41
"complex trauma," 56
concentration camps
    being shamed in, 128–29
connectedness
    importance of, xviii–xix
consciousness
    double, 20
    second, 4, 8–9
    split/dual, 92–93
    unitary, 20
*Coping with Trauma-Generated Dissocia-
    tion: Skills Training for Patients and
    Therapists,* 42
countertransference, 141
countertrauma
    described, 64
    "vicarious trauma" *vs.,* 64
Courtois, C.A., 41
critical agency, 132
criticism
    self- *see* self-criticism
cumulative trauma, 29

DA. *see* disorganized attachment (DA)
Dalenberg, C.J., 166
Davies, J.M., 141
declarative memory, 32
defense(s)
    attachment-based *see* attachment-based
        defense(s)
    "moral," 126
defensive exclusion, 119
dependence
    state, 179–80
depersonalization/derealization
    in traumatized people, 38
deprivation
    abuse and, 178–79
derealization/depersonalization
    in traumatized people, 38
determinism
    psychic, xx–xxi
    "subconscious," 6

unconscious, 6, 138
devaluation, 147
*Diagnostic and Statistical Manual of Mental
    Disorders* (DSM), 5
    inconsistencies on influence of trauma
        and dissociation, 55
*Diagnostic and Statistical Manual of Mental
    Disorders, Fifth Ed.* (DSM-5), 28, 29
    on exposure to traumatic events in US, 45
DID. *see* dissociative identity disorder (DID)
disconnection, 119, 176
    attachment and, 120–21
discrete behavioral states
    described, 177–78
    lack of association and, 176–77
    linked and not linked, 177–78
disorganized attachment (DA)
    behaviors related to, 100–1
    described, xxii, 99–102
    as dissociation, xxii, 97–109
    in dissociative clients, 102
    as precursor to BPD and DID, 101–2
    prevalence of, 97
    self-fragmentation covered over and,
        102–5
dissociated experience(s), 33–34. *see also*
    dissociation
    as absence or presence, 95
    described, 77
dissociated memories
    described, 77
dissociation
    ACEs with, xxi
    attachment-based, xviii, 120–21
    benefits of, 35–38
    body systems affected by, 45–57
    clinical examples, 79
    cognitive-psychoanalytic model of, 87
    DA as, xxii, 97–109
    defined, 26, 85, 86
    described, xxii, 33–34, 78–79, 85
    DSM inconsistencies related to, 55
    early studies of, 4–6
    embedded in our lives, 25–27
    example of, 36–38

in fostering survival, 35–36
as hidden, 26
hysteria and, 8–9
Janetian, 78
meanings of, 86
memory and, 31–35
mind/body link in, 47–49
mind-related effects of, 45–57
neglect by Freud, 20
new ways of thinking about, xx
pathological, 38
peri-traumatic, 26
prevalence of, 46–47
primary, 151
problematic, 38
process of, 26, 36–38, 86–87
professional confusion about effects on
    problems in living, 55–57
"psychoform," 47
psychological trauma and, xvii
reasons for, 38–39
recognition of, xix
repression and, 77–82
repression vs., 85
secondary, 151
somatoform, 23
as soothing, 36
spatial metaphors of, 80–82
as structure, 26
structure of, 86–87
tertiary, 151
trauma and, 22, 30
trauma as, xxi, 22, 25–44
trauma intertwined with, 25–44
traumatic experiences–related, 145
trauma treatment in reducing, 39–40
ubiquity of, xxi, 45–57
unconscious and, 77–96 see also
    unconscious
underrecognition of, 55
dissociation and repression theory, 20
dissociation-based structural models,
    139–45
dissociation-focused treatments
    in retraumatization prevention, 42–43

Dissociation in Children and Adolescents, 177
dissociation treatment, 39
"dissociative attunement," 73
dissociative clinical superego, 132–33
dissociative disorders
    nonspecified, 54
    prevalence of, 45–46
    psychosis confused with, 55–56
dissociative identity disorder (DID), xiv–
    xv, 10
    case example, 87–91, 94–95
    DA as precursor to, 101–2
    described, 10
    EPs and ANPs in, 151–54
    hippocampus size in persons with, 54
    prevalence of, 46
    state switches in, 56–57
    symptoms of, 55
    trauma therapy for, 42–43
dissociative multiplicity, 105–8
    case example, 107–8
    persistent, 108–9
dissociative organization
    structural, 38
dissociative personality structure
    models of, 136 see also specific types
dissociative phenomena, 4
dissociative processes, 26, 36–38
    described, 86
"dissociative" response
    hypoaroused, 116
dissociative self-states, xix
dissociative self-sufficiency, 163
dissociative structure, 26, 86–87
    in different personality organizations,
        137, 145–47
    superego structure resembling, 132
dissociative structure of the personality
    model of, 147–52
dissociative superego, 133
    clinical, 132–33
dissociative unconscious
    described, 93–94
    repressed unconscious vs., 93–94
dissociogenic shame, 126–30

distress
    trauma *vs.*, 28–31
dividedness
    case example, 157–59
    inner, 157–70
    interpersonal, 159–60
    intrapersonal, 159–60
dorsal vagal complex (DVC), 114–16
dorsal vagal parasympathetic response
    of ANS, 114–16
dorsal vagal response, 114–16
"double consciousness"
    in hysteria, 20
Douglass, F., 5
"Dr. Pencil"
    Janet as, 92
drama triangle
    Karpman's, 141
dream(s)
    case example, 183–86
    as healing, 182
dreamwork, 181–83
    case example, 183–86
"drive-structure" model, 137–39
DSM. *see Diagnostic and Statistical Manual
    of Mental Disorders* (DSM)
DSM-5. *see Diagnostic and Statistical Man-
    ual of Mental Disorders, Fifth Ed.*
    (DSM-5)
dual-instinct theory
    Freudian, 98
DVC. *see* dorsal vagal complex (DVC)
dyad(s)
    clinical as wounded, 59–75
dynamical systems theory, 177

early warning system, 125
earned secure attachment, 102
Educated, 107
ego
    "anti-libidinal," 143
    repressed and split parts of, 143
    as theoretical concept, 138
egocentric beliefs
    child's, 17–18

"either/or" polarization
    sexual trauma–related, 14–15
Electra Complex, 19
Ellenberger, H., 4–6, 10–11, 13
"embodied simulation," 122
EMDR. *see* eye movement desensitization
    and reprocessing (EMDR)
emotion(s)
    "vehement," 22
emotional arousal
    intensity of, 33
"emotional competence," 49
emotional personality (EP), 21
    described, 148–52
    in DID, 151–54
empathy
    importance of, 61
enactive models of relationships, 120
enactment(s)
    case example, 69–74
    described, 68–69
endopsychic model
    Fairbairn's, 143
engagement
    in infancy, 112–13
    sensitivity to ruptures in, 113
EP. *see* emotional personality (EP)
Epstein, O.B., 105, 163
Erdelyi, M.H., 83–84
exclusion
    defensive, 119
experience(s)
    dissociated *see* dissociated
        experience(s)
    staying close to, 63–65
"Expert Commentary: How the Dissocia-
    tive Structural Model Integrates DID
    and PTSD," 57
explicit memory, 32
exposure therapy, 40
expression(s)
    facial, 67
eye movement desensitization and repro-
    cessing (EMDR)
    described, 50

facial expression
  affects conveyed by, 67
  communication via, 67
Fadiga, L., 122
failure to thrive
  cases of, 113
Fairbairn, W.R.D., xxii, 45–47, 86, 125–26, 128, 130, 143, 157
Family Matters, 130
fatigue
  battle, 22
fear
  ABS in extinction of, 188
  attachment in reducing, 98–102, 106–7
  development dynamics of, 119–20
  "fear without a solution," 100, 144
Felitti, V.J., 51
Ferenczi, S., xiii, xv, xxii, 18, 26, 111, 121–23, 125, 130, 142–43, 146
fight/flight response, 48, 115
Fine, C.G., 41
Fitzgerald, M., 10, 13
"fixed ideas"
  subconscious, 7
  trauma as, 31
flashback(s), 34
Fleiss
  Freud's letters to, 13, 174
Fogassi, L., 122
Ford, J.D., 41
"forgetting" of trauma, 32
forgotten trauma
  importance and impact of, 6
Fortunoff Archives of Holocaust Testimony, 31
  at Yale University, 16
"fractionated abreaction," 41
Frankl, V., 128
Frawley, M.G., 141
freeze response, 115
Freud, A., 122
Freudian dual-instinct theory, 98
Freudian model, 60
  agency related to, xviii
Freudian psychoanalysis, xx–xxi

Freudian psychoanalysts
  Holocaust impact on, 15–16
Freudian psychoanalytic theory, 112
Freudian unconscious, 93
Freud, S., xiii–xiv, xxii, xxiii, 5, 6, 8–14, 20–21, 78, 91–93, 187–88
  on consequences of new narrative, 12–14, 17
  contributions of, 3–4
  in identifying child sexual abuse as cause of hysteria, 11–12
  inner conflicts of, 13–14
  letters to Fleiss, 13, 174
  neglect of trauma and dissociation by, 20
  Oedipal theory of, 19–20, 173–76
  repression theory of, 91
  roadblocks imposed by, 4
  seduction theory of, 12, 174
  self-contradictions of, 14–15
  sexual trauma–related "either/or" polarization of, 14–15
  from shame to superego, 130–32
  structural model of, 137–40 *see also* Freud's structural model
  trauma buried by, xx–xxi, 3–24
  visual metaphors for repression of, 81–83
Freud's structural model
  described, 138
  "drive-structure" model, 137–39
  as trauma–dissociation model, 140
Freyd, J., 119
"Further Remarks on the Neuro-Psychoses of Defense," 187

Gallese, V., 122
Gartner, R.B., 64
Gay, P., 11, 13–14
generative attachment, 166
Gilligan, C., xix
"glazed look," 116
Gödel, K., 161
"good me," 144
Great Mother, 188

Greek Demeter, 188

Grotstein, J.S., 20

"Group Psychology and Analysis of the Ego," 131–32

guilt
  described, 127
  shame *vs.,* 127

Hainer, M., xi

Hanks, T., 163

Harlow, H., 113

Harris, N., 53–55

healing
  from client being able to speak and hear her-/himself, xviii
  dreams as, 182
  psychological, xxiii–xxiv, 171–86

healthy multiplicity, 106

Heinimaa, M., 30

helplessness
  trauma model and, xviii
  trauma rooted in, xix

Herman, J.L., 22, 41, 59, 64

Hesnard, 11

Hilgard, E., 80

hippocampus, 32–33
  in DID, 54
  in nonspecified dissociative disorders, 54

Holmes, D., 84, 188

Holocaust
  Freudian psychoanalysts impacted by, 15–16

Holocaust trauma
  Oedipus overshadowing, 15–16

Hopenwasser, K., 73

"hospitalism"
  cases of, 113

Howell, E.F., 36–37, 54–55, 62–63, 66–67, 71–75, 83, 84, 86–91, 94–96, 123–25, 132, 133, 135–36, 139–40, 145–50, 157–60, 169–71, 174, 181–83

HPA axis. *see* hypothalamic-pituitary-adrenal (HPA) axis

human connectedness
  importance of, xviii–xix

human psyche
  described, 67–68

humor
  in softening shame, 130

Hunt, T., 95

hyperarousal
  impact on integration of traumatic memories, 7

hyperarousal pattern, 117

hypnoid, 9

hypnoid states, 9

hypnosis, 4

hypoarousal pattern, 116–17

hypoaroused "dissociative" response, 116

hypothalamic-pituitary-adrenal (HPA) axis
  dysfunction of, 53–54

hysteria
  basis of, 9
  child sexual abuse causing, 11–12, 17
  described, 5
  dissociation and, 8–9
  "double consciousness" in, 20
  studies on, 8–11 *see also Studies on Hysteria*

ICD-11. *see International Classification of Diseases, Eleventh Ed.* (ICD-11)

id
  as theoretical concept, 138

id, ego, and superego structure, 137–39

idealization
  primitive, 147

"identification with the aggressor," xv, 121–25
  Ferenczi's concept of, 142–43

identity-shapers
  roles as, 62

identity states
  switching between, 4

IFS model. *see* internal family systems (IFS) model

immobility
  "tonic," 116
implicit knowledge
  intuitive, 67–68
implicit memory, 32
infancy
  engagement during, 112–13
infant(s)
  DA among, 97
  mimicry in, 122
insecure attachment, 99
inside-out approach
  described, xxii
  outside-in approach *vs.*, 94–95
integration
  defined, 160
internal family systems (IFS) model
  Schwartz's, 43, 141–42
"internal saboteur," 143
internal working models (IWMs)
  Bowlby's theory of, 98, 101, 118–19,
    143–44
*International Classification of Diseases,
    Eleventh Ed.* (ICD-11)
  of WHO, 56
International Society for the Study of
    Trauma and Dissociation (ISSTD),
    xv
interpersonal dividedness, 159–60
interpersonal intersubjectivity, 164–70,
    181
interpersonal relationships
  intersubjective failure in, 164–70
interpretation(s)
  fallacy of, 63
  validity of, 63
intersubjective failure
  in interpersonal relationships, 164–70
intersubjectivity
  interpersonal, 164–70, 181
  intrapersonal, 164–70, 181
intersubjectivity theory, 61
intrapersonal dividedness, 159–60
intrapersonal intersubjectivity, 164–70,
    181

intuitive implicit knowledge, 67–68
Isis, 172–73, 188
  threat of self-reflection of, 181
isolation of affect, xiv
ISSTD. *see* International Society for the
    Study of Trauma and Dissociation
    (ISSTD)
Itzkowitz, S., xi
IWMs. *see* internal working models
    (IWMs)

Janetian dissociation, 78
Janet, P., xx, 5–6, 10–11, 18, 21, 22, 31,
    41, 87, 91, 92, 136, 145, 147
  body psychotherapy and, 7
  as "Dr. Pencil," 92
  phase-oriented trauma treatment and,
    6–7
  pioneering work of, 6–8
  PTSD and, 6
  trauma and dissociation theory of, 7
Jones, E., 19–20
Jung, C., 19
"jury-rigged self," 140–41

Kaiser health plan members
  study on, 51–52
Kalsched, D.E., 163, 167–68
Karpman, S., 141
Kernberg, O.F., xiv, 84, 146–47
kindling
  described, 40
Kiss Me, Kate, 19
Kluft, R.P., xiv, 41
  "rule of thirds" of, 41
knowing
  not knowing and, 83
knowledge
  intuitive implicit, 67–68
Kohut, H., xiv, 61, 80
Kuhn, T.S., 186
Kuriloff, E., 15–16

*Last Witnesses: Child Survivors of the Holo-
    caust,* 16

Laub, D., 16, 31, 97, 128
Leighton, J., 61
Levine, P.A., 8, 23, 25
Lewis, H.B., 127
linked
    not linked vs., 177–78
Liotti, G., 97, 101, 102
look(s)
    "glazed," 116
Lowe, C., 16
Luxemberg, T., 55
Lyons-Ruth, K., 95, 99, 120

magnetic resonance imaging (MRI)
    of brain, 54
"magnetic sleep," 4
malignant narcissism
    dissociative structure in, 146
masochism
    dissociative structure in, 146
    trauma and, xiv
    as trauma disorder, xv
Masson, J.M., 13, 187
Maté, G., 48, 49
McWilliams, N., 56, 84
medical model(s), 60
    trauma–dissociation model vs., xvii
melancholia
    described, 130–31
memory(ies)
    autobiographical, 32
    declarative, 32
    dissociated, 77
    dissociation and, 31–35
    explicit, 32
    implicit, 32
    narrative, 32, 35
    procedural, 32
    repressed, 77, 85
    trauma and, 7, 31–35
    traumatic experiences as, 32
Mesmer, F.A., 4
mesmerism, 4
metaphor(s)
    spatial, 80–82

Miller, J.B., xix
mimicry
    in infants, 122
mind
    dissociation of see dissociation
    trauma and dissociation effects on,
        45–57
mind/body link, 47–49
misery
    "psychological," 6
Mitchell, S., xv, 106
"moral defense," 126
Moskowitz, A., 30
Mourning and Melancholia, 130–31
MRI. see magnetic resonance imaging
    (MRI)
multiple selves, 105
multiplicity
    described, 105–6
    dissociative, 105–8
    healthy, 106
Myers, C., 21, 148
myth(s)
    of Osiris, xxiii–xxiv, 172–73

narcissism
    dissociative structure in, 146
    malignant, 146
narrative(s)
    new see new narrative
narrative memory, 32, 35
National September 11 Memorial and
        Museum
    in New York City, 135
neglect
    abuse and, 178–79
Neuman, E., 188
neurological system
    trauma effects on, 25
neurosis
    attachment-based dissociation vs., xviii
new narrative
    consequences of, 12–14, 17
    Freud's neglect of trauma and dissocia-
        tion in, 20

psychosexual and Oedipal theories,
12–14
Nijenhuis, E.R.S., 21, 23, 41, 47, 136
nonspecified dissociative disorders
hippocampus size in persons with,
54
normal personality
apparently *see* apparently normal personality (ANP)
not knowing
knowing and, 83
not linked
linked *vs.*, 177–78
"not-me," 144

"object usage," 168
Oedipal and repression-based theory
of psychoanalysis, xx
Oedipal doctrine
rigidified adherence to, 15–16
Oedipal-psychosexual theory, 4
Oedipal theory
Freud's, xxi, 18–20, 132, 173–76
giving cover to pedophiles, 19–20
new narrative, 12–14
no room for abuser in, 19–20
Oedipus, xviii, 171, 173–76
Holocaust trauma overshadowed by,
15–16
theory of, 16
Oedipus complex, 3, 4, 130, 132
Oedipus Rex, 174–76
Ogden, P., 8, 23
omnipotence, 147
"one brain: two selves," 152–55
one-person model
to two-person dyad, 60–61
open system(s), 160–64
Oresteia, 19
Orestes, 19
Orthodoxy
as armor, 16
Osiris
myth of, xxiii–xxiv, 172–73
Osiris Complex, 172

other
right-brain knowledge of, 67
ourselves
versions of, xviii
outside-in approach
described, xxii
inside-out approach *vs.*, 94–95
overwhelm
traumatic affective, xix

Pappenheim, B., 9–10, 23
Paracelsus, 4
pathological dissociation, 38
patterns of thinking
blame-other, xix
blame-self, xix
pedophile(s)
Oedipal theory giving cover to, 19–20
peri-traumatic dissociation, 26
Perlman, S., 65, 66
perpetrator role, 141
Perry, B., 23, 116–17
persecutory self-states
rageful, 125
persistent dissociative multiplicity
as maladaptive, 108–9
personal agency
in Freudian version of unconscious
determinism, 138
personality
apparently normal *see* apparently normal
personality (ANP)
emotional *see* emotional personality (EP)
model of dissociative structure of,
147–52
structure in, 137
theory of structural dissociation of,
147–52
personality configurations
dissociative structure in, 145–47
personality disorders. *see also* dissociative
identity disorder (DID); *specific types,
e.g.,* borderline personality disorder
(BPD)
self-states in, 145–47

phase-oriented trauma treatment
Janet and, 6–7
in retraumatization prevention, 41
physical health
ACEs impact on, 51–55
Piaget, J., 18
Pivnik, B., xi
polarization
"either/or," 14–15
polyvagal theory
Porges', 114–15
Porges, S., 114–16
Positive Element, 188
posttraumatic biological states, 114–17
case example, 114, 123
posttraumatic stress
founding father of field of, 6–8
psychosis confused with, 55–56
posttraumatic stress disorder (PTSD), 30,
34, 35
after Vietnam War, 22
BPD and, 56
complex, 40
Janet and, 6
prevalence of, 45
stressor event of, 28
in Vietnam veterans, 45
Waco disaster–related, 116–17
"Preliminary Communication"
in *Studies on Hysteria,* 8–9
pre-psychoanalytic period, 10
presence
dissociated experiences as, 95
Preston, L., 171
primary dissociation, 151
"primitive dissociation or splitting," 146
primitive idealization, 147
problematic dissociation, 38
procedural memory, 32
procedural unconscious, 95–96
process(es)
bottom-up, 49–51
dissociative, 26, 36–38, 86
psyche(s)
described, 67–68

fragmentation in BPD, 146
therapists' murky, 67–68
psychic determinism and repression,
xx–xxi
psychic trigger points
weighty interactions of universal, 60
psychoanalysis
Freudian, xx–xxi
Oedipal and repression-based theory
of, xx
originators of, 10
psychoanalyst(s)
blank screen, 166
Freudian, 15–16
"psychoform" dissociation, 47
psychological healing, 171–86
toward, xxiii–xxiv
"psychological misery," 6
psychological organization of traumatized
person
structural models of, 135–55 *see also specific types and* structural model(s)
psychological organization of traumatized
persons
structural models of, xxiii
psychological trauma, 27–28
dissociation of mind related to, xvii
as overwhelming, 30
psychoneuroimmunoendocrinology, 47, 49
psychopathy
dissociative structure in, 146
psychosexual theory
new narrative, 12–14
psychosis(es)
posttraumatic and dissociative symptoms confused with, 55–56
psychotherapist(s)
becoming real to client, 168–70
what clients know about, 66–75
psychotherapy
authority roles in, 61–63
body, 7
described, xviii
goals of, 140
structural change in, 137

PTSD. *see* posttraumatic stress disorder (PTSD)
Putnam, F.W., xv, xxiv, 41, 86, 136, 177–80
  SDLM model of, 144–45, 179–80

racism
  "unconscious," 5
rageful, persecutory self-states, 125
reconnection, 176
reenactment(s)
  described, 68–69
Regis, 11
Reinders, A.A.T.S., 152
rejection
  abuse and, 178–79
relational approaches
  to trauma, 43–44
relational bridge, 90
relationality, xviii–xix
  current concepts of, xix
  described, xix
"relational-structural" models, 139
relationship(s)
  enactive models of, 120
  intersubjective failure in interpersonal, 164–70
  therapeutic, 23–24
remembrance
  abreaction and, 9
repressed memories
  described, 77, 85
repressed unconscious
  agency in, 82
  described, 93–94
  dissociative unconscious *vs.*, 93–94
repression
  clinical examples, 79
  defined, 85
  described, xxii, 78–79, 85
  dissociation and, 77–82
  dissociation *vs.*, 85
  existence of, 84
  Freud's visual metaphors for, 81–83
  psychic, xx–xxi

spatial metaphors of, 80–82
  suppression and, 82–84
  trauma and, 14
  unconscious and, 77–96 *see also* unconscious
  uses and criteria of, 188
  willfulness in, 82
"Repression," 82
repression and dissociation theory, 20
repression theory
  Freud's, 91
rescuer role, 141
retraumatization prevention, 40–43
  dissociation-focused treatments in, 42–43
  phase-oriented trauma treatment in, 41
  reducing and controlling affect intensity in, 41–42
Richman, S., 16
right-brain knowledge of other, 67
right-brain-to-right-brain affectively responsive ways, 67
Rizzolatti, G., 122
role(s)
  authority, 61–63
  as identity-shapers, 62
  perpetrator, 141
  rescuer, 141
  victim, 141
Rosenfeld, H., 165
Ross, C.A., 57, 172
Rothschild, B., 8, 22–23
"rule of thirds"
  Kluft's, 41

saboteur(s)
  "internal," 143
safe place imagery, 42
Salpêtrière Clinic, 6
Scaer, R., 23
"schizoid dilemma," 126
Schneider, K., 55
Schore, A.N., 23, 50–51, 67, 95, 116
Schwartz, H.L., 121
Schwartz, R., 43
  IFS model of, 43, 141–42

SDLM model. *see* state-dependent learning
    and memory (SDLM) model
secondary dissociation, 151
second consciousness, 4, 8–9
secure attachment, 99
    earned, 102
seduction theory
    Freud's, 12, 174
self(ves)
    "jury-rigged," 140–41
    multiple, 105
    parts of, 43
    shame's focus on, 127
    split, 132
self-attack, xxii–xxiii
    case examples, 111–12, 114
    self-criticism and, 111–33
self-blame
    clients', 17
    curative power of, 117–18
"self-care system" (Kalsched)
    described, 163–64
self-contradictions
    Freud's, 14–15
self-criticism, xxii
    case examples, 111–12, 114
    self-attack and, 111–33
self-devaluation, 118
self-fragmentation covered over, 102–5
self-reflection
    Isis's thread of, 181
self-regulation
    ability for, 49
    learning, 178–79
self-state(s)
    dissociative, xix
    in personality disorders, 145–47
    rageful, persecutory, 125
self-sufficiency
    dissociative, 163
September 11, 2001 attack, 36–37, 135–36
sexual abuse
    child *see* child sexual abuse
sexual trauma
    "either/or" polarization and, 14–15

Shakespeare, W., 19
shame
    abuse and, 129
    case example, 126–27, 129
    compassion in softening, 130
    in concentration camps, 128–29
    described, 127
    dissociogenic, 126–30
    dissociogenic power of, 127–30
    distancing from, 128
    emergence in development, 128
    focus on self, 127
    guilt *vs.*, 127
    humor in softening, 130
    redemption from, 128
    split self due to, 132
    to superego, 130–32
    traumatic abuse–related, 129
    woundedness and, 74–75
Shapiro, F., 50
shell shock, 21, 22
Shell Shock in France, 21
shock
    shell, 21, 22
Siegel, D., 50–51
simulation
    "embodied," 122
Sinason, V., xi
"situation of tenderness," 18
sleep
    "magnetic," 4
SNS. *see* sympathetic nervous system
    (SNS)
Solzhenitsyn, A., 128
somatic states
    affects conveyed by, 67
somatoform dissociation, 23
Sophocles, 174
spatial metaphors
    of dissociation and repression, 80–82
Spiegel, D., 27–28
Spitz, R.A., 113
split/dual consciousness
    unconscious *vs.*, 92–93
split self, 132

splitting
  BPD and, 56–57, 146
  defenses of borderline personality orga-
    nization related to, 146–47
  described, 146–47
Stanford Prison Experiment
  Zimbardo's, 62
state(s). *see also* somatic states; *specific types,*
    e.g., behavioral-mental states of being
  behavioral-mental, 177–78
  discrete behavioral, 176–78 *see also* dis-
    crete behavioral states
  hypnoid, 9
  identity, 4
  posttraumatic biological, 114–17
  somatic, 67
state dependence, 179–80
state-dependent learning and memory
    (SDLM) model
  Putnam's, 144–45, 179–80
state space
  strange attractors in, 177
state switches
  in DID, 56–57
Steele, K., 21, 41, 42, 47, 136
  "theory of the structural dissociation of
    the personality" of, 21
Stern, D.N., 78, 113
still-face experiment
  Tronick's, 113
strange attractors
  in state space, 177
Strange Situation, 99, 100
"strangulated affect," 9
stress
  chronic, 54
  effects of, 54
  posttraumatic *see* posttraumatic
    stress; posttraumatic stress disorder
    (PTSD)
  toxic, 54
stress response(s)
  dysregulation of, 53–55
structural change
  in psychotherapy, 137

structural dissociation of personality
  theory of, 147–52
structural dissociative organization, 38
structural model(s)
  Bowlby's attachment models of IWMs,
    143–44
  defined, 137
  dissociation-based, 139–45
  dissociative structure in different per-
    sonality organizations, 145–47
  "drive-structure" model, 137–39
  Fairbairn's endopsychic model, 143
  Freud's, 137–39 *see also* Freud's struc-
    tural model
  "identification with the aggressor"
    model, 142–43
  Karpman's drama triangle, 141
  of psychological organization of trauma-
    tized person, 135–55 *see also specific*
    types
  purpose of, 137
  Putnam's SDLM model, 144–45
  Schwartz's IFS model, 43, 141–42
  Structural Model of the Dissociation of
    the Personality, 147–52
Structural Model of the Dissociation of
    the Personality
  theory of, 147–52
structure(s)
  authority, 61–63
  dissociative *see* dissociative structure
  dissociative personality, 136
  id, ego, and superego, 137–39
  superego, 132
Studies on Hysteria, 8–11, 82–83, 92, 93
  "Preliminary Communication" in, 8–9
subconscious
  described, xxii
"subconscious" determinism, 6
subconscious "fixed ideas," 7
submission, 47, 116
Sullivan, H.S., 86, 128, 144
superego
  described, 130
  dissociative, 132–33

superego (*continued*)
   dissociative clinical, 132–33
   from shame to, 130–32
   as theoretical concept, 138
superego construct
   problems associated with, 138–39
superego structure
   dissociative structure resembling,
     132
suppression
   repression and, 82–84
survival
   dissociation in fostering, 35–36
sympathetic nervous system (SNS), 115

Taming of the Shrew, 19
TAT (Thematic Apperception Test), 103
Terr, L., 23
tertiary dissociation, 151
"The Aetiology of Hysteria," 11, 12, 14,
   175
"the body keeps the score," 23
*The Deepest Well: Healing the Long-Term
   Effects of Childhood Adversity,* 53
"the dissociative nature of the human
   mind," 46
"The Ego and the Id," 132
The Haunted Self, 47, 148, 154–55
Thematic Apperception Test (TAT), 103
theory(ies). *see* psychosexual theory; *specific
   types, e.g.,* Oedipal theory
theory of attachment
   Bowlby's, 97–98
theory of Oedipus, 16
theory of the structural dissociation of the
   personality, 147–52
   Steele's, 21
therapeutic relationship(s)
   developments in, 23–24
therapist(s)
   becoming real to client, 157–70
   clients' awareness of murky psyches of,
     67–68
   what clients know about, 66–75
"the talking cure," 9–10, 23

*The Way We Are: How States of Mind Influ-
   ence Our Identities, Personality, and
   Potential for Change,* 177
thinking
   blame-other patterns of, xix
   blame-self patterns of, xix
"Three Essays on the Theory of Sexuality,"
   187–88
Tompkins, S., 128
"tonic immobility," 116
top-down verbal therapies, 49–51
   described, 49
"total submission," 47, 116
Towson University, 42
toxic stress
   effects of, 54
transference(s), 141
   traumatic, 68
trauma
   abuse and, 27
   ACEs with, xxi
   adverse impacts of, xx
   "betrayal," 119
   body systems affected by, 25, 45–57
   "complex," 56
   counter-, 64
   cumulative, 29
   defined, 27–31
   denial of, 173
   depersonalization/derealization due to,
     38
   described, 27–30
   as dissociation, xxi, 25–44
   dissociation due to, 22, 30
   dissociation intertwined with, 25–44
   distress *vs.,* 28–31
   DSM inconsistencies related to, 55
   embedded in our lives, 25–27
   as fixed idea, 31
   "forgetting" of, 32
   forgotten, 6
   Freud's burying of, xx–xxi, 3–24
   hallmark of, 128
   Holocaust, 15–16
   masochism and, xiv

measurement of, 28–31
memory and, 7, 31–35
mind/body link in, 47–49
mind-related effects of, 45–57
neglect by Freud, 20
neurobiological result of, xx
neurological system effects of, 25
new ways of thinking about, xx
objective view of, 29
as overwhelming, 27–28, 128
prevalence of, 46–47
professional confusion about effects on
    problems in living, 55–57
psychological *see* psychological trauma
recognition of, xix
relational approaches to, 43–44
repression and, 14
rooted in helplessness, xix
sexual, 14–15
ubiquity of, xxi, 45–57
underrecognition of, 55
"vicarious," 64
as wound, 27
trauma and dissociation informed
    approach
described, xvii–xviii
trauma and dissociation theory
Janet's, 7
trauma disorder
masochism as, xv
trauma–dissociation model
described, xvii
Freud's structural model as, 140
medical model *vs.,* xvii
trauma–dissociation theory, 91, 92
trauma experience(s)
staying close to, 63–65
trauma model
helplessness recognized by, xviii
trauma theory
attachment theory and, 98
traumatic abuse
shame related to, 129
traumatic affective overwhelm, xix
"traumatic bonding," 120

traumatic events
DSM-5 on exposure to, 45
traumatic experiences
dissociative consequences of, 145
as memory, 32
processed in brain, 32–33
traumatic transferences, 68
traumatized persons
psychological organization of, xxiii
structural models of psychological orga-
    nization of, 135–55 *see also specific
    types and* structural model(s)
trauma treatment
for DID, 42–43
forms of, 39–40
in reducing dissociation, 39–40
types of, 39–40
Trevarthen, C., 171
triggered
by clients, 65
trigger points
weighty interactions of universal psy-
    chic, 60
Tronick, E.Z., 113, 115
Truman, H.R., Pres., 62
two person dyad
from one-person model to, 60–61

unconscious, 91–94
agency in repressed, 82
described, xxii, 77, 91
dissociation and, 77–96 *see also*
    dissociation
dissociative, 93–94 *see also* dissociative
    unconscious
early studies of, 4–6
Freudian, 93
procedural, 95–96
repression and, 77–96 *see also* repressed
    unconscious; repression
split/dual consciousness *vs.,* 92–93
unconscious determinism, 6
personal agency in Freudian version of,
    138
"unconscious racism," 5

unitary consciousness, 20
universal psychic trigger points
    weighty interactions of, 60
Urkel, S., 130

Vaillant, G.E., 84
Van Derbur, M., 108, 153
Van der Hart, O., 6, 21, 23, 30, 41, 42, 47, 86,
    92, 93, 102, 116, 136, 147–51, 154–55
Van der Kolk, B.A., 8, 23, 33, 40–42
vehement, 7
"vehement emotions," 22
ventral vagal complex (VVC), 115
verbal therapies
    top-down, 49–51
Vermetten, E., 54
vibe(s)
    in communication, 95–96
vibration(s)
    in communication, 95–96
"vicarious trauma"
    countertrauma vs., 64
victim role, 141
Vietnam veterans
    PTSD in, 22, 45
Vietnam War
    PTSD after, 22, 45
Virgin Mary, 188
visual metaphor(s)
    for repression, 81–83
vulnerability
    recognition of, xix
VVC. see ventral vagal complex (VVC)

Waco disaster
    PTSD patterns in children after,
    116–17
Westover, T., 107
When the Body Says No, 48
WHO. see World Health Organization
    (WHO)
willfulness
    in repression, 82
Wilson (volleyball), 163
Winnicott, D.W., 160, 168–69
Women's Institute, xiv
Women's Movement
    advent of, 22
World Health Organization (WHO)
    ICD-11 of, 56
World Trade Center (WTC) attack
    on 9/11/2001, 36–37, 135–36
wound(s)
    trauma as, 27
wounded dyad, xxii
    clinical dyad as, xxi–xxii, 59–75
woundedness
    shame and, 74–75
WTC. see World Trade Center (WTC)
    attack

Yale University
    Fortunoff Archives of Holocaust Testi-
    mony at, 16
Yehuda, N., 36

Zimbardo, P., 62